Marketing Models: Multivariate Statistics and Marketing Analytics

Dawn Iacobucci

Acknowledgments

I am grateful to Pankaj Aggarwal, Ulf Böckenholt, Anand Bodapati, Katherine Burson, Wayne DeSarbo, Jeff Dotson, Hubert Gatignon, Kent Grayson, Dominique Hanssens, Geraldine Henderson, Nigel Hopkins, Lawrence E. Jones, Michael Lewis, Prashant Malaviya, Charlotte Mason, Vincent Onyemah, Gabriele Paolacci, Deidre Popovich, Mark Ratchford, David Schweidel, Siddharth Singh, Rob Smith, and Patti Williams for their insightful, smart, kind and generous comments.

Notes to the Reader

Content. This book presents a number of models for analyzing multivariate data. The examples are set in the context of marketing questions and customer data, but the material should be accessible to students in other management disciplines and even those in fields outside of business schools.

Level. This book is written for students in MBA programs or advanced undergraduates who seek to strengthen and refine their analytical abilities, Ph.D. students of both the quantitative and behavioral varieties, and academics or practitioners who find they were not exposed to a technique that they now need. I've tried to write about these techniques in a clear manner, at least avoiding the stuffy nature of many stats professors. My hope is that you will find the tone of the writing to be as if I'm sitting down with you, explaining the techniques to you, and coaching you. None of which is to say the book is an easy read—there are sections of most chapters that are pretty intense. But readers who are motivated (and willing to turn off media that compete for their attention) will come away being very highly trained in some really amazing analytical methods. Finally, a rare author's offer: if you find some material confusing or incomplete, please email me and I'll try to address your issues.

Table of Contents

Chapter 1
Introduction to Marketing Models: Multivariate Statistics and Marketing Analytics

It's a wonderful time to be a geek and use statistics if you work in the business world. Companies are spinning off more data and collecting it as never before, and smart businesspeople are increasingly using that data. Information is gathered to understand customers and the marketplace better, and to be more competitive.

Why Go Quant?

Business decisions are strengthened with empirical evidence. As we consider any proposed strategy or tactic, it is helpful to have information that suggests whether or not it's a good idea to engage in that action. Without such information, the decision is a guess. Instead, if there are supportive data, the decision is greatly substantiated. If, on the other hand, the data indicate that the proposal is not a good idea, it is still better to know, and to know sooner rather than later, to save money, time, and other resources. In addition, strategic choices are more persuasive when they are "fact-based," that is, based on information and evidence. The strategies are also more believable when communicated, and therefore it is easier to get people on board, from employees to investors to customers.

Subsequently, when some strategy is implemented, managers will want to know whether doing so was worth it—what was the return on the investment (ROI) for that set of actions. The ROI question is exacerbated in times of tight budgets, but even in good times, no one wants to waste money. If other corporate functions are held accountable, it seems equally fair to ask the same of marketing. We marketers can bemoan the fact that many of our goals are long-term (e.g., building brand equity) or difficult to measure (e.g., attitude enhancement attributed to our social media plan), but that doesn't mean we shouldn't try. Indeed, doing so can be quite rewarding; e.g., a comprehensive set of studies affirmed the importance of marketing, from demonstrating that marketing positively affects firm performance more strongly than R&D or operations, to showing that effective advertising has a sustained and growing impact.[1] The philosophy of seeking empirical support has permeated top management:

- "If you pretest your product with consumers, and pretest your advertising, you will do well in the marketplace." (Ogilvy)
- "Do we think, or do we know? . . . [let's run] an experiment." (Harrah's)
- "We never throw away data." (Amazon)
- "Do you have evidence to support that hypothesis?" (Xerox)

Many business and marketing questions may be answered by statistics, numbers that characterize the state of some market or the preferences of some customer segment. We certainly use statistics in this book, but a model is more than a collection of numbers.

What is a Model?

If a model is more than just statistics, let's begin with the question, "What is a model?" A model is a simplified representation of the world built to help us understand the world and make predictions about it. In this book, we focus on mathematical models of various forms, but strictly speaking, models don't have to be mathematical. You've probably seen many "boxes and arrows" sorts of models—box A leads to box B which in turn causes box C, etc. In developing models, we might also begin at that rough conceptual level, but we will strive to put good measures and data in the boxes to help us understand the relationships among them. For example, we might pose questions about the real world in terms of differences between customer segments, which would suggest models to compare those groups' means on some variables. Alternatively, we might pose a question about the real world regarding the correlation between ratings of customer satisfaction and firms' financial performance, which would prompt us to begin our modeling with correlations.

In modeling, we don't believe that the model captures all the elements of the real world—we have characterized models as simplified versions of the world. We hope to build a model that captures the essence of what is relevant for the business and marketing questions at hand.

Here's an example. As a kid, you probably knew someone who built model airplanes (perhaps that kid was you!). A model airplane kit contains pieces of plastic to glue together and paint. The little model airplane is likely to

---

[1] Hanssens, Dominique (2009), *Empirical Generalizations about Marketing Impact.* Boston: MSI.

have rubber wheels, a pair of wings, clear plastic for windows, maybe seats inside, etc. It might have doors that open, a rudder that moves, and perhaps even an engine that works. That is, the model airplane has some elements that are like those of a real plane. Yet they aren't the same; the model is a metaphor for, or represents, the real thing. Both planes might fly, but even if they do, the model plane doesn't go as fast as the real plane. If the model plane flies, it does so by radio control, and it doesn't carry passengers or packages. And yet, so what? The model plane flies around the yard, zooming here and zipping there, and it's fun, and it's cool.

Models in marketing and business are analogous. Say we fit a little regression model to predict likely numbers of purchases of our brand as a function of just two things: customers' stated preferences and their past brand purchases. Our model is like a plastic plane. We don't really believe that customers think like a regression—as if they determine their preference, multiply it by a beta weight, add it to their past brand purchases (similarly weighted), and then predict for themselves which brand to purchase.

We also don't believe that the only considerations in the real world for the customer's brand choice are their preferences and their past behaviors. We know the real world is far more complicated—there are contextual factors (state of the economy, customer confidence), competitive actions (features or price promotions of competitors' brands or the retailer's own brand), customer personality idiosyncrasies (biases about a brand's country of origin), etc., all of which contribute, to a great extent or subtly, directly or indirectly, always or only occasionally, to customers' brand choices.

We acknowledged that our model airplane doesn't fly fast, and it doesn't carry passengers or packages, and we said, so what. We can also acknowledge that our statistical model of likely customer brand choice doesn't fully capture all customer decision variables either, and again we say, so what. Even with just our two independent variables, we can make predictions and acquire more information than we had before we created the model.

The ultimate question in assessing a model is whether the model is useful. Is it true that the little plastic plane doesn't incorporate all of the features of a real airplane? Yes. Yet does it help us understand some basic structures about planes or some basic properties about aerodynamics? Yes.

In addition, the question about whether a model is useful is often best answered in comparison to another, competing model. So, for example, the little plastic plane is closer to the reality of an actual plane than a piece of paper folded into a paper airplane that we throw through the air. Similarly, our model with two predictors (using preference and past purchases to predict their next brand choice) will provide better predictions than a model that uses something like a customer's citizenship to predict brand choice, and certainly our model predictions are better than a guess.

In addition, frequently in business, we want models to offer predictions. If we have a strong analytical understanding of the customer or market phenomenon, and we've formulated it into a comprehensive yet parsimonious model, which we've populated with reasonably valid data, then we should be able to forecast, with some confidence, scenarios that are more (or less) likely to unfold. Sometimes we can watch and see whether a scenario unfolds and then we can evaluate the goodness of the model (e.g., if we predict sales and then gather those sales data). Sometimes it will be less clear (e.g., we might use a model to decide whether to launch a new product, but if the forecast looked grim, we wouldn't launch), and in such a circumstance, we gain confidence in our models and modeling ability through experience over many scenarios.

It's Hip to B²

For these sorts of reasons, management has become more science-like. We use data—empirical evidence—to build models. We use the models to understand and forecast.

Naturally a career as a marketing analyst would mean working steeped in data. However, it's also true that when the CEO or CMO commissions research from in-house providers or consultants, it's important to understand what to ask for and what to look for so as to be smart consumers of the resulting research.

The push for quants has so fully permeated the business ethos that interviewers and recruiters are also coaching applicants to strengthen their résumés by quantifying their experiences, e.g., "My project increased sales by 24% in just 3 months" rather than "My project contributed greatly to the company's bottom line." The quantification lends objectivity and precision to otherwise vague claims of grandeur.

Management is not alone.[2] Models and equations for predicting success have permeated many realms of life previously thought to be immune. A fabulous example is the surprisingly successful book by Michael Lewis, *Moneyball*,

---

[2] Here's a business model for you. If you add the Mars company's candy to the McDonald's arches, you get the post-it notes company: m&m + **ጠ** = 3M. Nyuck nyuck nyuck.

which narrates the decision to use statistics and simple winning strategies in baseball. Analogously, the movie *21* depicts students counting cards to beat the house odds while gambling in casinos.

One might argue that gambling is naturally akin to probability, and that baseball is notorious for generating mountains of statistics, but modeling and forecasting are being used in still more industries. For example, models help movie studios estimate likely commercial success at the box office, domestically and internationally, DVD sales, and the popularity and revenue of downloads. Music is being deconstructed to understand the elements of success for both genre and artist, and to help producers determine where to allocate their production and marketing dollars. Simple extracts of demographic data including age, zip codes, and median household incomes help health care centers choose site locations to establish their geriatric services. And of course, the world of finance took off when Wall Street began importing physicists for their math skills. One might argue that they haven't been entirely successful, and using the marketing models in this book would lead to better financial modeling and predictions than those that have been implemented to date.[3]

Which Marketing Models to Cover?

There are many techniques that we could examine, so to guide my choice about which methods to include in this book, I did what any good marketer would do—I conducted a poll. I queried MBA alumni and executives (in each sample, approximately half of the respondents had been out 3.5 years, and half 15 years or longer). I asked them quite simply, "What are your biggest business headaches?" and "What do you want your new hires to be able to do, to hit the ground running?"

The business questions that arose are listed in the 1st column of Table 1.1. The questions and issues were classified into the themes listed in the 2nd column. For example, the first question is: "I get the concept of '80:20'…so, who are my '80' customers—which ones are they and how do I reach them?" This question is about identifying and profiling customers. That customer information is the essence of a segmentation study in marketing. The marketing concepts are listed in the 3rd column of the table. The statistical methods are presented in the 4th column, and it's the ties between the marketing issues (3rd column) and the modeling methods (4th column) that are the essence of this book.

While theoretically, most statistical models can be used to answer many kinds of substantive questions, it's true that in practice, there are some sweet spots in terms of matching the marketing questions posed with the strengths of a particular modeling technique to provide answers. For example, we'll see in Chapter 2, that the marketing question of "segmentation" (finding groups of similar customers) is perfectly amenable to the technique of cluster analysis (which groups together similar entities). Thus, to emphasize the book's perspective as a user's resource, each chapter covers a marketing topic using the optimal methods.

The flow of the chapters follows the business concerns:

- In Chapter 2, we begin with the question, "Who are my customers?," the marketing technique of segmentation, and the modeling approach of cluster analysis.
- In Chapter 3, we are motivated by the question, "Are my customers loyal—what factors feed into their brand choices?" We'll look at brand loyalty and brand switching tables, and we'll work toward logit models and logistic regressions—models for dependent variables that are categorical, like brand choices.
- In Chapter 4, we then puzzle, "If customers are loyal, great, but why, and if they prefer a competitor, why? We need to measure customer attitudes, like on customer satisfaction surveys." We'll see that factor analysis helps us measure attitudes as cleanly as possible.
- In Chapter 5, we might posit that we have reasonable measures of customer satisfaction and other metrics, and now the focus is on the question, "What are the drivers of our customers' satisfaction?" We'll see path analysis, an impressive generalization of regression models, as a means of understanding those driving factors.
- In Chapter 6, we want to get a sense of customers' perceptions and preferences, and not just with respect to our own brand but relative to the competition. We'll use multidimensional scaling to create perceptual maps (we'll also consider a related technique called correspondence analysis). We'll get a view of the market structure, e.g., where there is a lot of competition and where there is little.
- In Chapter 7, we might wish to take advantage of the spaces in the perceptual map where there were few competitors, and plan to develop a new product in any of those spaces. Most businesses are savvy enough to be able to create many new products, so the question is, which of the potential opportunities should they pursue?

---

[3] And of course, using models well is not the same as making good ethical choices for customers and citizens instead of only for oneself or one's financial company! But that's a topic for another book.

Conjoint analysis helps us design new products with the attributes that customers will appreciate.

- In Chapter 8, we might proceed to take a new product to market, and to do so we might run a test market. It is also the case that in many business scenarios, we're very interested in assessing ROI. While superficially, these may look like different questions, the pursuits of their answers share the methodologies of experimentation and analysis of variance.
- In Chapter 9, in contexts such as a new product launch, or even in times of budgeting and planning, businesses frequently ask for forecasts and estimates of sales scenarios. A tried and true marketing model for diffusion is described, along with forecast models for repeat purchasing after initial trial purchases.
- In Chapter 10, we look at social networks. The mechanism underlying diffusion models relies upon word-of-mouth, which flows through networks. In addition, obviously social networks and social media have permeated our lives, and it's worthwhile to understand some basic concepts and means of analyzing them.
- In Chapter 11, we look backward to consider several classic marketing models.
- In Chapter 12, we look forward. We look at what we're facing in current and future models with respect to "big data," and we'll see some resources for data to model in the future. [4]

Table 1.1: The Relationships between the Business Concerns, Marketing Questions, and the Modeling Techniques Selected for *Marketing Models*

Business Questions	Business Themes	Marketing Questions	Modeling Techniques	See Chapter
• "I get the concept of '80:20'…so, who are my '80' customers—which ones are they and how do I reach them?" • "When I ask them for a marketing plan, MBAs need to know how to start off with a good segmentation study."	Identify and profile customers	Segmentation	Cluster analysis	2
• "Are our customers loyal?" "What decision factors go into their decisions to buy our brand vs. a competitor's?"	Brand choice	Brand choice, loyalty, switching	Logit models and logistic regression	3
• "<Our main competitor> runs frequent customer satisfaction surveys. We'd like to do some. Where do we start?"	Capturing customer and marketing metrics	Measuring customer attitudes	Factor analysis	4
• "What are the main drivers of customer satisfaction or dissatisfaction (so we know what to maintain or what to fix)?"	Factors that impact marketing and business metrics	Customer satisfaction, customer lifetime value	Path models, structural equations	5
• "How do customers 'see' our brand?" "We think customers see us <in some way>. Is that true?" • "How do we compare to our competitors?" "Who are our competitors, really?" "What's our position in the market, our strengths vs. our competitors'?"	Perceptions about our brand or company vis-à-vis the competition	Perceptual maps, positioning, preferences, market structure	Multidimensional scaling, correspondence analysis	6
• "There are so many kinds of new products we could be developing. Which direction should we take?"	Opportunities	New product development	Conjoint analysis	7

---

[4] A final class of concerns came from experienced managers who rued of their young hires, "We have a lot of in-house white papers and data, but they don't show initiative in finding data." We address this concern also in Chapter 11.

Table 1.1, continued

Business Questions	Business Themes	Marketing Questions	Modeling Techniques	See Chapter
• "Definitely ROMI (or ROI); when I do something to reach my customers, am I getting my money's worth?" • "With all these media choices, where do I spend my ad budget?"	Financial testing and accountability	RO(M)I, market tests, resource allocation	Experiments and analysis of variance	8
• "If we go ahead and launch, can we achieve our goals; how well can we expect to do?" "How big is this market?" or "What's the up-side potential on sales here?"	Market capture	Diffusion and forecasting, market sizing	Diffusion models	9
• "What are we supposed to do on Facebook?"	Social media	Word-of-mouth	Social networks	10

Philosophy of *Marketing Models: Multivariate Statistics and Marketing Analytics*

Modeling books seem to be written in one of two styles. On the one hand, some books are written by authors who underestimate the reader's intelligence and treat modeling techniques as proverbial black boxes: "here are the basics, don't worry about the details or what the model or computer is really doing." On the other hand, some books are written by authors who overestimate the reader's interest in the establishment of the veracity of the methods, and present endless pages of proofs. In this book, I'm aiming for the strengths of both and trying to avoid the weaknesses of either. I'm going to take a bunch of very cool models and open up the black boxes so you can see all the details. I want this book to be useful, and I don't think you can be an informed user unless you know precisely what the model is doing. If you really want to learn these techniques, this book is for you.

At the same time, per my comment about proofs (what a yawn!), I realize that in some circles people seem to be rewarded for doing bigger, better, louder math, but I'm not impressed with math for math's sake. I want this book to be practical, so even if I know there is research developing that builds on some technique, I'm not going to present the complicated, esoteric math version unless it has been proven to be substantially superior to existing models. What I prize is a really good model that is strong, clear, robust and powerful in performance, and accessible in terms of readings and software. IRL, the ultimate assessment of a model is whether it's useful.

I like succinct writers and I also believe that readers are more likely to read if the book doesn't go on and on. So, to keep this book succinct, and therefore more useful, I have assumed some basic knowledge. First, I'm assuming readers have taken at least an introductory marketing management course, so that I can dive right into discussing "how to do segmentation" rather than having to persuade you, "here's why segmentation is important." If you're coming at this material from another angle or a different science, don't worry, you can handle the material (it's just that you'll find the examples weird). Second, I'm writing this book assuming that readers will have had a basic course in statistics. Even if you had trouble with that course, this book should still be accessible, but it helps if I can say, "that t-statistic is significant," without having to define a t-statistic or significance tests.[5] And if you actually liked your previous stats classes, then you're in for a treat—welcome to geeks-R-us. ☺

---

[5] If you need help, see Iacobucci and Churchill, *Marketing Research: Methodological Foundations*, 11th ed.

Chapter 2: Segmentation and Cluster Analysis

Marketing Concepts: Segmentation, Recommendation Engines
Modeling Concept: Cluster Analysis

Chapter Outline
1. Introduction
2. Input Variables
3. Measures of Similarity
4. Clustering Algorithms
    a. Hierarchical Clustering Models
        i.   Single-Link
        ii. Complete-Link
        iii. Average-Link
        iv. Ward's Method of Clustering
    b. k-means Clustering
5. Interpretation and Verification
6. Recommendation Agents and Collaborative Filtering

Introduction

Segmentation, targeting, and positioning (STP) comprise the strategic arm of marketing that precedes the tactical 4Ps. A market must be segmented before we can choose which segment(s) to target and how to position our market offering. Thus, to be good marketers, we will start with segmentation.

The goals of a good segmentation scheme are two: first, we wish to identify groups of customers who are similar to each other, perhaps with regard to their demographics or psychographics, but ultimately with respect to their preferences and purchases regarding our brand. When we have a group of similar customers, we can proceed fairly confidently that the features and benefits sought in our products and brands are shared across the group, that is, if we can satisfy one customer in the segment, we stand a good chance of satisfying most of the customers in that segment. Second, we look for segments to be different from group to group. If one group likes all the same brands that another group likes, for our purposes, we might as well combine the groups and have one segment rather than two.

Consider these examples. Cluster analyses have been helpful in deriving segments of retail channel preferences (e.g., women without kids like stores, catalogs, and online; women with kids like catalogs or online; men like online except for gifts, for which they prefer stores to get assistance from employees). Clustering identified investors who were confident in their own judgments, sought low trade commissions, and didn't want to pay for advisor services, vs. people who were unsure and willing to pay for advice, vs. people who were fairly confident but would pay for advice because they liked the personal touch. The assets of these classes of advisors were not appreciably different. Clustering helped a large computer firm identify its business customers who cared only about power and performance, vs. those who were price conscious vs. those who wanted user-friendly interfaces. These segments were comparable in size and firm valuation.

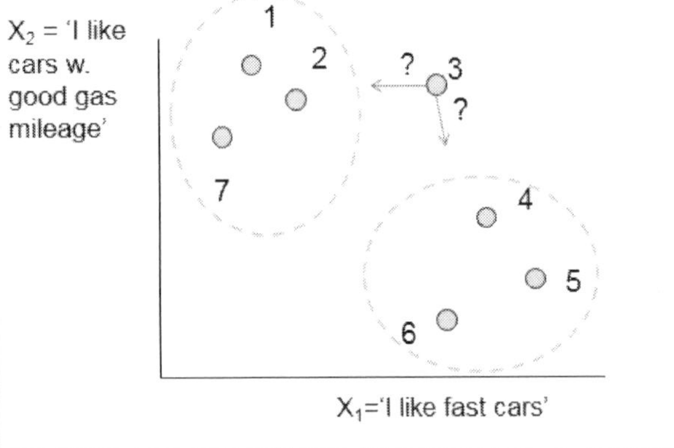

Cluster analysis is fabulous and easy, so let's see how it's done. Figure 2.1 shows a simple example, using only 2 input variables—customer ratings of the extent to which they value fast cars, or cars with good gas mileage (or

Figure 2.1: The Goal of Cluster Analysis: identify clouds of data points where objects represented by points in a tight cluster are similar to each other.

X_2 = 'I like cars w. good gas mileage'

X_1 = 'I like fast cars'

both, or neither). In the scatter plot, we can see two rather distinct groups, which we'll call clusters (or segments). The idea is that the resulting clusters will indicate that the customers 1, 2, and 7 appreciate gas mileage, whereas the preferences in the 4, 5, 6 segment are for fast cars. Given our brand's positioning, we will target one group or the other, but probably not both, at least not with the same product. These clusters may look fairly obvious, but cluster analysis will help us with cases such as customer 3—to which cluster does this customer belong, if either? Cluster analysis will also help us with real world cases, in which far more variables are involved than just the 2 plotted, and far more customers are involved than 7.

These goals are perfectly suited to and easily attained by cluster analysis. A cluster analysis algorithm will take the input variables we feed it, compute a measure of similarity between the entities (e.g., customers), and group together the entities that are most similar, keeping those that are more different in different clusters. The term "entities" is intended to be general, e.g., we can cluster brands, if we have data on the perceptions of multiple brands, but for segmentation purposes, entities are customers—consumers or businesses. We want to find groups of customers who are similar with respect to the variables we believe are important to our business.

Input Variables

It is important to remember that statistical methods are simply procedures. They crunch whatever data you give them. That's great, because it means that we can cluster just about anything. For example, biologists use cluster analysis to create zoological taxonomies and classify new creatures or fossils, whereas literature scholars use cluster analysis to identify the likely authors of ancient manuscripts. Marketers have clustered households by zip code, websites by clickstream data, shoppers by grocery cart contents, loan applicants by financial risk profiles, consumers by media viewing habits, and so on.

Figure 2.2 contains the beginning of a marketing dataset, in which customers (people, households, businesses, etc.) form the rows, and the columns are the variables measured on the customers. This snapshot includes variables that indicate how recently the customer has purchased from the firm ("recent"), the value of the items purchased then ("value"), the customer's zip code (derived from loyalty cards, credit cards, or manual input at check-outs), the median house value for that zip code (which we obtain from databases online), and counts of SKUs (stock-keeping units) the customer bought. Promo variables reflect whether the customer redeemed a coupon, a rebate, and two email offers. Supplemental survey data yielded the customers' favorite TV shows and Internet sites. The data set continues in both directions—many more customers, and many more variables. Any or all of these variables potentially may be included in a cluster analysis—the set we use depends on our objectives.

Figure 2.2
Potential Segmentation Variables for Inclusion in Clustering

Customers
↓ Variables:

ID	Recent	Value	Zip	House	Bought 1 2 3 4 5 6 7...	Promo C R E1 E2	Survey media TV1 TV2 TV3 I1 I2 I3 I4...
1057	5	199	02134	450	3 2 1 0 0 0 0	0 1 1 0	1 0 0 1 0 1 1
0143	1	25	78712	259	6 4 2 0 0 0 0	0 0 1 1	0 1 1 1 1 1 1
1552	3	317	94304	550	0 0 0 1 1 1 1	1 1 0 0	1 0 0 0 1 1 0
0094	2	54	10203	640	0 0 0 1 1 0 0	1 0 0 1	1 1 0 0 0 0 0
8744	1	19	50102	259	0 0 0 0 0 1 1	0 1 1 0	1 1 1 0 0 1 0

N

The fact that statistical methods are simply procedures also comes with the responsibility to use each method appropriately. For example, we know we're not supposed to compute means on categorical variables, such as country of citizenship or brand of car ownership. This reminder to "model responsibly!" got a nickname of its own when statistical computing first became possible. The acronym "gigo" stands for "garbage in, garbage out," meaning, if the variables you're putting into the model are ugly ducklings, you can't expect the model to produce results that are beautiful swans.

The variables that marketers use can be indicators that are geographic (country, climate, urban vs. rural), demographic (age, gender, income, education, household composition, number of cars owned), behavioral (online purchases and downloads, loyalty programs, cable and magazine subscriptions), and attitudinal (brand awareness, category knowledge and involvement, price sensitivity, prestige aspirations). If the customers being segmented are businesses, the variables can similarly be geographic (store coverage), demographic (account size, company size, NAICS industry), behavioral (technical requirements, order sizes, preferred vendors), and attitudinal (purchase and job-bidding policies). Here are a few real examples:

- The "Prizm" segmentation scheme is based on zip codes (see the Claritas service at Nielsen). Zips convey location (e.g., rural vs. urban) and approximate income levels. For example, rich city dwellers are called *Urban Uptowns*, and people in the city with less money are called *City Blues*. The logic is that well-off families with two kids, an SUV, and a dog are pretty similar in what they consume, what deals will appeal to them, what movies they'll Netflix, etc., whether they live in Austin, Columbus, or Indianapolis.
- For marketers interested in nonprofits, the book *Seven Faces of Philanthropy* presents a segmentation study of donors' behaviors and motivations. They found, for example, that there are people who earned their money as entrepreneurs and now they want to give to their local community, in part to be recognized as a big fish in that small, local pond—these givers are called *Communitarians*. There are *Socialites*, who enjoy going to fund-raising events; *Devouts*, who give as part of their spiritual beliefs and religious stewardship; *Dynasts*, who inherited wealth and were taught to provide for those less fortunate, and so on.
- As a final example, consider the *Fortune* article (by Taylor, vol.131, p.24) that featured Porsche segments. Porsche found that there are several types of guys who buy their cars: *Top Guns* are ambitious and expect to be noticed in these powerful cars. *Elitists* are old-money blue-bloods; the car is just a car. *Proud Patrons* are guys who had worked hard and consider the car a well-earned trophy, etc.

If many types of variables can be used in a cluster analysis, how does the marketer choose which to include? We'll illustrate 5 issues on the data in Figure 2.2. First, look around and see what data you already have in-house, but be sure not to limit your cluster analysis to these variables—not all of them should go in, and there may be far more interesting and important variables that you should include that you simply have no data on, yet. Huge amounts of data are available online, much of it for free. For example, a lot of demographic data on people and businesses await you at census.gov (you'll know you're a geek when you can proudly say that it's one of your favorite websites). If you have extracted all the data you can from within the company and online, you might find that some of your questions have been answered. You will almost also certainly find that not all of them have been, so with that realization, spend the money for at least a small data collection effort to supplement the current data so that the cluster analysis results can be as meaningful and useful as possible.

For example, we might compile the following database: first, from internal sales data and our CRM (customer relationship management) database, we pulled three behavioral measures (how recently a customer has bought from us, how much they spent during that purchase, and how many times the customer bought every one of our SKUs) and one demographic variable (the customer's zip code). The recency and value data would be easy to obtain for any company (online, retailers, service providers, etc.). The number of times each item was ever purchased would exist if the company kept historical records; if not, the measure might be modified, perhaps to convey the number of times each item was bought over the past 2 years. The zip code would exist if the customer's billing, shipping, or loyalty card information was captured.

Second, we can supplement our data with free secondary data online, e.g., finding the median household income for each customer's zip code. This approach avoids the difficulty of asking our customers for their incomes, and their possibly refusing to provide the information, inflating it, or reacting badly to our company for having asked. Of course nothing comes without a price, and imputing an average for a household data field obviously makes an assumption that the value holds true, at least roughly, for that customer.

Third, perhaps our interest was in our customers' media habits, so that we might make smarter use of our advertising budget. We could not derive this information from our customers' interactions with us, and it is unlikely to already exist in some database we might access, or at least certainly not in the form we'd like. So we drew a small ($N = 100$) sample of our customers and sent them a survey. It was short, so we got a reasonably good response rate (~67%). Those questions asked the selected customers to report their TV and Internet habits and the magazines to which they subscribe. A snippet of these data appear toward the end of the list on the right in Figure 2.2, for five customer households. We'll use these data in a moment.

Fourth, we'll do a little "pre-processing," beginning with checking the simple descriptive statistics on each variable before tossing it into the mix. The useful variables have to exhibit some amount of variance. To illustrate why, consider this example: a large insurance company ran an online survey and found that for the question, "Do you carry all of your insurance policies with one company, or do you have your car insurance with a different company from your home owner's insurance?" almost all the respondents enjoy the convenience of dealing with just one company. On a 1 to 5 rating scale, 80% of the responses were "5" (one company), and the remaining 20% of respondents were split over the categories 1–4. This variable would not be a good candidate for cluster analysis, because, recall the goal, we're seeking similarities within and differences between customer groups. In this case, there was very little variance. Most of the customers were the same, so they would land in the same segment. Unless we believe there is only one segment out there (and if we truly believed that, why would we be conducting a segmentation study?), then that conclusion would be misleading, and the variable not useful.

In contrast, that same survey posed another question, "How likely is it you would switch to another insurance company if they offered you a 10% discount?" For this question, the histogram showed a bimodal plot—about 40% of the sample said, "1 = Very unlikely," another 40% of the sample said, "5 = Very likely," and the remaining 20% fell in the categories in between. This variable is a great example of information that is likely to be useful in a cluster analysis because it is already showing similarities and differences (the group of 1s, and separately, the group of 5s). The results are beginning to lend insight into how customers think—the 1s appear to be brand-loyal and the 5s appear to be price-sensitive.

In final preparation for the clustering, we double-check the variables we propose. Just as we want to include variables that actually convey distinguishing information, we also don't want to include too many variables that convey the same information. The cluster analysis doesn't really care how many variables of any type go in; that's not the problem. The issue is that redundant variables implicitly get weighted more. Consider the following example. Say we were planning to segment our CRM database. Our boss might say, "be sure to include all 5 variables that measure recency," those questions being: "How recently has this customer purchased from us," where the 5 variables capture "within the last week," "month," "quarter," "6 months," or "year." In addition to these variables, say the boss wants us to include the variable that captures annual sales to that same customer, what direct marketers call "monetary value." We would be inputting 6 variables, where 5 measure something really similar—granted, they won't be perfectly correlated, but the recency variable will be overly influential compared to the monetary value variable simply because the latter is on its own.

Luckily, the fix is easy. Before contemplating the cluster analysis, most marketing analysts run a factor analysis to look for those redundancies. We'll see factor analysis in detail in Chapter 4, but for the moment, we can note that in a way, cluster analysis and factor analysis are analogous—in cluster analysis, we're looking for similar groups of customers to form segments, whereas in factor analysis, we'll look for groups of highly correlated variables that co-vary together as if they were driven by a single factor. For example, if the 5 recency variables captured the same information, they would all reflect one factor. We could then go forward with an aggregate of the 5 (e.g., their average or some other index), or one of the 5 variables that we believe is most representative, and then the monetary value variable would have a better chance of having an equal footing in influencing the clusters found.

Measures of Similarity

Once we have determined the variables that will form the basis of the segmentation, the first thing the computer does is to compute some measure of similarity among all the customers. A natural measure is a correlation coefficient.

Correlations range from +1 (2 customers have identical patterns) to –1 (2 customers have the exact opposite patterns). Very roughly speaking, a cluster analysis begins by looking for the customers who are highly correlated (e.g., 1.0 and 0.9). The model puts those customers together into a group to reflect their similarity. In the next iterations, the clustering algorithm brings in customers whose data were a little less similar (e.g., correlations of 0.8s and 0.7s, etc.), and so on (more details shortly).

Correlations are often fine, and they're very frequently used, in part because many people understand them. Yet while correlations reflect relative patterns, they don't reflect mean differences. Recall the calculation: $r_{xy} = [\sum (x_i - \bar{x})(y_i - \bar{y})]/(S_x S_y n)$. Check out the numerator—we literally get rid of information about the means (for that matter, we also divide out information about the scale).

In Figure 2.3, we zoom in on the purchase data of the 5 customers in Figure 2.2. Customer 1057 is a guy who bought 3 spy novels in the last quarter, 2 business books, and 1 do-it-yourself guide. Customer 0143 has the same tastes, but he bought twice as many of each. The correlation between these two customers is a perfect 1.0 because the correlation is sensitive to the pattern of which categories of books were bought (which is the same), but not the quantities they

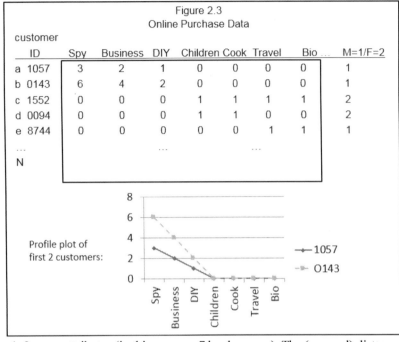

Figure 2.3
Online Purchase Data

customer

ID	Spy	Business	DIY	Children	Cook	Travel	Bio	...	M=1/F=2
a 1057	3	2	1	0	0	0	0		1
b 0143	6	4	2	0	0	0	0		1
c 1552	0	0	0	1	1	1	1		2
d 0094	0	0	0	1	1	0	0		2
e 8744	0	0	0	0	0	1	1		1
...			...			...			
N									

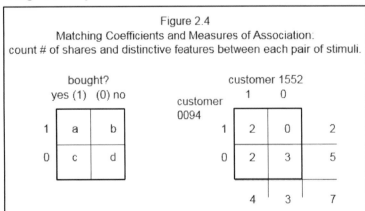

Profile plot of first 2 customers: — 1057, — 0143

purchased (which are different). Both profiles peak upward on spy novels and business books (they co-vary), yet profile 1057 is higher than the other.

For some purposes, the patterns are the most important information, such as if we were segmenting consumers by what kinds of books they read, so that we could send them the appropriate direct mailing literature. For other purposes, volume differences between customers matter (e.g., how many books of each type had been bought), such as segmenting by "low" vs. "high" frequency or monetary value.

When volume matters, we don't want to subtract out the means (as is done in the correlation coefficient). Instead, we'd compute a (Euclidean) distance between each pair of customers. For customers a and b, we'd measure how close or far apart they are on each of k = 1, 2, …, r attributes (in this case, r = 7 book genres). The (squared) distance is computed: $d_{ab}^2 = \sum_{k=1}^{r}(x_{ak} - x_{bk})^2$, and it captures the elevation information (means) as well as the (relative) pattern information in calculating the similarities and differences between the two customers' purchases.

In terms of the correlations, customers 1 and 2 had the highest (r = 1.0), customer 3 was correlated with customer 4 (r = .55) and also with customer 5 (r = .55), and the smallest correlations were between customers 1 and 3 (r = -.88) and 2 and 3 (r = -.88). By comparison, in terms of distances, customers 4 and 5 were each most similar to 3 (d = 1.41), customers 1 and 2 were next closest to each other (d = 3.74), and the distance or difference between customers 2 and 3 was the greatest (d = 7.75). Notice that the ordering of pairs of customers, in terms of who is similar to whom, changes depending on whether the r or d is calculated. Thus, as always, be thoughtful modelers, not just number crunchers.

There's one last wrinkle. Suppose these purchase data come from Amazon, a shop that offers a zillions SKUs. Imagine their spreadsheet—it has millions of customers as rows and the zillion SKUs as columns. When we compute a correlation or distance, we zoom in on a pair of customer rows, and there is no customer who buys everything at Amazon. Even a customer who has bought 1000 spy novels will simply have a zillion minus 1000 or so zeros in their row. If we included all SKUs when computing r or d, most customers would be computed to be very similar, because the numerous "did not buy"s would overwhelm the "did buy"s.

It's ok: geeks to the rescue. Figure 2.4 shows a 2×2 matrix cross-classifying the purchases of customer 0094 (the rows) and 1552 (the columns). The table entries are counts of the number of shared and distinctive purchases, where "1" labels the "did buy" and "0" labels the "did not buy." Note the cell labels, a, b, c, and d, in the matrix to the left. A measure of similarity called the "simple matching coefficient" compares the diagonal numbers to the total: $S_{MC} = (a + d)/(a + b + c + d)$. For

Figure 2.4
Matching Coefficients and Measures of Association:
count # of shares and distinctive features between each pair of stimuli.

bought?
yes (1)   (0) no

	1	0
1	a	b
0	c	d

customer 1552

customer 0094

	1	0	
1	2	0	2
0	2	3	5
	4	3	7

these data, $S_{MC} = 5/7 = 0.714$. The range on S_{MC} is 0.0 (there are no common purchases) to 1.0 (the purchases were identical), so this S_{MC} is fairly strong.

Suppose we had also included 10 more categories of SKUs—other genres of books, or altogether different products—and say neither of these customers bought anything in any of the 10 new categories. Then cell d becomes 13 rather than 3. Then $S_{MC} = 15/17 = 0.882$, even higher than the 0.714. Yet, we can sense that the increase is spurious, an artifact of including many zero cells. There is a "fix"—we compute the "Jaccard Coefficient," which is like S_{MC} but it ignores the d cell in both the numerator and denominator. Thus, any SKUs that appear in neither customer's shopping histories do not influence the measure. The coefficient is: $J = a / (a + b + c) = 2/4 = 0.50$ (whether we include the last 10 categories or not). Thus, while S_{MC} is dependent on a good selection of attributes, J is a bit less so (which is a good thing).

In practice, you'll see correlations used the most, then distances. That proportion probably ought to be switched, but it's a tough battle to fight, given that people are more likely to understand correlations than distances. If a matching coefficient is desired, it's better to use J than S_{MC}.

Clustering Algorithms

Once we have some measure of similarities (e.g., r is higher for more similar pairs) or differences (e.g., d is higher for more different pairs), we are ready to use cluster analysis. There are many clustering algorithms. We'll look at the most popular ones, so that you will know what people are talking about 99% of the time. One class of algorithms produce "hierarchical" clusters, which means that once two customers are put into the same segment, they are always together. That is, the clusters formed at one stage in the model are carried forward, so if A and B are put into a cluster, then in subsequent stages, others might join the A-B cluster, but A and B would never be broken into separate clusters. For example, if C joins, then the A-B cluster gets subsumed into or nested within the A-B-C.

Other algorithms are not constrained by this quality—if we ask for 5 segments, then customers A and B might be in the same segment, but if we ask for 6 or 4 segments, they might be in separate segments. Hierarchical clustering models tend to be more frequently used because computationally they're faster, but we'll look at examples of both kinds.

Hierarchical Clustering Models

Hierarchical clustering techniques may also be further categorized by whether they are agglomerative or divisive. In agglomerative techniques, every customer starts in his or her own segment, and with each iteration, the model puts together customers who are similar, either by forming a new cluster with two similar customers, or by adding a customer to an already existing cluster because he or she seems to be like the customers in that segment. The formation of clusters, or blending customers into clusters, or clusters into other clusters, continues until the very end, when all customers are in the same segment.

Divisive techniques go in the other direction—all customers begin in one segment, and each iteration breaks off the customer, customers, or cluster segment that is the most different and should probably be in its own group. Here too, this breaking off continues over many iterations, until the end when everyone is in his or her own cluster.

Which way you go doesn't really matter. Also, note that the extremes in either approach—everyone in the same cluster or everyone in a separate cluster—are referred to as "trivial" solutions, and as the term implies, those results are uninteresting and not helpful. We wouldn't be conducting a segmentation study if we really believed everyone was the same (one segment), and even if "one-to-one" marketing were ideal, the truth is, companies need some scales of economy and cannot operate efficiently if every customer is in a separate segment.

So, for all the talk of "finding groups," how does cluster analysis do it? Recall Figure 2.1. A very small subset of data are plotted here, only 7 customers from a sample of 2000 people who filled out a survey about their car preferences. The survey had 15 questions on it, but this scatter plot uses only the 1st and 2nd items, to keep things easy visually. If we were to try to identify clusters by just eyeballing these data, we might agree that customers {1, 2, 7} look like a cluster. Customers {4, 5, 6} aren't quite as tight as the first three, but they look like another cluster.

The question that remains is what to do with customer 3. We have three options: 1) put 3 with {1, 2, 7} because they all like good gas mileage; 2) put 3 with {4, 5, 6} because they all like fast cars; or 3) leave customer 3 all alone, in a third cluster. It is possible that customer 3 represents a segment distinct from the other two—someone who wants both speed and good gas mileage.

Single-link clustering is the name of the model or algorithm that puts a customer into a segment if he or she is similar enough to at least one member in the existing cluster. In this example, look for the customer in each cluster who is closest to 3—in the cluster {1, 2, 7}, that customer is 2. In the cluster {4, 5, 6}, the customer is 4. The algorithm chooses to put customer 3 into the cluster {1, 2, 7} if customer 3 is closer to 2 than 4, or into the cluster {4, 5, 6} if 3 is closer to 4 than 2. Customer 3 has to have something in common with customer 2 or 4, but 3 might not be very similar to customers 1, 7, 5, or 6. Single-link gets its name because only a single link from within the whole cluster needs to be similar or close to the customer potentially being added (for this reason, the technique is also sometimes referred to as "nearest neighbor analysis," but "nna" is a vague term that is imprecisely used to refer to other models and techniques as well, so we will not use it—we aim to be precise).

Complete-link clustering uses the opposite criterion. In this approach, customer 3 joins a cluster only if he or she is similar to all the other members; i.e., the customer is completely linked to (or similar to, or close to) all the members in the group. Another way to think about this criterion is that we begin by looking into each cluster for the customer who is farthest from, or most different from, customer 3. In cluster {1, 2, 7}, that is customer 7; in cluster {4, 5, 6}, it's customer 6. Now the question is whether customer 3 is closer to 7 or 6—if 7, then 3 joins {1, 2, 7}; if 6, then 3 joins {4, 5, 6}. If the customer is closer to 7, presumably the whole cluster is closer, because 7 was the farthest away (or most different).

Average-link clustering looks not at the minimum distance (or maximum similarity) like single-link, nor at the maximum distance (or minimal similarity) like complete-link, but as its name implies, it looks at averages. Specifically, take customers 1, 2, 7, find their means on X_1 and X_2, and plot that point. That point is referred to as the cluster centroid— where centroid is a just a fancy term for a multivariate mean, or a mean along more than one dimension. After the means are computed, customer 3 joins whichever cluster is closer—the averages on X_1 and X_2 for {1, 2, 7} or the means on X_1 and X_2 for {4, 5, 6}. Figure 2.5 depicts the conceptual distinction between single-link, complete-link, and average-link clustering regarding the similarity thresholds in cluster formation.

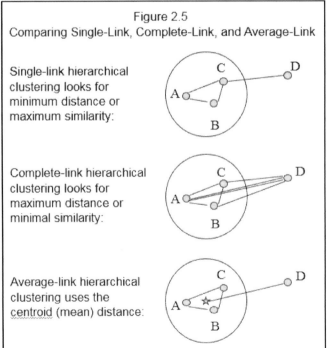

Figure 2.5
Comparing Single-Link, Complete-Link, and Average-Link

Single-link hierarchical clustering looks for minimum distance or maximum similarity:

Complete-link hierarchical clustering looks for maximum distance or minimal similarity:

Average-link hierarchical clustering uses the centroid (mean) distance:

As an example to compare these techniques, let's walk through an example to see what the computer is doing when it's crunching our data. Figure 2.6 contains a matrix of co-ownership data. Such data arise in a number of ways, for example, it's not unusual for marketers to read scanner data looking for items that people tend to buy together (e.g., chips and dip, cookies and ice cream, sunscreen and bug spray, etc.). In this case, imagine taking a large consumer sample and asking respondents to list the vehicles their family owns. The index f_{ij} would be the number of households that owned a car of type i (the row) as well as a car of type j (the column).

Some of these classes of vehicles are more popular than others, and we don't want that to bias the results. For example, if 100 households owned both a sedan and SUV, that wouldn't be terribly impressive because there are a zillion sedans and SUVs, so it wouldn't be that unusual to see them coincide. It would be more impressive if we found 100 households that owned a hybrid and convertible, since each is rarer. Thus, to correct for the differences in market shares, we divided the frequency, f_{ij}, by the row and column sums, f_i and f_j respectively. The data in Figure 2.6 are the adjusted co-ownerships, c_{ij}, of vehicles i and j: $c_{ij} = f_{ij} / (f_i + f_j)$.

Figure 2.6

What's in Your Garage? Household Vehicle Co-Ownership:
Proportion of Households Owning Vehicles
of Both the Row i and Column j Types

	Sports car	Sedan & coupe	Hybrid	Luxury vehicle	Pickup truck	4WD / AWD	Convertible	SUV	Single-link: Use Max Sim
Sports car	-	.108	.010	.019	.014	.005	.007	.037	.108
Sedan & coupe	.108	-	.030	.144	.075	.043	.017	.110	
Hybrid	.010	.030	-	.033	.007	.003	.005	.049	.033
Luxury vehicle	.019	.144	.033	-	.030	.053	.022	.051	
Pickup truck	.014	.075	.007	.030	-	.033	.031	.020	.075
4WD/AWD	.005	.043	.003	.053	.033	-	.021	.019	.053
Convertible	.007	.017	.005	.022	.031	.021	-	.012	.022
SUV	.037	.110	.049	.051	.020	.019	.012	-	.110

The largest index in Figure 2.6 is the 0.144 between luxury vehicles and sedans and coupes. Note that these data do not convey similarities per se—a high c_{ij} doesn't mean that a luxury vehicle is similar to a sedan. But the numbers are similarity-like in that larger numbers mean the pairs of vehicles are more frequently co-owned and thus should be clustered together. And yes, that's the first iteration through the data. The algorithm sorts through the indices, identifies 0.144 as the most similar, and puts luxury vehicles and sedans together as the first cluster formation. Woohoo—we have a cluster!

Recall that this procedure is hierarchical, so going forward into subsequent iterations, luxury cars and sedans will always be in the same cluster. Furthermore, to go forward, the algorithm treats the two as a unit. To do so, the matrix needs to be updated. There are two rows and columns—one for luxury vehicles and one for sedans and coupes—that now need to be reconciled and simplified down to a single representation. In single-link clustering, we examine the two columns (or rows) for sedans and luxury cars and merge the columns (and rows) by taking the maximum similarity index (or the minimum dissimilarity index) as representing the pair. Co-occurrences are like similarities, so the maximum for each pair is listed in the column to the right in Figure 2.6.

Figure 2.7
Single-Link Updated Matrix: Round 2

	Sports car	Sedan & Luxury	Hybrid	Pickup truck	4WD / AWD	Convertible	SUV	Single-link: Use Max Sim
Sports car	-	.108	.010	.014	.005	.007	.037	.108
Sedan & Luxury	.108	-	.033	.075	.053	.022	.110	
Hybrid	.010	.033	-	.007	.003	.005	.049	.049
Pickup truck	.014	.075	.007	-	.033	.031	.020	.075
4WD/AWD	.005	.053	.003	.033	-	.021	.019	.053
Convertible	.007	.022	.005	.031	.021	-	.012	.022
SUV	.037	.110	.049	.020	.019	.012	-	

Figure 2.7 shows the updated matrix, in which sedans have merged with luxury cars. We begin the process again. The largest numeric value is the 0.110, between the cluster we just formed and SUVs, so the algorithm adds SUVs to the cluster. To update again, the pairs of data columns are compared, and the maximum similarities are noted in the column at the right.

Figure 2.8
Single-Link Updated Matrix: Round 3

	Sports car	Sedan & Luxury & SUV	Hybrid	Pickup truck	4WD / AWD	Convertible	Single-link: Use Max Sim
Sports car	-	.108	.010	.014	.005	.007	
Sedan & Luxury & SUV	.108	-	.049	.075	.053	.022	
Hybrid	.010	.049	-	.007	.003	.005	.049
Pickup truck	.014	.075	.007	-	.033	.031	.075
4WD/AWD	.005	.053	.003	.033	-	.012	.053
Convertible	.007	.022	.005	.031	.012	-	.022

Figures 2.8 through 2.11 continue this process until, in Figure 2.12, there is only one possible step remaining, and that is to add convertibles with what had become an ever-expanding cluster. Figure 2.13 represents the cluster analysis in a "dendrogram," a tree-like structure that shows the steps during which each car class combined with the others ("dendron" is Greek for tree). The numbers inserted at each step, 0.144, 0.110, etc. are called "fusion coefficients" and we shall discuss them shortly. We shall also comment on the form of this dendrogram, but that is easier to do when you have something for comparison.

Figure 2.9
Single-Link Updated Matrix: Round 4

	Sedan & Luxury & SUV & Sports car	Hybrid	Pickup truck	4WD / AWD	Convertible	Single-link: Use Max Sim
Sedan & Luxury & SUV & Sports car	-	.049	.075	.053	.022	
Hybrid	.049	-	.007	.003	.005	.049
Pickup truck	.075	.007	-	.033	.031	
4WD/AWD	.053	.003	.033	-	.012	.053
Convertible	.022	.005	.031	.012	-	.031

Figure 2.10
Single-Link Updated Matrix: Round 5

	Sedan & Luxury & SUV & Sports & Truck	Hybrid	4WD / AWD	Convertible	Single-link: Use Max Sim
Sedan & Luxury & SUV &Sports &Truck	-	.049	.053	.031	
Hybrid	.049	-	.003	.005	.049
4WD/AWD	.053	.003	-	.012	
Convertible	.031	.005	.012	-	.031

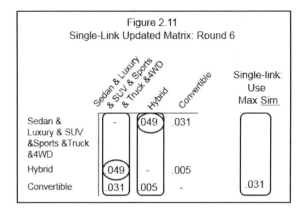

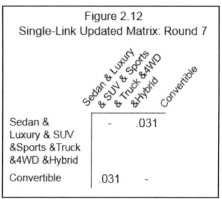

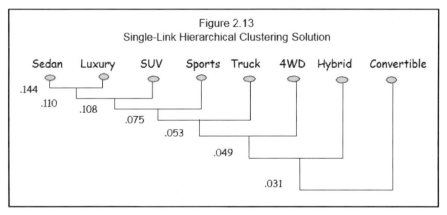

In complete-link clustering, the algorithm begins the same way—with the data in Figure 2.14 (which are the same as in Figure 2.6). We note that the 0.144 is the largest number, hence sedans and luxury cars comprise the first cluster for the complete-link approach as well. The difference in the algorithm comes next in how the matrices are updated. In complete-link, we take the minimum similarity (or maximum dissimilarity) index to represent the pair. Refer to the conceptual illustrations in Figure 2.5—in single-link, whether an object will join a cluster is determined by the most similar item, and in complete-link, an object joins a cluster as a function of the most different (least similar) item. These concepts are translated into the matrix updates by taking the maximum similarity for single-link, and the minimum similarity for complete-link.

In Figure 2.14, note that the numbers in the right column are different from those in Figure 2.6, and hence the updated matrix in Figure 2.15 is not quite the same as the matrix in Figure 2.7. Figures 2.16 and 2.17 proceed with the same logic, but watch the difference in the solution unfold. In the next step, at the top of Figure 2.16, we don't just add another vehicle to the growing cluster—we form a brand new cluster—woohoo, things are getting exciting now! Trucks combine with 4-wheel drives (4WDs), which kind of makes sense—tough cars? Then hybrids join sedans, and the algorithm continues until, in Figure 2.18, there is a dendrogram that looks rather different from that in Figure 2.13. Let's finish off with average-link and then we'll compare the solutions.

Figure 2.15
Complete-Link Updated Matrix: Round 2

	Sports car	Sedan & Luxury	Hybrid	Pickup truck	4WD / AWD	Convertible	SUV	Complete-link: Use Min Sim
Sports car	-	.019	.010	.014	.005	.007	.037	.019
Sedan & Luxury	.019	-	.030	.030	.043	.017	.051	
Hybrid	.010	.030	-	.007	.003	.005	.049	.030
Pickup truck	.014	.030	.007	-	.033	.031	.020	.020
4WD/AWD	.005	.043	.003	.033	-	.021	.019	.019
Convertible	.007	.017	.005	.031	.021	-	.012	.012
SUV	.037	.051	.049	.020	.019	.012	-	

Figure 2.16
Complete-Link Updated Matrix: Rounds 3 and 4

	Sports car	Sedan & Luxury & SUV	Hybrid	Truck	4WD	Convertible
Sports car	-					
Sedan & Luxury & SUV	.019	-				
Hybrid	.010	.030	-			
Pickup truck	.014	.020	.007			
4WD/AWD	.005	.019	.003	.033	-	
Convertible	.007	.012	.005	.031	.021	-

	Sports car	Sedan &Luxury &SUV	Hybrid	Truck,4WD	Convertible
Sports car	-				
Sedan & Luxury & SUV	.019	-			
Hybrid	.010	.030	-		
Pickup truck & 4WD	.005	.019	.003	-	
Convertible	.007	.017	.005	.021	-

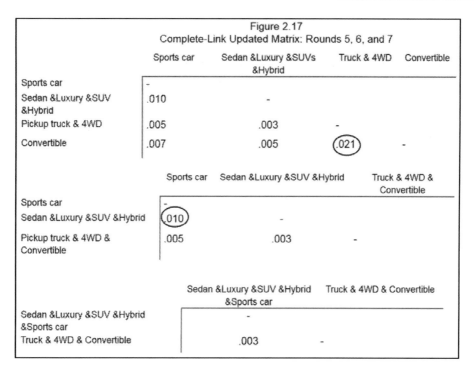

Figure 2.17
Complete-Link Updated Matrix: Rounds 5, 6, and 7

	Sports car	Sedan &Luxury &SUVs &Hybrid	Truck & 4WD	Convertible
Sports car	-			
Sedan &Luxury &SUV &Hybrid	.010	-		
Pickup truck & 4WD	.005	.003	-	
Convertible	.007	.005	(.021)	-

	Sports car	Sedan &Luxury &SUV &Hybrid	Truck & 4WD & Convertible
Sports car	-		
Sedan &Luxury &SUV &Hybrid	(.010)	-	
Pickup truck & 4WD & Convertible	.005	.003	-

	Sedan &Luxury &SUV &Hybrid &Sports car	Truck & 4WD & Convertible
Sedan &Luxury &SUV &Hybrid &Sports car	-	
Truck & 4WD & Convertible	.003	-

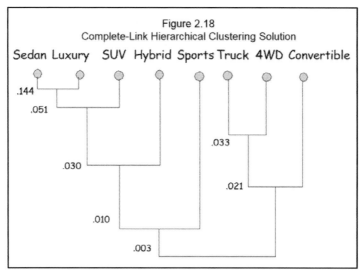

Figure 2.18
Complete-Link Hierarchical Clustering Solution

Average-link begins by comparing sedans and luxury vehicles, and the updating is done by simple averages—not maximum this or minimum that, but just take the two previous indices, average them, and continue. Figures 2.19, 2.20, and 2.21 show the iterations toward the solution depicted in Figure 2.22.

Figure 2.19
Average-Link Updated Matrix: Rounds 1 and 2

	Sports	Sedan &Luxury	Hybrid	Truck	4WD	Convertible	SUV
Sports car	-						
Sedan & Luxury	.0635	-					
Hybrid	.010	.0315	-				
Pickup truck	.014	.0525	.007	-			
4WD/AWD	.005	.048	.003	.033	-		
Convertible	.007	.0195	.005	.031	.021	-	
SUV	.037	.0805	.049	.020	.019	.021	-

	Sports	Sedan &Luxury &SUV	Hybrid	Truck	4WD	Convertible
Sports car	-					
Sedan &Luxury &SUV	.0502	-				
Hybrid	.010	.0402	-			
Pickup truck	.014	.0362	.007	-		
4WD/AWD	.005	.0335	.003	.033	-	
Convertible	.007	.0158	.005	.031	.021	-

Figure 2.20
Average-Link Updated Matrix: Rounds 3 and 4

	Sedan &Luxury &SUV &Sports	Hybrid	Truck	4WD	Convertible
Sedan &Luxury &SUV &Sports	-				
Hybrid	.0251	-			
Pickup truck	.0251	.007	-		
4WD/AWD	.0192	.003	.033	-	
Convertible	.0114	.005	.031	.021	-

	Sedan &Luxury &SUV &Sports	Hybrid	Truck &4WD	Convertible
Sedan &Luxury &SUV &Sports	-			
Hybrid	.0251	-		
Pickup truck &4WD	.0222	.005	-	
Convertible	.0114	.005	.026	-

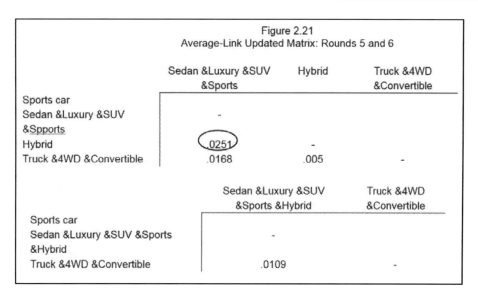

Figure 2.21
Average-Link Updated Matrix: Rounds 5 and 6

	Sedan &Luxury &SUV &Sports	Hybrid	Truck &4WD &Convertible
Sports car Sedan &Luxury &SUV &Spports	-		
Hybrid	.0251	-	
Truck &4WD &Convertible	.0168	.005	-

	Sedan &Luxury &SUV &Sports &Hybrid	Truck &4WD &Convertible
Sports car Sedan &Luxury &SUV &Sports &Hybrid	-	
Truck &4WD &Convertible	.0109	-

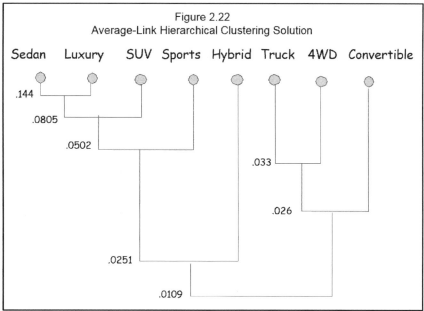

Figure 2.22
Average-Link Hierarchical Clustering Solution

Obviously in the future, we'll have the computer do these cluster analyses, and we will see only the final solutions. But it is easy to simulate the iterations, and doing so helps give a sense of the data and the model. To look at a dendrogram like that in Figure 2.22, begin by covering most of the figure with a piece of paper so that only the labels at the top and their initial dots are showing. Then move the paper slowly down so that each linking or clustering is revealed, step-by-step, just as the cluster analysis created them, iteration by iteration. (There! You've just played "computer," a game of artificial intelligence!)

For example, in the average-link solution just derived and presented in Figure 2.22, we see that sedans and luxury cars are frequently co-owned. If we stopped at this point, we would have 7 clusters, sedan and luxury cars together, and each of the remaining vehicles representing distinct segments. That result is not very parsimonious. To continue, move the paper down to reveal the next iteration, which adds SUVs to the existing cluster, and so on.

The solution at any stage is referred to as a partition. We can write these solutions in set theory notation given that each entity belongs to one cluster or set. Thus, the second iteration (where we just paused) is written: {sedan, luxury, SUV}, {sports}, {hybrid}, {truck}, {4WD}, {convertible}. Skip ahead to the 5th step, during which convertibles are added to the truck segment, and the partition is written: {sedan, luxury, SUV, sports}, {hybrid}, {truck, 4WD, convertible}.

Now the only remaining question is which partition is most useful to us, or, "What's the right number of clusters?" We can dismiss the beginning point (8 clusters) and end point (1 cluster) as trivial solutions, and perhaps by the same logic, any number close to these (7 or 2). Still, aiming for a solution "in the middle" gives us a lot of wiggle room. We'll address this question more systematically in a moment, but looking at Figure 2.22, it would appear that there are either 2 or 3 clusters—that on the left (sedans et al.) and that on the right (trucks et al.), and the question is whether hybrids belong to the first cluster or should they represent a distinct segment, a car that is unique and infrequently co-owned with anything. This case is interesting because a marketing manager could imagine arguing it either way. It may well make sense to go forward playing with both solutions (hybrids in and out of the first cluster), and make the choice later once we see which makes more sense in subsequent analyses.

Let's back up a moment and examine the complete-link solution in Figure 2.18 and the single-link result in Figure 2.13. Complete-link looks a bit like average-link, a fairly typical result. Yet, there are differences—hybrids are clustered into the sedan group, and we have to decide whether or not to include the class of sports cars in the cluster. The {truck, 4WD, convertible} cluster seems robust, appearing pretty cleanly in both solutions. Figure 2.13 is altogether different in structure. This solution illustrates "chaining," a typical result of single-link. Sometimes you'll see chaining drawn as one member (e.g., car) connected to another connected to another, etc., e.g., X-Y-Z. Other times, chaining is represented as concentric circles—the first circle encloses the sedans and luxury vehicles, then a larger circle brings in the SUVs, etc. Regardless of the depiction, chaining is a characteristic that renders the single-link technique not greatly useful—the conclusions would typically be, "some number of customers, 2, 3, 10, depending on where you stop, are in 1 cluster, and everyone else is in his/her own cluster." By comparison, complete-link or average-link yield tighter clusters. The more compact clusters of complete-link and average-link are much more useful for segmentation, so they are used more frequently.

Ward's method is a hierarchical clustering technique that proceeds very differently from single-, complete-, and average-link.[6] It operationalizes the intuition that if segments or clusters are indeed groups of similar customers, then the variability within a group should be smaller than the variability across the groups. The technique is often called "Ward's method of minimum variance," implying its objective of seeking to assign customers to segments so as to minimize the variance within clusters.

The next question is, "How do we know when minimum variance is achieved?" We'll measure the extent to which this goal is met by using an R^2 index like in regression. In a standard regression, R^2 is a measure of fit that tells us the amount of the total variance that is explained by the regression model in proportion to the total variance. An equivalent way of saying that maximum variance is explained is to say that error variability is minimized.

In Ward's method, the index is defined as: $R^2 = (SS_{total} - SS_{error}) / SS_{total}$. The total sum of squares measures how close every customer is to the overall means on all the variables used in the analyses. Say the clustering is proceeding on p = 5 variables whose means are 3, 5, 14, 650, and 1200. To compute SS_{total}, we take each respondent i regardless of what cluster they're in, and calculate the difference between that person's score on each of the 5 variables and the means on each of those variables: $\sum_{i=1}^{N} \sum_{j=1}^{p} (x_{ij} - \bar{x}_j)^2$. The value x_{ij} in the dataset represents customer i (i = 1, 2, ..., N = sample size) on variable j (j = 1, 2, ..., p = number of variables in analysis, here p = 5). The $\bar{x}_j$'s are the means (3, 5, 14, etc.) on the variables. The differences are squared and then summed (hence, "sum of squares").

The error sum of squares is computed by comparing each individual customer to the means of only the other observations in the customer's cluster (again on all p variables). The SS_{error} is small (relative to SS_{total}) when the individual customers are fairly close to their cluster means, implying that there is similarity within the cluster. $SS_{error} = \sum_{i=1}^{N} \sum_{j=1}^{p} \sum_{k=1}^{r} (x_{ijk} - \bar{x}_{jk})^2$. The term x_{ijk} refers to the ith customer on the jth variable located in the kth cluster. The term $\bar{x}_{jk}$ refers to the mean on the jth variable in the kth cluster.

Ward's method begins with each of the N sample units (e.g., each customer) in his or her own cluster. We begin with N different clusters, each of size 1. At this point, we calculate the beginning SS_{total}, and given that the number of clusters, r, is the same as the sample size N, then SS_{error} would equal SS_{total}, meaning that, at the moment we cannot do worse—we have maximum error, when we want minimum error.

---

[6] Because the technique is so different, now might be a good time for a cup of coffee... just sayin'.

We begin forming clusters. We'll form one cluster of size 2, and leave all the other customers in their own clusters (with cluster size 1). Thus, instead of N clusters, we'll have N − 1 of them. Let's say we begin by putting customers 1 and 2 together (with 3 through N in their own clusters). We compute R^2 again, and set it aside. We then try a different cluster solution; we put customers 1 and 3 together (with 2 and 4 through N in their own clusters), compute R^2, set it aside, etc. We go through the entire data set in this manner, to customers 1 and N, and then start again, combining customers 2 and 3, then 2 and 4, through 2 and N, and continue, all the way to combining customers N − 1 and N (with all others in clusters of size 1). At this point, we can see all options. The pair of sample units (e.g., customers) that yields the smallest error sum of squares, or equivalently, the largest R^2 value, forms the first cluster.

Next, we form N − 2 clusters. This next cluster might be a new cluster of size 2, or it might be that a customer joins the cluster of size 2 that we just formed. We'll use whatever combination yields the highest value of R^2.

At each step in the algorithm, the customers and clusters are combined when they minimize the error sum of squares or maximize the R^2 value. The algorithm keeps going and going, stopping when all sample units are combined into a single large cluster of size N.

If that was a little abstract, check out Figures 2.23 to 2.25. In Figure 2.23, we see 4 customers and the number of movies, DVDs, and plays that each has seen over the past year. The SS_{total} is computed at the right: each data point 6, 31, 2 in the 1st row, 4, 29, 1 in the 2nd, etc. is compared to its respective column mean—5, 33.25, 1.5. The differences are squared, then summed. The number $SS_{total} = 47.750$ doesn't have any inherent meaning as large or small—the question is how large is SS_{error} relative to SS_{total}. We haven't seen SS_{error} yet, so we proceed to Figure 2.24.

Figure 2.23
Entertainment Data: Preparation for Ward's Method

Customer	Movies	DVDs	Plays	Computing Sum of Squares (SS)
A	6	31	2	$(6-5.00)^2 + (31-33.25)^2 + (2-1.50)^2 =$ 6.313
B	4	29	1	$(4-5.00)^2 + (29-33.25)^2 + (1-1.50)^2 =$ 19.313
C	5	36	1	$(5-5.00)^2 + (36-33.25)^2 + (1-1.50)^2 =$ 7.813
D	5	37	2	$(5-5.00)^2 + (37-33.25)^2 + (2-1.50)^2 =$ 14.313
Means:	5.00	33.25	1.50	$SS_{Total} = 47.750$

In Figure 2.24, all possible cluster solutions in the first round are listed in the first column: we could put A &B together and leave C and D separate, all the way to the bottom where we could put C&D together and leave A and B on their own. For each, the means for movies, DVDs, and plays are updated, and the error sum of squares is listed for that particular cluster solution. To compute SS_{error}, we again sum over all variables and all individuals. We compare each individual's data on each variable to the cluster mean for that variable (if a customer is in his or her own cluster, then the cluster mean equals his or her own data point on that variable, so the difference is 0).

Figure 2.24
Ward's Method: 1st Iteration

Possible Cluster	means for	Movies	DVD	Plays	Error SS	R^2
{A&B} {C} {D}	A&B	5.0	30.0	1.5	4.50	0.906
{A&C} {B} {D}	A&C	5.5	33.5	1.5	13.50	0.717
{A&D} {B} {C}	A&D	5.5	34.0	2.0	18.50	0.613
{B&C} {A} {D}	B&C	4.5	32.5	1.0	25.00	0.476
{B&D} {A} {C}	B&D	4.5	33.0	1.5	33.00	0.309
{C&D} {A} {B}	C&D	5.0	36.5	1.5	1.00	0.979 ←min error, max R^2

When the SS_{error} is small, it tells us that the data are close to their cluster means, implying that we have a cluster of similar units, and that's when R^2 is maximized ($R^2 = (SS_{total} - SS_{error})/SS_{total}$). In Figure 2.24, we can see that SS_{error} is minimized, or R^2 maximized, when the first cluster to form is C&D, leaving A and B on their own.

Figure 2.25 shows all possible cluster solutions and their fits for the next iteration. Customers C&D are treated together, and the cluster possibilities include only whether A joins, or B joins, or A&B go together (but separately from C&D). The means for the variables (movies, DVDs, plays) are updated, and then the SS_{error} and R^2 are similarly recomputed. This second iteration tells us that it is optimal to form a second cluster, such that we have A&B in one, and C&D in another. The final iteration would combine the two clusters, if we wished to do so.

Figure 2.25
Ward's Method: 2nd Iteration

Possible Cluster	means for	Movies	DVD	Plays	Error SS	R^2	
{C&D&A} {B}	C&D&A	5.33	34.67	1.67	22.00	0.539	
{C&D&B} {A}	C&D&B	4.67	34.00	1.33	39.33	0.176	
{C&D} {A&B}	A&B	5.00	30.00	1.50	5.50	0.885	← min error, max R^2

In these data, C&D came together because of their similarity—their highest numbers on DVDs and middle numbers on movies. Plays had little effect in the computations, because the numbers showed so little variability. We cannot control the variability among customers, but we could normalize all the variables (i.e., create z_{movies}, z_{dvds}, and z_{plays}) before clustering them (though note that doing so implies new assumptions).

While Ward's method optimizes a different objective function, it is still hierarchical like single-, complete-, or average-link. Specifically, once two or more units are joined into a cluster, they remain together to the end of the modeling.

In tests of Ward's method, it has been noted that it tends to find or create clusters of relatively equal sizes. That quality may have some appeal in application to segments. It would be as popular and frequently used as complete-link and average-link methods except when analyzing big data because Ward's method requires large numbers of combinations to be computed in early iterations.

k-Means Clustering

An altogether different approach to putting customers (units) into segments (clusters) is a technique called k-means clustering, an iterative procedure that is not hierarchical. Instead, it's referred to as a "partitioning" technique.

Recall that a partition is simply the description of which customers belong in which cluster, for as many clusters as deemed appropriate. Each of the previously considered hierarchical approaches yielded a new partition at each iteration, but they are contained in a nested structure:

- For example, in a data set of 5 customers, we denote the beginning clusters, wherein all customers are in segments of size 1 as: {1},{2},{3},{4},{5}.
- Next, say in round 1, if a cluster formed that combined customers 1 and 2 to be a set {1,2}, then the partition would be denoted: {1,2},{3},{4},{5}.
- In round 2, say customer 3 joined that cluster, then the partition would be: {1,2,3},{4},{5}.
- In round 3, say customers 4 and 5 combined, then we'd have the partition: {1,2,3},{4,5}.
- In the final round, these 2 clusters would combine: {1,2,3,4,5}.

Each step of the hierarchical procedures results in a partition for that iteration.

In k-means, we don't get all the partitions from N clusters to 1 cluster. Rather, we tell the model, "I want there to be 3 clusters,"; then the model sets $k = 3$ and proceeds. If we also wish to examine the partition of customers into clusters for 4 or 5 or 20 segments, we run additional models, in which we specify k to be 4, then 5, then 20. Each k-means solution starts over, so there is no reason to expect any hierarchical quality; the 4 clusters when $k = 4$ might not be 4 of the 5 clusters when $k = 5$, for example.

Here's how k-means is done. We tell the computer that we want $k = 3$ clusters (or whatever we wish). The computer begins by randomly assigning each customer to 1 of 3 clusters (segments).

Once all N customers are in 1 and only 1 cluster of the k clusters, the centroids of each of the k clusters are computed. Remember a centroid is just a fancy name for the multivariate means, or the means on all the variables used as input to the cluster analysis. Thus, we'll get the means on variable 1, 2, 3, ..., p (say 5), for each cluster. For $k = 3$ clusters and $p = 5$ variables, there would be $k \times p$ or 15 means computed.

Next, compute the distance between each customer and the centroid of all 3 clusters. If customer 1 is currently assigned to cluster 1, and he or she is closest to the cluster 1 means, then the customer stays in cluster 1. However, if the distance between customer 1 and the centroid of cluster 3 (say) is less, then we reassign customer 1 to belong more sensibly in cluster 3. Note we are employing the objective of putting customers (units) into the segments (clusters) to enhance similarity (closeness).

The k-mean iterations continue, with new cluster membership assignments, compute new centroids as well as distances between customers and centroids. Iterations cease when there are no more new optimal reassignments to be made—all customers are in the segment whose data most closely resembles their own.

In Figures 2.26 to 2.28 we use the 4 customers and their entertainment data to illustrate k-means. We have a hypothesis (or guess) that the number of clusters or segments is 2, so we'll tell the computer, k = 2. Figure 2.26 shows a random number drawn on the 0–1 scale, and we (the computer) use the cut-off of .5, assigning customers with a random draw less than .5 to the 1st cluster, and customers with a random draw greater than .5 to the 2nd cluster.

Given that initial assignment, we compute the means on all p = 3 variables for the customers in the randomly assigned clusters. They appear at the top of Figure 2.27. The distance between each customer and both of the clusters is computed, e.g., for A, the distance to the cluster AD is 9.25 units, and the distance to the cluster BC is 5.50. Thus, A has not been optimally assigned, so we move A to the other cluster. We make these comparisons for all customers, and reassign them wherever necessary. In Figure 2.28, we have the new clusters, A&B and C&D, the new means, and the new distances, and we see that in every case, the customers are now in their appropriate clusters—where their data are closer to that cluster's means than the other cluster's means.

The idea behind any clustering model is to put customers (or any units) into clusters such that within a cluster, the units are similar to each other, and across clusters, the units in different clusters are different. This is known as minimizing the variability within clusters, and maximizing the variability between clusters.

Figure 2.26
k-Means Method: Starting Configuration

Customer	Random Number*	Assign to
A	0.884	cluster 2
B	0.292	cluster 1
C	0.376	cluster 1
D	0.639	cluster 2

*The rand() function in excel returns numbers on a uniform distribution 0≤ x <1.0.

Figure 2.27
k-Means Method: 1st Iteration

Means for		Movies	DVD	Plays
A&D	5.5	34.0	2.0	
B&C		4.5	32.5	1.0

Customer	and Cluster	Distance²	
A	A&D	9.25	
A	B&C	5.50	move A to join B&C
B	A&D	28.25	
B	B&C	12.50	keep B in B&C
C	A&D	5.25	
C	B&C	12.50	move C
D	A&D	9.25	
D	B&C	21.50	keep D

Figure 2.28
k-Means Method: 2nd Iteration

Means for	Movies	DVD	Plays
A&B	5.0	30.0	1.5
C&D	5.0	36.5	1.5

Customer	Cluster	Distance²	
A	A&B	2.25	
A	C&D	31.50	keep A
B	A&B	2.25	
B	C&D	57.50	keep B
C	A&B	36.25	
C	C&D	0.50	keep C
D	A&B	49.25	
D	C&D	0.50	keep D

Interpretation and Verification

Once clusters have been derived, we must make sense of them. Interpretation begins by examining the means on each variable we used, for each segment. Doing so provides a profile as to how the customer segments vary. We might find that segments 1 and 2 are high on variable X, compared with segment 3, and segments 2 and 3 are low on variable Y, compared with cluster 1. We then understand and can communicate to others that cluster 1 is "high X, high Y," cluster 2 is "high X, low Y," and cluster 3 is "low X, low Y," albeit with more imaginative labels (an occasion to which marketers always rise!).

Creating a table or plot of the 95% confidence intervals for all k segments by all p variables tells us immediately which of the differences that appear visually distinct are truly statistically significantly different. To be pure, we should correct the Type I error rate, from $\alpha = 0.05$ to $\alpha = 0.05/(k \times p)$. Statistically, a stronger alternative to the confidence intervals would be to run an analysis of variance (ANOVA), one for each input variable used as the dependent variable, and cluster membership of all the customers in the database as the predictor variable (see Chapter 8). It is quite probable that the input variables are correlated among themselves, and a procedure that would incorporate these properties would be a MANOVA (multivariate ANOVA; also Chapter 8).

The comparison of confidence intervals or the ANOVAs on the input variables helps determine which segment differences that appear to exist do indeed statistically exist. The next step of the best segmentation studies is to compare the segments on customer data that were not used to derive the clusters. For example, if the clusters were formed by examining similarities among patterns of SKU purchases, this next step of interpretation may involve demographics and media usage. The idea is that we have a feel for segment purchase behavior, and now we want to know who these people are (gender, income, geo) and how we can reach them (ESPN, *New Yorker*, cnn.com).

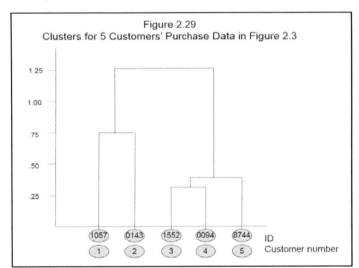

Figure 2.29
Clusters for 5 Customers' Purchase Data in Figure 2.3

For example, recall the book genre purchase data of Figure 2.3. Its dendrogram (from an average-link cluster analysis on correlations) is drawn in Figure 2.29. If we selected 2 clusters, customers 1&2, and customers 3–5, we'd find that these segments correlate fairly highly with gender ($r = 0.67$), with the men preferring the spy novels, business books, and DIY guides, and women buying the kids' books, cookbooks, travel books, and biographies.

Recommendation Agents and Collaborative Filtering

For marketers, cluster analysis is a "two-fer!" It is useful for finding segments, and it is also the model underlying online recommendation agents or "collaborative filtering." Recall the discussion regarding customers and a company's database of the SKUs they have purchased (e.g., Figure 2.2).

A recommendation agent clusters customers by their purchases to find groups who have bought similar sets of merchandise. From those sets, the algorithm can detect which of the SKUs some customers in that segment have purchased that other customers have not (segments are collections of similar customers, but almost never are they precisely identical). The agent then makes suggestions regarding the as-yet-unpurchased items.

Collaborative filtering is the same thing. It gets its name from the social medium element—other customers' data are used to formulate the recommendations. The filtering terminology is akin to saying a segment is likely to find SKUs of set X (say, mystery novels) of interest, but not SKUs of set Y (hip hop music downloads). Thus, the recommendations are filtered by priority—don't bother showing the Ys, just show the Xs. Filtering underlies the web links and articles presented to anyone who is online from their personal computers, i.e., those that store their histories and preferences in cookie files. Cluster analysis is the analytical tool that drives product recommendations at Amazon, movie recommendations at Netflix, and music recommendations at iTunes Genius or Pandora Radio.

Cluster analysis is also the analytical mechanism that underlies Match.com and similar dating sites. People seeking others will sign up and answer a lot of questions about themselves. Then the model makes recommendations about likely satisfactory matches. The system uses the self-report data, but it also knows which attributes people are likely to exaggerate, and it also attaches more statistical weight to what people do (e.g., what they click on to meet certain types of people) than what they say they'll do (e.g., people often claim they know their desired type of person, and that type isn't always consistent with the people they select to meet).

Summary

In marketing segmentation, we want to find groups of customers who are similar to each other on characteristics we care about, and we want the groups themselves to be different (otherwise, we'd combine the segments). Cluster analysis is perfectly suited to this goal, and you saw how easy it is.

There are many, many (many!) clustering models and algorithms available. The ones presented in this chapter are very frequently used and have good performance qualities. Other clustering methods have characteristics that are interesting and potentially quite useful, depending on one's needs. For example, in overlapping clusters, a customer might belong to more than one cluster at the same time. There also exist models based on fuzzy set theory that are essentially probabilistic; e.g., a customer belongs in cluster A with 75% probability and in cluster B with 25% probability. Finally, latent class models push that logic further—they work from known prevalence indices (e.g., market shares) and assign customers to different classes (e.g., representing different brand loyalties) with probabilities that are estimated and then inferentially tested.

Regarding cluster analysis, here are the issues to consider: 1) Be smart in your choice of variables. 2) There are many clustering models—k-means, Ward's, and complete-link and average-link are probably the most frequently used (you probably never want to use single-link). 3) It's very important to try to validate the interpretation of the clusters, ideally with data that weren't already used to derive the clusters.

Segmentation is important. Cluster analysis can find segments. Cluster analysis is easy.

Table 2.1: Helpful Tips for Cluster Analysis

What does cluster analysis do?

- □ Seeks groups of similar entities (of respondents like customers, or of stimuli like brands)—think about the variability within a cluster as being small relative to the differences between clusters.
- □ Clustering respondents is the best way to conduct a customer segmentation.
- □ Clustering often provides a view complementary to perceptual maps derived from multidimensional scaling.

What decisions need to be made?

- □ Which variables should be included in a segmentation study? Often only demographics are included, but attitudinal data (so-called psychographics) such as perceptions and preferences should also be included to help explain the data better and contribute to a deeper understanding of customer behavior.
- □ Choose one of these algorithms (and play with more than one): complete-link, average-link, k-means, or Ward's method. If you receive a white paper in which someone conducted a single-link clustering, bounce it back to them with a sneer.
- □ Use ANOVA to validate the cluster profile interpretations.

References

Cluster analysis texts:
- Aldenderfer, Mark S. and Roger K. Blashfield (1984), *Cluster Analysis*, Newbury Park, CA: Sage. (Great intro.)
- Hartigan, John (1975), *Clustering algorithms*, NY: Wiley. (Has fortran code for many clustering algorithms.)
- Sneath, Peter H. A. and Robert R. Sokal (1973), *Principles of Numerical Taxonomy*, San Francisco: Freeman. (Solid, examples are from biology.)

Determine number of clusters:
- Krolak-Schwerdt, Sabine and Thomas Eckes (1992), "A Graph Theoretic Criterion for Determining the Number of Clusters in a Data Set," *Multivariate Behavioral Research*, 27 (4), 541-565.
- Milligan, Glenn W. and Martha C. Cooper (1985), "An Examination of Procedures for Determining the Number of Clusters in a Data Set," *Psychometrika*, 50 (2), 159-179.
- Steinley, Douglas and Michael J. Brusco (2011), "Choosing the Number of Clusters in K-Means Clustering," *Psychological Methods*, 16 (3), 285-297.

Other clustering topics articles:
- Goodman, Leo A. and William H. Kruskal (1954), "Measures of Association for Cross Classification" *Journal of the American Statistical Association*, 49, 732-764. (Presents measures like correlations but for categorical data.)
- Hartigan, John A. and M. A. Wong (1979), "A K-Means Clustering Algorithm," *Applied Statistics*, 28, 100-108. (Source of k-means.)
- Hubert, Lawrence and Phipps Arabie (1985), "Comparing Partitions," *Journal of Classification,* 2, 193-218. (Compute an index showing similarity between two cluster solutions.)
- Johnson, Stephen C. (1967), "Hierarchical Clustering Schemes," *Psychometrika*, 32 (3), 241-254. ("Hierarchy" is defined, single-link & complete-link are introduced.)
- Lance, G. N. and W. T. Williams (1967), "A General Theory of Classificatory Sorting Strategies, I. Hierarchical Systems," *Computer Journal*, 9, 373-380. (Presents an equation for a family of clustering algorithms, subsuming single, complete, average, Ward's, etc.)
- Milligan, Glenn W. (1979), "Ultrametric Hierarchical Clustering Algorithms," *Psychometrika*, 44 (3), 343-346.
- Ward, Joe H., Jr. (1963), "Hierarchical Grouping to Optimize an Objective Function," *Journal of the American Statistical Association*, 58 (301, March), 236-244. (The Ward of Ward's method)

Related techniques:
- McCutcheon, Allan L. (1987), *Latent Class Analysis*, Newbury Park, CA: Sage.
- Smithson, Michael and Jay Verkuilen (2006), *Fuzzy Set Theory*, Thousand Oaks, CA: Sage.

Thumbnail sketch regarding software:
- SAS: for hierarchical methods, use proc cluster, specify method=average, create output outtree=outxx to use in proc tree; for k-means use proc fastclus. For help: support.sas.com/documentation/
- SPSS: go to analyze, classify, hierarchical cluster. Choose to cluster cases or variables, display statistics and plots. For help: search "IBM SPSS documentation," and open the "statistics base" manual.
- XLStat: for hierarchical methods, choose menu dropdown of agglomerative hierarchical, and use the defaults. For k-means, follow analyzing data, k-means, enter k (#clusters) in dialog box. For help: www.xlstat.com, click on "support" and then "tutorials."

Chapter 3: Brand Choice and Logit Models

Marketing Concept: Brand Choice, Brand Loyalty, Brand Switching, Scanner Data
Modeling Concept: Logit Models and Logistic Regressions

Chapter Outline
1. Introduction
2. Brand-switching Matrix
3. Chi-Square
   a. Standardized Residuals
   b. Log Linear Model Extension
4. Logit Models
   a. Odds Ratios
   b. Logit Example
   c. Logit Logic from a Different Angle
   d. Logistic Regressions
5. A Bit of Database Marketing and Direct Marketing and CRM and RFM

Introduction

Brand managers live and breathe their brand. They hope their customers will too, and some do, forming brand communities online or IRL, generating positive "buzz" as zealots, etc. At the least, brand managers are hoping for loyalty. The question is, "How should we define loyalty?" Definitions and measurements are often intertwined, so we might alternatively ask, "How should we measure loyalty?"

Consider the consumer packaged goods (CPGs) that we buy at grocery and drug stores. In any category—soft drinks, chips, gum, shampoo, pens—the brands a customer purchases over time may comprise a sequence such as: brand A at time 1, brand A at time 2, brand B at time 3, brand A at time 4, etc. In the same product category, another customer's purchases may be: A, B, C, B, D, A, D, and so forth. Comparing these sequences, most people would claim that the first customer exhibits greater brand loyalty.

Note that we don't expect that 100% of the purchases must be of one brand to characterize a series of purchases as relatively more loyal than another. Note too that we have no idea why the first sequence included the brand B—was B on sale? Was brand A out of stock? We also don't know if the first customer is passionate about brand A or simply finds A to be good enough and it's not a purchase the customer deems worthy of complex reconsideration. It's also no crime to work in a product category that lends itself to variety seeking, as exhibited by the second consumer—candy bars and vacation destinations are two such classes of purchases. The variance in the sequence might not mean the customers find a particular brand lacking; instead, perhaps customers don't want to do the same thing repeatedly.

Even with all these questions, it is obvious that the first customer's purchase pattern is different from the second customer's purchases. Marketing research firms used to ask panel samples of customers to keep diary records of the purchases they made. Now large marketing research firms such as Nielsen and IRI (Information Resources Inc.) have integrated the scanned purchase data from grocers and other vendors with complementary marketing information such as household media viewing, coupon redemption, grocer retailer promotions, etc. into what is called "single source data." The resulting longitudinal panel data have become an extremely important type of data for marketers to assess customer behavior.

To study brand loyalty, and its obverse phenomenon, brand switching, we'll take the sequences of brand purchases, and study them in a "Markov" (just a fancy Russian name for two steps) pair of sequences. For the first customer's data, A, A, B, A, we use a sliding window of 2 purchases to derive the pairs: (A,A), (A,B), (B,A). For the second consumer, the string A, B, C, B, D, A, D yields the pairs: (A,B), (B,C), (C,B), (B,D), (D,A), (A,D). Next, we'll aggregate over all households in our panel sample to create a brand-switching matrix.

Brand-switching Matrix

Figure 3.1 presents the brand-switching matrix for our data. The four brands comprise both the rows and the columns, the difference being that the rows denote the brands purchased last time, $t-1$, and the columns represent the brands purchased this time, t. For example, the pairs (A,B), (B,C), etc. are pairs of brands purchased at (time 1, time 2), (time 2, time 3). Thus, the (A,B) pair is counted among the 26 in the first row and second column. The (B,C) pair is one of the 42 data points in the second row and third column.

Figure 3.1
Brand-Switching Transition Matrix

		Brand purchased at time t				
		A	B	C	D	
Brand purchased at time t-1	A	119	26	20	19	184
	B	19	45	42	21	127
	C	13	41	45	18	117
	D	14	17	15	26	72
		165	129	122	84	500

For the purposes of modeling brand loyalty and switching, the times need only be recorded sequentially. Thus, time 1 for household 1 might be Monday morning, 9 a.m., time 2 might be 2 weeks later, Tuesday afternoon, time 3 might be the following evening, etc. Furthermore, the times for household 1 need not correspond to the times for household 2. (We would align the timing to look at whether a marketing campaign launched at some particular time had an impact on subsequent purchasing.)

How might you define loyalty in Figure 3.1? For most, the intuition is that the diagonal values contain this information—these are the A-A, B-B, etc. purchases, where what someone bought last time is the same as what they're buying this time.

This intuition is right, but the statistics are off just a bit. The numbers on the diagonal, 119, 45, etc., aren't a clean indicator of loyalty because they also reflect the differential market shares of the 4 brands. The right-hand margins are the brand shares at time $t-1$, and the bottom row contains the brand shares at time t. The row and column sums aren't identical, but both essentially say that A is the market leader, B and C are comparable, and brand D has the smallest share.

To understand the problem with the information being confounded, consider Brands B and C, both of which have 45 repeat purchasers. The 45 is more impressive on the smaller base of brand C's share than on B's somewhat larger share. So we need a technique to separate the effects of loyalty and brand share. We can view this switching matrix as a special kind of cross-tab, and apply the chi-square to it.

Chi-Square

Cross-tabulations, cross-tabs for short, are familiar as the collection of the frequencies with which the ith level of the row variable occurs in a sample with the jth level of the column variable. They're also known as transition matrices (or Markov matrices) when time is involved, as in Figure 3.1.

Cross-tabs are suited to categorical variables—those that are already nominal (e.g., gender, ethnicity, political party) or ordinal (e.g., ranking one's favorite brands), or those that are categorized versions of underlying continuous variables (e.g., high, medium, low income groups). The Pearson X^2 tests for an association between two categorical variables. If the variables were continuous (interval or ratio), we'd use a correlation coefficient to assess the relationship.

The notation for these cross-classifications will be $i = 1, 2, ..., I$ for the rows, and $j = 1, 2, ..., J$ for the columns. The particular table entry, o_{ij}, is the "observed" frequency in the ith row and j^{th} column. Cross-tabs are sometimes referred to as contingency tables because each cell value o_{ij} provides the number of observations in the sample with characteristic column $= j$, contingent upon row $= i$.

Row sums (or row margins) are denoted n_{i+} for row i (the $+$ represents the fact that we collapsed over, or summed over, the j columns). The column sums (or column margins) are denoted n_{+j}, and n_{++} denotes the grand total.

When we run a correlation on continuous variables and conclude "it's significant," that means we can reject the null hypothesis of no linear relationship. Analogously, the null hypothesis for the X^2 is that the row variable is independent of the column variable. Other expressions include "no association," "no interaction," "no contingency," or "no relationship." While this null is analogous to saying there is no correlation, strictly speaking, that phrase is not proper because we are not testing a correlation coefficient. The alternative hypothesis is that there is some kind of association present.

If the null is that the row variable is independent of the column variable, we'd expect the frequencies in the table to be distributed randomly, in proportion to the margins. If the null hypothesis were true, then knowing the brand that a customer bought last time would not help us predict, better than chance, what brand the customer would buy this time.

Recall from your basic stat course that if two events are independent, then the joint probability is simply the product of the two marginal probabilities: $p_{ij} = p_{i+} \times p_{+j}$. In words, the probability that a consumer is in cell (i,j) would be simply the probability of being in row i times the probability of being in column j. We estimate: $p_{i+} = n_{i+}/n_{++}$, that is the row proportion (the row sum over the grand sum), and $p_{+j} = n_{+j}/n_{++}$ to estimate p_{ij}:

$$p_{ij} = p_{i+}p_{+j} = \left(\frac{n_{i+}}{n_{++}}\right)\left(\frac{n_{+j}}{n_{++}}\right).$$

The X^2 operates on frequencies, not probabilities, so we multiply the right-hand side by n_{++} to obtain the frequency we would expect ("e") in cell (i,j) if i and j were independent:

$$e_{ij} = \left(\frac{n_{i+}}{n_{++}}\right)\left(\frac{n_{+j}}{n_{++}}\right)n_{++}$$

and note that one pair of n_{++} cancels, leaving:

$$e_{ij} = \frac{n_{i+}\,n_{+j}}{n_{++}}.$$

In words, the frequency e_{ij} we would expect, derived from a model of independence, is the row sum times the column sum over the grand sum. For example, the value 60.72 in Figure 3.2 is the result of $(184 \times 165)/500$.

To assess how well a model of independence fits the observed data, the χ^2 fit statistic is computed:[7]

$$X^2 = \sum_{i=1}^{I} \sum_{j=1}^{J} \frac{(o_{ij} - e_{ij})^2}{e_{ij}}.$$ Thus, cell by cell, the values in Figure 3.1 are compared to their counterparts in Figure 3.2.

For these data, $X^2 = 156.00$. For any 2-way table, the degrees of freedom are $(I-1)(J-1)$. Given the X^2 and df, Excel's chidist function returns a p-value less than .0001. The statistic is significant, so we reject H_0 as implausible and conclude that the row variable (brand bought at time t − 1) and the column variable (brand bought at time t) are indeed probably associated (as, of course, we'd expect).

Figure 3.2
Expected Frequencies

Brand purchased at time t

		A	B	C	D
Brand purchased at time t-1	A	60.72	47.472	44.896	30.912
	B	41.91	32.766	30.988	21.336
	C	38.61	30.186	28.548	19.656
	D	23.76	18.576	17.568	12.096

Standardized Residuals

Computing the X^2 is somewhat like assessing an R^2 in regression—it's interesting and informative at a macro level: does the model fit or not?—but there's more to do. Cell by cell, we can look at the residuals, which are simply the differences between our data (o_{ij}) and the expected frequencies (e_{ij}): $(o_{ij} - e_{ij})$. In fact, we look at the standardized residuals, $(o_{ij} - e_{ij})/\sqrt{e_{ij}}$. If you look at the equation for the X^2, you'll see we've already computed these pieces (they're the square roots of the pieces we summed to get X^2). As a quick self-test, what does it mean if a residual, or standardized residual, equals zero? What would it mean if $X^2 = 0$? (Hint: it rhymes with "the model fits _erfectly.")

Figure 3.3
Standardized Residuals

Brand purchased at time t

		A	B	C	D
Brand purchased at time t-1	A	7.479	-3.116	-3.716	-2.143
	B	-3.539	2.137	1.978	-0.073
	C	-4.122	1.968	3.079	-0.374
	D	-2.002	-0.366	-0.613	3.998

The standardized residuals will enable us to understand what's going on in the data at the micro level, cell by cell. If any standardized residual exceeds 1.96 in magnitude, it is significant, signaling that the model of independence is particularly problematic for that cell. Figure 3.3 shows the brand-switching matrix of standardized residuals. We may now inspect the diagonal to assess the brand loyalties, as had been our intuition, because we've corrected for the market shares. That is, at this point, the different margins have been factored out, via $(o_{ij} - e_{ij})/\sqrt{e_{ij}}$.

In terms of loyalty, we can first note that all brands enjoy significant loyalty—in every case, the diagonals are positive and significant. There are more A-A (and B-

---

[7] The theoretical value and distribution is denoted with the Greek symbol, χ^2. The sample value is denoted X^2.

B, etc.) purchases in the data than random brand choices (relative to market share) would predict. Once a customer finds a particular brand, they will most likely buy that same brand next time.

The standardized residuals are interpretable in terms of magnitude and sign, including in relation to each other. The standardized residuals are obviously not probabilities—they can exceed 1, and they can be negative. But we can use terms such as "likely" when the numbers are large and positive, and "unlikely" when the numbers are large and negative. Hence, the brand manager for brand A enjoys the strongest brand loyalty. (These data describe a CPG—consumer packaged goods—in which brand A is also that with the largest share—a not uncommon finding. Further, it is priced a little higher than the others and enjoys a position of high quality.)

Brands B and C have significantly loyal customers also, but not as much as A, and not even as much as D. Brand D is the store brand, and it's highly likely that its loyal customers are seeking better prices. Brands B and C are between A and D—not as premium as A, but not as cheap as D.

In fact, the data suggest that brands B and C are essentially substitutable brands. The standardized residuals indicate that there are significant B→C and C→B patterns. If a customer purchases brand B, the most likely thing they'll do next time is buy B again, but right behind that behavior is to purchase C. If a customer buys C, then next time they'll probably buy C again, but they also dabble with B.

There are also significant negative values in the table. In the first row, we see that a customer who has purchased brand A is highly (significantly) unlikely to purchase B, C, or D. The reverse is also true: in the first column, we see that customers of B, C, or D are unlikely to buy A next round. It might seem that we've covered that ground after we saw the strong A-A pattern, and it's true that there are constraints in the table as captured by the notion of degrees of freedom. Nevertheless, the results of strong loyalty and strong (lack of) switching are distinct. To understand, look at brand D. It has several values in its row and column that are not significant—once a customer buys D, they might or might not buy B or C, essentially randomly. The two insignificant values in the D column say that a B or C customer might or might not buy D, essentially randomly.

There's another analogy with regression—in regressions, sometimes R^2 can be relatively low, yet some b-weights are significant (e.g., a strong predictor, but the overall model is too simple to capture much of the variance), and sometimes R^2 can be fairly high, yet few if any of the b-weights are significant (e.g., often occurs in small samples or when there is a lot of multicollinearity). In the cross-tab situation, sometimes X^2 may be relatively low, yet there may be some significant values among the standardized residuals. This result indicates that overall the model fits pretty well, and yet one or more cells within the table doesn't fit very well and we'd want to look at those cells to figure out why they're peculiar. Conversely, X^2 may be high and significant, indicating that the model of independence does not fit, yet none of the standardized residuals are significant. This scenario occurs when all of the cells aren't fit terribly well, but neither are they fit terribly badly. Each cell contributes some non-significant amount of lack of fit, which cumulates into a large X^2. Of course it is most intuitive when X^2 is large and there exist several significant standardized residuals, or when the X^2 is small and the standardized residuals are not significant, but if either of the other scenarios occurs, it doesn't mean you did something wrong.

Log Linear Model Extension

Cross-tabs are not just for brand switching. Cross-tabs are used to study associations between pairs of all kinds of categorical (nominal or ordinal) variables—marketers might compare preferences of Brands A, B, C, etc. across segments formed by gender, age, usage frequency, etc. And of course, cross-tabs can easily be extended beyond 2-way tables, such that we might look at brand preference, gender, age, and usage frequency all at the same time. Once the tables get bigger than 2-dimensional, the X^2 needs to be generalized as well—say hello to log linear models.

The model underlying the X^2 is that of independence (no association), and that assumption was the starting point that gave rise to the equation for the expected frequencies: $e_{ij} = \frac{n_{i+} \, n_{+j}}{n_{++}}$. This formula is multiplicative, which can make it hard to handle. If we take the natural logarithm of both sides, we'd get: $\ell n(e_{ij}) = \ell n(n_{i+}) + \ell n(n_{+j}) - \ell n(n_{++})$, so now the equation is linear (i.e., add or subtract, but not multiply or divide) in the log scale. So it's "log linear." Neat, right?

This new log linear model shows that the expected frequencies are a function of three terms: a term associated with the row effects (i), a term associated with the column effects (j), and the grand total. Thus, fitting the statistical model of independence to a two-way table is analogous to estimating a main effect for the row variable and a main effect for the column variable, and a grand mean or intercept-like term.

If the cross-tab were more complicated, say brand preference by gender by ad exposure, we would build a model with more terms to capture the new complexities. For example, we'd be curious to see if there were associations between brand preference and ad exposure, to assess marketing effectiveness or brand preference and gender, to study segments, etc. Cross-tabs can be as big as you want, cross-classifying as many variables as you want, and each variable can take on 2 or more levels. Log linear models can be used to analyze these multidimensional tables.

As an example, Figure 3.4 presents a 3-dimensional cross-tabulation of television viewing habits. A production company was curious to understand what TV shows people tended to watch in real time on TV vs. those they would watch on the production sites (e.g., ABC.com), vs. those they would catch on another provider (e.g., Hulu). The company's expectations were that people want to watch sports in real time (TV) or as close to real time as possible (provided after regularly scheduled airing on production sites like ABC.com). They expected this time urgency due to both true fandom, and because of not wanting to feel left out the next day at work in discussions about the game over the proverbial water cooler. The company expected that there was less time urgency for other standard TV shows and series, so viewers could wait a week or so to catch up on their favorite *CSI* or sitcom until they were available on a site like Hulu.

The company hired a marketing research firm to obtain the cooperation of a panel of 1000 consumers. Those consumers were screened to meet a criterion of watching at least 2 hours of TV per day, and they had to agree to have a type of spyware put on their computers and hardware on their televisions to record what TV shows they watched where and when. The recordings were captured for 9 months, at the end of which 619 participating households remained in the panel. Their data are shown in Figure 3.4.[8]

	< 30 years old			30 years +		
	TV	ABC.com	Hulu	TV	ABC.com	Hulu
Timely shows	43	39	16	40	34	21
Standard shows	81	61	53	90	67	74

Figure 3.4
TV Viewing Data: What do We Watch and Where?

The first cross-classifying variable is whether the TV show that was watched had an element of time urgency, such as a sports show. We'll see that timeliness did matter, as the production company had anticipated. What they hadn't anticipated was the kind of TV shows for which an urgency was felt by the viewer—sports, yes, but also shows of the contest variety like *American Idol, Dancing with the Stars* and *Survivor*, etc. Thus, the data were first coded and analyzed as sports shows vs nonsports shows, but they had to go back and code for sports and contests (and other "timely" shows) vs nontimely (or "standard" shows) programming.

The second factor was the age of the panelist, classified only roughly into younger (not yet 30 years old) and older (30 years and older). The third factor was whether the TV show was viewed (or recorded) during its regularly scheduled airing time, or from the website of the production company (e.g., ABC.com, Fox.com), or from a third-party channel host (all online sources except for the named production companies, so these included Hulu or similar service providers, most of which were legal sites).

To illustrate how log linear models can be used, we began by first fitting the main effects model to these data:

(1) $\ln(e_{ijk})$ = intercept + show_type$_i$ + age$_j$ + host$_k$.

In this model, show_type and host were significant. There was no significant effect of age.

Next, we added 2-way interactions, one at a time, to see whether any explained a significant additional amount of the data. The only term that popped up as significant was the show_type $\times$ host interaction. Specifically, we fit the following model:

(2) $\ln(e_{ijk})$ = intercept + show_type$_i$ + age$_j$ + host$_k$ + show_type$_i \times$ host$_k$

and compared its fit to the fit of model (1). The fit statistics in log linear models are like X^2's.) The difference between the fits of the two models was 8.698, which is distributed X^2 on 2 degrees of freedom, and that yielded a p-value < 0.05. Thus the addition of the show_type $\times$ host interaction in the second model was significant, and it contributed a significant improvement in understanding this data set. Model 1 was too simple, and model 2 is preferred.

No other interactions were significant, so model (2) was deemed to be the best model. It fit the best and was simultaneously most parsimonious. Adding additional terms to the model helped improve the model fit slightly, but not

---

[8] In the full data set over 9 months, each of the 619 households watched an average of 1350 TV shows (about 3.5 hours a day, roughly 5 shows a day). We could analyze the data at the unit of N = 619*1350 TV shows, but there is not independence among these observations, given that each set of approximately 1350 shows was selected by one household. Thus, the data in Figure 3.4 are a random sample of 1 TV show per household.

significantly, so additional terms would only complicate the model without significantly enhancing fit. Stated another way, model (2) was best because it contained the significant show_type × host interaction, and yet it was the simplest of all models to contain that term.

Figure 3.5 contains the parameter estimates for model (2). The main effect for show_type has a positive value for regular programming, and a negative value for sports shows and other timely shows. This main effect simply means that of all the 619 shows captured in the cross-tab in Figure 3.4, more of them were regular TV shows than sports and timely shows. Next, the age coefficients indicate there were slightly more older people in the panel than younger, but recall that this effect was not significant, so it's best not to interpret it at all. Next, the main effect of the medium on which a TV show was watched was significant, and it indicates that people are still watching shows primarily on TV (or DVRs), then sources like ABC.com, and least of all via sources like Hulu.

The main effects for the type of TV show and the host are moderated by their 2-way interaction. The interaction coefficients may be interpreted within rows; thus for timely shows, production sites like ABC.com were more popular than TV, and Hulu-like sites were the least popular. For regular, nontimely shows, Hulu was the most popular, then regular TV, and lastly, the ABC.com-like sites. Alternatively, the coefficients may be interpreted within columns. Managers of sites like Hulu might be interested to know that they pull a lot of viewers for regular TV shows and far fewer for sports or timely contest shows. Managers of ABC.com sorts of sites pull the reverse profile (but not quite as extremely different). TV is used to watch timely shows more than regular shows, but there is barely a difference. The production company was happy with the research—it confirmed some of their expectations and yet taught them things they didn't know. In general, Figures 3.4 and 3.5 illustrated how to analyze a 3-d table, and how to use log linear modeling to analyze contingency tables that were not inherently about brand choices, loyalty, or switching.

Figure 3.5
TV Viewing Data Parameter Estimates

Show Type	a=1 (regular programming)		0.4196
	a=2 (timely shows, sports & contests)		-0.4196
Age	b=1 (older; 30+)		0.0534
	b=2 (younger; <30)		-0.0534
Viewing Host	c=1 (TV regularly scheduled air time)		0.2539
	c=2 (ABC.com)		0.0449
	c=3 (Hulu)		-0.2988

Show Type × Viewing Host interaction:

	c=1 (TV)	c=2 (ABC.com)	c=3 (Hulu)
a=1 (regular)	-0.0582	-0.1388	0.1970
a=2 (timely)	0.0582	0.1388	-0.1970

Logit Models

Some cross-tabs are set up with an implicit causal order in mind. For example, obviously a brand-switching matrix structure uses past purchases to predict future purchases. Perhaps less obvious is a cross-tab that classifies brand preferences (A or B) by some segmentation variable (e.g., male or female), but they tend to imply that we're studying whether gender helps us understand and predict brand choices, rather than the reverse. Not all cross-tabs have a causal aim, as the TV viewership table just illustrated. However, it's true that in marketing, we're frequently trying to predict something.

If we're working with cross-tabbed data and we want to make predictions, we use logit models. The relationship between log linear models and logit models is analogous to the relationship between correlations and regression. In correlations, we look at symmetric (linear) relationships among variables, whereas in regression, we use some variables to predict another. Log linear models are like the correlations, in that no particular variable has a unique status—we're not trying to predict anything, we're just trying to understand the patterns in the tables. If we want to predict something, we turn to logit models.

Logit models are like regressions in that we'll have 1 or more predictors, and 1 dependent variable we're trying to understand. The difference is that in regression, the dependent variable is supposed to be continuous (interval or ratio) like a rating scale, whereas for logit models, the dependent variable is categorical.

Categorical variables are also called discrete variables. They might be nominal or ordinal, and they might comprise 2 or more categories. Examples include consumers' brand preferences or choices (e.g., Tide, Cheer, Yes, Wisk, etc.), anticipated transportation for the Labor Day weekend (such as plane, train, or automobile), or questions asking for consumers' knowledge or agreement, allowing for responses such as "yes," "no," or "don't know." In any case, all the choices are mutually exclusive, and the customer chooses only one of the options.

We will focus on the case where our dependent variable is binary. Examples include: a survey question that is answered yes or no, a customer who bought our brand or didn't, predicting a vote for a Democrat or Republican, etc.

Odds Ratios

In regular regression, we interpret model coefficients along the lines of, "as this predictor increases by a unit, we expect to see the dependent variable increase by b units." The same logic holds in logit models, but the data are categories, not continuous measures. So if we were to say, "as this predictor increases by a unit," what we really mean is, "as this predictor changes from 0 = young to 1 = old," for example. It's not a continuous increase—it's a jump from being in one category to another. So in this framework, we'll talk about odds. We'll use predictor variables to answer the question, "For customers with this profile, what are the odds that the customer will buy our brand vs. another brand?"

You've probably heard of "odds" with respect to betting on horses at a racetrack. The odds express a guess about the likelihood that a horse will win a race—50 to 1 odds means it's unlikely whereas odds like 2 to 1 means it's more likely (and therefore will pay less abundantly). In logit models, we'll use odds to pose questions like, "What are the odds that the customer bought our brand vs. they did not?"

Say we have a binary dependent variable, Y (1 = bought our brand vs. 0 = did not) and 2 predictors: X_1 (age, coded 0 = young, 1 = old) and X_2 (loyalty card owner, coded 1 = yes, 0 = no). As in regular regression, logit models have intercept terms, and as in regression, we need them but they're not usually very interesting. In a logit, the intercept will answer the simple question, "What are the odds that a customer bought our brand vs. they didn't?" but we already know overall sales and market shares. What will be more interesting are the logit parameters that answer the questions, "What are the odds that a customer buys our brand (vs. doesn't), given that they're younger (vs. older)," "What are the odds a customer buys our brand given that they're members of our loyalty program (vs. they're not)," and "What about if they are young as well as loyalty members, or some other combination?"

Thus, to really understand logit models, it's good to be facile with odds. Figure 3.6 presents a simple 2x2 cross-tab, of gender and preferences for brands X and Y. We designed the study to sample an equal number of men and women, and hence the row marginals are equal, at 100. We cannot control people's preferences, but overall, that is to say, without looking at gender yet, the sample showed a preference for brand Y over X on the order of 3:1. (Presumably our results resemble the relative market shares if our sample was random and representative.)

In the top table in Figure 3.6, we see our data. Row percentages may be computed: the 100 men prefer brand Y a bit, and in comparison, the 100 women prefer brand Y a lot. Conversely, if we were the brand manager, we could focus on the column percentages, which tell us that men are more likely to be the customers for brand X (4:1), and women the customers for brand Y (9:6 or 3:2).

In the bottom table in Figure 3.6, we see how 200 people would be distributed across the 4 cells "randomly," at least in proportion to the row and column margins. You should recognize this randomness as the computed expected frequencies—if the data were random, that is, if gender and brand preference were not related, then the 100 men should be distributed simply in proportion to the column margins, the brand shares (X:Y = 1:3). The same would hold true for the women. Once again, the logic is symmetric, so we could say that if the data were random, then the 50 people in the sample who like brand X should be approximately 50:50 male:female (according to the row margins). Similarly, the 150 people who prefer brand Y should be half male and half female.

We know how to analyze these data—compare the o's and e's via a X^2, etc. Using the logic of odds, we'd characterize the table as follows. Data in a cross-tab would demonstrate independence of the row and column variables if the pattern we observed across columns (rows) were constant over the rows (columns). For example, in row 1, we take 100 people and divide them into 25% and 75%, and we do the same thing in row 2. (Conversely, in column 1, we take 50 people and divide them into 50% and 50% across the rows, and do that for column 2 as well.)

Figure 3.6
Odds Ratios

Our Data→	Brand X	Brand Y	
Men	40	60	100
Women	10	90	100
	50	150	

H_0: Equal Odds→	Brand X	Brand Y	
Men	25	75	100
Women	25	75	100
	50	150	

We can state that more succinctly if we compute an "odds ratio." Instead of asking, "What are the odds in row (column) 1 vs. 2?," we will directly compare the odds by dividing one by the other. The odds ratio, or the "O.R.," puts all the people in column 1 in the numerator and compares the odds that they're in row 1 vs. 2, and puts all the people in column 2 in the denominator and compares their odds of being in row 1 vs. 2: $O.R. = \dfrac{o_{11}/o_{21}}{o_{12}/o_{22}}$.

Given this equation, it's easy to see that if we have a cross-tab in which the row and column variables are independent, then the odds in the numerator will be about the same as the odds in the denominator, and the ratio, O.R. will be approximately 1.0 in value.

If we flip the terms around a little, then $O.R. = \dfrac{o_{11} \times o_{22}}{o_{12} \times o_{21}}$, which is the product of the main diagonal (upper left to lower right) in the numerator relative to (divided by) the product of the off-diagonals in the denominator. This version should remind you of a correlation—if the 1,1 and 2,2 cells have the greatest frequencies, then the O.R. will indicate a positive association. If the off-diagonal cells (1,2 and 2,1) have the greatest frequencies, there is a negative association.

Odds ratios are attractive because they're easy to compute and understand. Unfortunately, the index is encumbered by the fact that there is no upper-bound. The minimum value for O.R. is zero, but the maximum is ∞. A small odds ratio ranges from 0 to 1, and a large odds ratio ranges from 1 to ∞. It just seems a little lopsided. So instead, people use Yule's Q:[9]

$$Q = \frac{(O.R.-1)}{(O.R.+1)} = \left[\frac{o_{11}o_{22}}{o_{12}o_{21}} - \frac{o_{12}o_{21}}{o_{12}o_{21}}\right] \Big/ \left[\frac{o_{11}o_{22}}{o_{12}o_{21}} + \frac{o_{12}o_{21}}{o_{12}o_{21}}\right] = \frac{o_{11}o_{22} - o_{12}o_{21}}{o_{11}o_{22} + o_{12}o_{21}}$$

Q ranges from –1 to 1, and equals 0 where there is no association. Thus Q operates much like the correlation coefficient.

For the data in Figure 3.6, O.R. = 6.0 and Q = 0.714. The Q tells us that there is a strong positive association between gender (men to women) and brand (X to Y). If we recoded the data or reassembled the table such that the position of men and women were switched (or the brands were switched), then the Q would be –0.714, so we just need to keep clear which direction we're testing and how we coded all the variables.

Logit Example

Let's see how the principle of odds leads us to logits. We'll work with a sample data set from a large auto company, depicted in the 4-way table in Figure 3.7.[10] The company wants to understand the segment of consumers who might be interested in "green" cars (all electric or hybrid). The variables we have include: i) age (coded as 30 or younger = 0, and 31 and older = 1), ii) education (coded as 0 = high school graduate, 1 = some college or college graduate, 2 = post-graduate degree), iii) involved in community activities (coded as 0 = no, 1 = yes), and iv) consumer says they're interested in buying a green car (0 = no, 1 = yes).

This example illustrates the difference between the log linear and logit approaches, mentioned previously as being analogous to correlations vs. regressions. We might find it interesting to simply explore and poke around and analyze the various relationships among these 4 variables, but it's more likely that we have a mission—that we want to understand how age, education, and community involvement may be used to predict and understand consumers who want green cars vs. those who don't. Thus, we'll create a logit model with the green car variable as the dependent measure. For every combination of age, education, and community, we'll compare the odds that the consumer wants to buy a green car or not. We'll do this in every cell—for young, least educated, no community participation (comparing the 122 vs. 114), all the way to older, most educated, and involved (comparing the 10 vs. 24).

---

[9] Yule the mathematician, not the Christmas tide greetings.

[10] These data are like those in Knoke and Burke, *Log-Linear Models*, Sage, p.23.

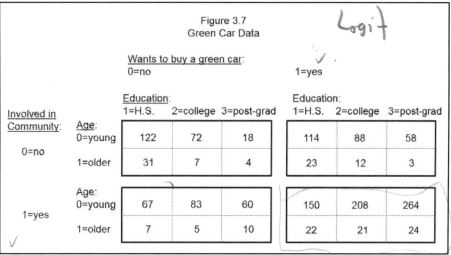

Figure 3.7
Green Car Data

Wants to buy a green car:
0=no   1=yes

Involved in Community: 0=no	Age:	Education: 1=H.S.	2=college	3=post-grad	Education: 1=H.S.	2=college	3=post-grad
	0=young	122	72	18	114	88	58
	1=older	31	7	4	23	12	3
1=yes	Age: 0=young	67	83	60	150	208	264
	1=older	7	5	10	22	21	24

Here's how we proceed. If we're curious about the probability that a consumer wants a green car, $p(Y = 1)$, vs. the probability that the consumer doesn't, $p(Y = 0) = [\,1 - p(Y = 1)\,]$, then the odds of going green are $p(Y = 1) / [\,1 - p(Y = 1)\,]$. In the X^2 discussion, we needed expected frequencies, rather than probabilities, and that's true of logit models too, so let's translate to be consistent. If the probability of wanting a green car is $p(Y = 1)$, then for a sample of size N, the number of consumers who we would expect to want a green car would be: $e_{ijk1} = N \times p(Y = 1)$, for age i, education level j, and membership k. The number of consumers we'd expect to have a response of "no" or "0" would be $e_{ijk0} = N \times [\,1 - p(Y = 1)\,]$. These relationships tell us that while we work with e's, it's very easy to obtain the p's, if we wish.

Next, we'll compare the odds of wanting a green car or not, computed just like the other odds ratios we've seen: e_{ijk1}/e_{ijk0}. We've also seen that it's easier to work with linear models than multiplicative ones, so let's take the natural logs of the odds ratio: $\ln(e_{ijk1})/ \ln(e_{ijk0})$. That is, we have the odds ratio, and then we log it. Log-it. Logit. Get it? Hmm.[11] (The next section is just algebra, so you can skip to *** if you wish.)

To model either e_{ijkm} (m = 1 for green = yes, and m = 0 for green = no), we need to capture effects in the data (e.g., marginals) of age (i), education (j), membership (k), and all their relationships (all main effects and interactions among the predictors). Remember, we're going cell by cell to look at the odds of wanting a green car or not, so we have to capture the descriptions of each cell. Let's call age variable A, education E, membership M, and going green G. Say we believe that wanting to go green is a function of age, education, and membership, as well as an interaction between age and education.

In the category m = 1 (want to buy a green car), the model would say:
$$\ln(e_{ijk1}) = \text{intercept} + A_i + E_j + M_k + G_1 + A_i{*}E_j + A_i{*}M_k + E_j{*}M_k$$
$$+ A_i{*}E_j{*}M_k + A_i{*}G_1 + E_j{*}G_1 + M_k{*}G_1 + A_i{*}E_k{*}G_1$$
and for the category m = 0 (not interested in the green car), the model would say:
$$\ln(e_{ijk0}) = \text{intercept} + A_i + E_j + M_k + G_0 + A_i{*}E_j + A_i{*}M_k + E_j{*}M_k$$
$$+ A_i{*}E_j{*}M_k + A_i{*}G_0 + E_j{*}G_0 + M_k{*}G_0 + A_i{*}E_k{*}G_0.$$
Working with natural logs, we know that $\ln(e_{ijk1}/e_{ijk0}) = \ln(e_{ijk1}) - \ln(e_{ijk0})$, so to compare the odds of going green or not, in each of the cells in the table, we study the logit and subtract those sets of terms:
$$\ln(e_{ijk1}/e_{ijk0}) = \ln(e_{ijk1}) - \ln(e_{ijk0})$$
$$= (\text{intercept} + A_i + E_j + M_k + G_1 + A_i{*}E_j + A_i{*}M_k + E_j{*}M_k$$
$$+ A_i{*}E_j{*}M_k + A_i{*}G_1 + E_j{*}G_1 + M_k{*}G_1 + A_i{*}E_k{*}G_1)$$
$$- (\text{intercept} + A_i + E_j + M_k + G_0 + A_i{*}E_j + A_i{*}M_k + E_j{*}M_k$$
$$+ A_i{*}E_j{*}M_k + A_i{*}G_0 + E_j{*}G_0 + M_k{*}G_0 + A_i{*}E_k{*}G_0).$$
Lots of terms cancel, leaving only those with the green variable in them:
$$= (G_1 + A_i{*}G_1 + E_j{*}G_1 + M_k{*}G_1 + A_i{*}E_k{*}G_1)$$
$$- (G_0 + A_i{*}G_0 + E_j{*}G_0 + M_k{*}G_0 + A_i{*}E_k{*}G_0)$$
Rearranging terms gives us:
$$= (G_1 - G_0) + (A_i{*}G_1 - A_i{*}G_0) + (E_j{*}G_1 - E_j{*}G_0)$$

---

[11] Actually, logit is short for log (natural log) of a probability unit.

$+ (M_k*G_1 - M_k*G_0) + (A_i*E_k*G_1 - A_i*E_k*G_0).$

We know the response variable is binary (interest in green cars or not), so when the model provides a parameter estimate for a term like green=1, it will be the same as for green=0 except that they'll have opposite signs (there's only 1 degree of freedom for a binary variable). So, if the estimate for "interest in green" is $green_1 = 0.35$, then the estimate for "not interested in green" is $green_0 = -0.35$. As a result, the logit equation can be further simplified. For example, the first term $(green_1 - green_0)$ can be written as $(green_1 - -green_1) = 2 \times green_1$. This final simplification results in the following:

$$= 2 (G_1 + A_i*G_1 + E_j*G_1 + M_k*G_1 + A_i*E_k*G_1)$$
$$= 2 (green_1 + age_i*green_1 + education_j*green_1 + member_k*green_1 + age_i*education_k*green_1).$$

***

Our green car logit model looks like this (we don't even have to write the green term—it's implied because it is the dependent variable):

$$\ln(e_{ijk1}/e_{ijk0}) = c + c_1\ age_i + c_2\ education_j + c_3\ member_k + c_4\ age_i*education_j.$$

When we fit the model to our data, we obtain the parameter estimates in Figure 3.8.

Figure 3.8
Green Car Parameters

Age:		Education: 1=H.S. 2=college 3=post-grad			Community:	
0=young	.072				0=no	-.384
1=older	-.072	-.308	.134	.174	1=yes	.384

	Education: 1=H.S. 2=college 3=post-grad			
Age: 0=young	-.038	-.288	.326	
1=older	.038	.288	-.326	& logit intercept = 0.636

What do the parameters mean? In general, the interpretation of logit coefficients is a lot like that done in regular regression; as the independent variable increases by one unit, the logit changes by the amount of the logit coefficient associated with that predictor. A positive coefficient means that the independent variable enhances the (log of the odds on the) dependent variable, thus making a green car purchase more likely. A parameter near zero means the predictor variable doesn't contribute much to the (log of the odds of the) dependent variable. A negative coefficient means that the independent variable decreases the (log of the odds of the) dependent variable.[12]

Specifically for our data, being involved in the community probably enhances a person's worldview, and in any event, raises the odds of going green a great extent (0.384). In addition, being young raises the odds of going green (albeit only slightly, 0.072), and consumers with more education have higher odds of going green (–0.308 for H.S., 0.134 for college, 0.174 for postgrads), but for both age and education, the interpretation of these main effects (one variable at a time) is tempered by the fact that there is an age by education interaction (higher order interactions always dominate in data interpretations). The interaction tells us that greater education enhances the odds of going green, but only for the younger people—it actually is detrimental among the older cohort. Alternatively, viewing the coefficients from the columns, we could say that for high school graduates, age matters very little, if at all, in distinguishing people who will go green vs. not. The older people in the sample with a college degree are more likely to go green than the younger college grads, and the older people with postgrad degrees are less likely to do so than their younger counterparts. (Don't

---

[12] Recall that regular regression has standardized regression coefficients, βs—as the predictor increases by one standard deviation, the dependent variable changes by β of its standard deviations. Logits have standardized coefficients also. In a standard normal curve, the mean and standard deviation of z are 0 and 1. The standard deviation of a standard logistic curve is a very weird $\pi/(\sqrt{3}) = 1.8138$. The standardized coefficient = the unstandardized coefficient (we've been calling them c's to keep them separate from regression's b's) × the standard deviation of the predictor × 1.8138. These factoids are lively fodder for your next cocktail party.

forget that in a one-time survey, younger people with postgrad degrees would have just earned them compared to older people who may have received their postgrad degrees decades ago—thus, be careful about a cohort effect.)

We can also put the model to work. For example, take the case of older people (age i = 1), college grads (education j = 2), and involvement in community networks (community k = 1), and plug in the appropriate coefficients:

$$\text{logit} = \text{intercept} \quad \text{age} \quad \text{college} \quad \text{community} \quad \text{age} \times \text{education}$$
$$\ln(e_{1211}/e_{1210}) = 0.636 \quad -0.072 \quad +0.134 \quad +0.384 \quad +0.288 = 1.37.$$

For a comparison, consider younger people (age i = 0), college grads (education j = 2), and those not involved in community networks (community k = 0), and plug in the appropriate coefficients:

$$\text{logit} = \text{intercept} \quad \text{age} \quad \text{college} \quad \text{community} \quad \text{age} \times \text{education}$$
$$\ln(e_{0201}/e_{0200}) = 0.636 \quad +0.072 \quad +0.134 \quad -0.384 \quad -0.288 = 0.17.$$

The values 1.37 and 0.17 are analogous to predicted values in regression—these are the predicted log odds.

If "log odds" seems like a weird scale to interpret, we can solve for the odds by taking $e^{\text{logit}} = e^{1.37}$ and $e^{0.17}$, which equal 3.9354 and 1.1853, respectively. The first odds, 3.9354, says that older people with college educations and involved in their communities are likely almost 4:1 to be interested in a green car vs. not being interested in a green car. The second odds, 1.1853, says that younger college grads not involved in their community are pretty much on the fence— they're not particularly interested in green, but they're not particularly rejecting the idea either—1 is like saying the odds of going green or not are 50:50.

Finally, if odds are still not your thing, we can translate the odds back to probabilities: we defined the odds as $p(Y = 1)/[1 - p(Y = 1)]$, so the $p(Y = 1) = \text{odds}/(1 + \text{odds})$. Thus, the probability that an older person, college grad, involved in the community would get a green car is 3.9354/4.9354 = 0.797, and the probability that a younger person, college grad, not involved in the community would go green is 1.1853/2.1853 = 0.542. By the way, the relationship written in this form, $p(Y = 1) = \text{odds}(Y = 1)/(1 + \text{odds}(Y = 1))$ is the reason you'll sometimes see these various equations written in still other ways, such as:

$$\text{logit}(Y) = c + c_1 \, \text{age}_i + c_2 \, \text{education}_j + c_3 \, \text{member}_k + c_4 \, \text{age}_i {*}\text{education}_j,$$

which enhances the similarity in appearance between the logit model and regular regression. Given that $e^{\text{logit}(Y)} = \text{odds}(Y = 1)$, and therefore, $\text{odds}(Y = 1) = e^{(c + c1\,\text{age} + c2\,\text{education} + c3\,\text{member} + c4\,\text{age}*\text{educ})}$, the probability that Y = 1 is therefore also written as:

$$p(Y = 1) = \text{odds}(Y = 1)/(1 + \text{odds}(Y = 1)) = \frac{e^{c+c1\,age+c2\,education+c3\,member+c4\,age*educ}}{1+e^{c+c1\,age+c2\,education+c3\,member+c4\,age*educ}}.$$ Really, it's not all that complicated. Math people just like making things look worse so that they can seem smarter. <Eye roll.>

For simplicity, we have been assuming that the dependent variable is binary. When it is discrete with more than 2 categories, logits still work on odds ratios, which compare 2 numbers, so the polynomial categories must be combined in some way. Depending on the questions posed about the data, we might compare the odds of responses in the 1st category vs. all others combined. We might follow up that model with models that contrast the 2nd category to all others (or to all others except the 1st), and so on. Sometimes there is a special category, such as a control group or a benchmark of some sort, and we'd fit several logits, each of which contrasts a category to that special category, such as category 1 vs. category k, category 2 vs. k, 3 vs. k, etc.

The logic for these models is no different, but there is more to keep track of, so be careful in interpretation. These are sometimes referred to as multinomial choice models (when the number of categories is 3 or more), because underlying assumptions about binomial distributions can be extended to the use of multinomial distributions. But to communicate clearly to the most people in your audience, just refer to them as logit models, regardless of whether the dependent variable is binary or more extensive.

Logit Logic from a Different Angle

We zoomed in on logit models from a perspective of generalizing simple cross-tabs and odds ratios. There are two other vantages from which logits are frequently developed, and it should further strengthen your understanding to see them in comparison. The first perspective shows how logit models are related to regular regression. The second perspective shows how logits are related to utility models.

First, think about regular old regression. We set up a model to predict $Y = b_0 + b_1 X_1 + b_2 X_2 + \varepsilon$ and proceed just fine if Y is continuous. There are no particular restrictions on the X's, b's, or ε's, so the model's predicted values, $\hat{Y}$'s, can vary in theory from $-\infty$ to $+\infty$, although, of course, in reality the range is much narrower for the Y's and $\hat{Y}$'s. If the dependent variable is not continuous but binary, taking on only values 0 or 1, we could use regression (the b's are unbiased, but their standard errors are not the smallest, hence the approach is statistically inefficient and underpowered, albeit conservative), but many $\hat{Y}$'s would be < 0 or > 1. That is, they wouldn't map onto the true nature of the data.

Instead of trying to model that binary Y, we could model the odds, $p(Y = 1)/[p(Y = 0)] = p(Y = 1)/[1 – p(Y = 1)]$. If we look at that odds equation as the probability that $Y = 1$ increases, the odds will blow up—officially, we say that the odds of $Y (= 1)$ are not bounded and may range in theory toward $+\infty$. The odds are still bounded, at the lower end, at 0, but we can fix that too. To do so, we model the natural log of the odds, specifically, $\ell n\{p(Y = 1)/[1 – p(Y = 1)]\}$. This transforms our binary Y into values that are unbounded at both ends, in theory ranging from $-\infty$ to $+\infty$, and then we can crunch. Thus we model not Y in a regression but the logit transform of Y in the logit model.

That exercise, of showing how logits and regressions are related, provides a statistical reason for using logit models for binary dependent variables and regressions. This second perspective shows how logits are related to choice models. The simple underlying assumption of choice models is that customers will (or should) choose a brand from among a consideration set that maximizes their utility. We'll call v_{ij} the true utility that consumer i has for brand j, and we'll acknowledge, like in most statistical models, that the data we see are a function of that underlying truth and some noise (sampling error, measurement error, the consumer is in a funny mood, whatever): $u_{ij} = v_{ij} + e_{ij}$. We'll model the true, deterministic part as a function of attribute k (k=1, 2, …,k): $v_{ij} = b_1X_{1i} + b_2X_{2i} + \ldots + b_pX_{pi} = \sum_{k=1}^{p} b_kX_{ki}$.

For example, say a local shopping mall has two anchor stores, Nordstrom's and Sears. On 7-point rating scales, one consumer rates Nordstrom's quality at 6 and its overall prices at 6. By comparison, the consumer rates Sears at 4 on quality and 3 on prices. Furthermore, the consumer values quality more than price, reflected in a larger weight (b) attached to the quality scores than to the prices. Consumer i's predicted utility would be: $v_{i,Nordstrom's} = 0.7(6) + 0.3(6) = 6$, and $v_{i,Sears} = 0.7(4) + 0.3(3) = 3.7$. Comparing the utilities for the two stores, we'll predict that this consumer will prefer to shop at Nordstrom's. Of course, in reality, we obtain store preferences (consumers' estimations of v_i's) and their perceptions of the attributes (the means on quality and price), and then we would estimate the relative importance of the attributes (the b's). When the consumers' estimates are continuous preferences, we can model the v_i's via regression. When the consumers provide choice data, the v_i's are discrete, and we model those categorical data via logit models.

Logistic Regressions

Many people use the terms "logit models" and "logistic regressions" interchangeably. That's ok, it's not the end of the world. The models certainly share the fact that their dependent variables are categorical. But more precisely, a logit model is one in which all of the predictors are also categorical, whereas a logistic regression is more general in that the predictors may be categorical or continuous, or both. In addition, and again quite precisely, $p(Y = 1) = \frac{e^{c+c_1 X_1+c_2 X_2}}{1+e^{c+c_1 X_1+c_2 X_2}}$ is known as the "logistic function" (it's an s-shaped curve, similar to the cumulative normal).

A Bit of Database Marketing and Direct Marketing and CRM and RFM

In this final section, we're going to look at a realm of marketing that at first glance seems very different and at second glance seems a huge opportunity for logit modelers. Specifically, let's consider the task of database marketers (a more contemporary term for direct marketers), who try to forecast the likely effectiveness of running some individually tailored and targeted promotion. In the aggregate, across customers, marketing and business questions are often about forecasting sales, but the database marketer is more interested in predicting at the individual customer or household level, such as, "yes, they'll redeem the coupon I just emailed them" or "no they won't," or "they'll choose brand A, B, or C."

Traditionally, direct marketing is done by scoring customers on RFM. RFM stands for recency, frequency, and monetary value. Recency is a variable or set of variables that captures how recently the customer bought from us, over some duration covered in our database, e.g., last year, last quarter, prior to our promotions, etc. Frequency captures how frequently the customer has bought from us. Monetary value is a measure of the average value in price, or even better, in contribution margin, of the SKUs the customer has purchased. RFM indicators are all interesting and important measures of a customer's worth. One can imagine bringing any of these back to the questions that opened the chapter— how might R, F, and M be used to help us define and identify loyal customers vs. those who are vulnerable to switching vs. those who have switched who may be amenable to returning vs. those who we'd do anything to keep vs. those who we don't want back, etc.

Recency is naturally captured as a date and time of purchase. In database or direct marketing, the dates are transformed to codes. For example, a histogram of purchases might show customers grouped into 5 categories: those who have purchased as recently as within the past month, those who have bought in the time frame of 1 to 3 months prior, 3 to 6 months, 6 to 9 months, and those who haven't purchased more recently than 9 months ago. Direct marketers score these categories as 5 = "within past month," to 1 = "9 months or prior." Larger scores are used for customers who are more valuable.

Similarly, frequencies of purchases, which are naturally captured as numbers like 1, 2, …, 100, etc., are scored. There might be 3 categories here: 1 for people who bought "0 to 10," 2 for customers who bought "11 to 39," and 3 for customers buying "40 or more." Finally, monetary value is also coded, say, 1 for customers who spent "$100 or less," 2 for those spending "$101–$250," 3 for those spending "$251–$500," and 4 for those spending "$501 or more."

Imagine the spreadsheet. We have recency, frequency, and monetary value information as well as their recoded counterparts, R, F, and M.

Next, the resulting coded scores for R, F, and M are then weighted, using managerial insights. For example, someone might argue that monetary value is the most important and so the M scores should be attached the weight of 5, whereas recency is less important, say a 3, and frequency is the least important, say a 2. In the spreadsheet, we would create a 4th new variable: CustomerWorth = 5R + 3M + 2F, a rough, back-of-the-envelope kind of prioritization. Then database marketers target the customers with the top scores on customer worth for their best programs.

It's great to get the R, F, and M data. No question. This pursuit has morphed into today's concerns about CRM, and no one would question its importance.

The oddity is in the data treatment. First, data that were continuous have been transformed into categorical variables that are a little rougher and less precise than they had been in their original form. Second, we create a weighted combination, but where did the weights come from? Yeesh.

If we're trying to predict some continuous measure such as customer valuation in dollars, we can use a regression. If we're trying to predict some categorical variable, we'd use logit or logistic regression models as presented in this chapter. We could use R, F, and M as predictors, along with whatever other variables interest us. And we'd obtain logit or logistic regression coefficients that would reflect the relative importance of those predictors (without our having to guess). The forecasting challenges of the direct and database marketers are met very nicely by the logit and logistic regression models.

The bottom line is that old direct marketing and database marketing techniques are just that—old. It's a little weird to substitute real numbers with codes, and it's a lot weird to attach arbitrary weights when we have easy and accessible ways to obtain precise weights and weights that are data-driven, not clouded by our well-meaning but subjective intuition. It is best to get the RFM data, but use the information in its natural form, rather than recoding it, and it's infinitely better to obtain optimal weights via regressions or logits rather than making them up.

Summary

Marketers often find themselves working with categorical data. The simplest approach for analysis is a cross-tab, and that analysis will suffice for many questions. Nevertheless, it's always better to be armed with more analytical tools, and log linear modeling and logits offer much more power and flexibility.

We began with an examination of brand loyalty and switching, which is increasingly important for CRM managers who wish to understand customer attraction and retention. Here are two recent examples. First, a databased casino tracked their players via customers' electronic ID and gaming cards, so as to offer the customers incentives and see if they couldn't get the gambling customer to "switch" into more profitable categories for the casino. Second, a large national department store used its CRM data in a logit to obtain probabilities of purchase across several speculative scenarios (one was a new clothing line, another assessed the attractiveness of a new promotion, etc.). They used the logit-predicted probabilities, multiplied those by the customers' respective historical monetary values (in their CRM database), and multiplied again by the average margin on the SKUs in question to obtain a really solid estimate of customer profitability.

The possible applications for switching matrices, using cross-tabs more generally, and, of course, using logits and logistic regressions are endless. These are simply statistical techniques, so just as regression may be applied to countless data sets, logits can also be useful in numerous applications.

References

Texts:
- Knoke, David and Peter J. Burke (1980), *Log Linear Modeling*, Sage. (Great, succinct intro.)
- Fienberg, Stephen E. (1980), *The Analysis of Cross-Classified Categorical Data*. (2nd ed), Cambridge: MIT Press.

- Kennedy, John J. (1983), *Analyzing Qualitative Data: Introductory Log-Linear Analysis for Behavioral Research*. NY: Praeger.

Thumbnail sketch regarding software:
- SAS: use proc logistic (list categorical predictors, e.g., class A B; then write a model statement with the dep var as a function of the categorical predictors and any continuous variables not listed in the class statement, e.g., model y = A B x;). For help: support.sas.com/documentation/
- SPSS: go to analyze, regression, binary logistic, and choose binary dependent variable and predictor variables. For help: search "IBM SPSS documentation," and open the "advanced statistics" manual.
- XLStat: choose menu dropdown of modeling data, choose logistic regression, response variable is your dep var, then select qualitative predictors for logit, and if you want, add quantitative predictors for logistic regression. For help: www.xlstat.com, click on "support" and then "tutorials."

Chapter 4: Measuring Customer Satisfaction and Factor Analysis

Marketing Concept: Measuring Customer Satisfaction and Customer Attitudes
Modeling Concept: Factor Analysis

Chapter Outline
1. Introduction
2. Measurement Theory
   a. Reliability
   b. Validity
3. Eigenvalues and Eigenvectors
4. Factor Analysis
   a. Selecting "r," the Number of Factors
   b. Orthogonal Rotations (but Use an Oblique Rotation instead)
   c. Oblique Rotations
   d. Confirmatory Factor Analysis

Introduction

There's an expression that has been popular among managers, "If you can't measure it, you can't manage it." This sentiment encourages quantitative assessments of business practices—for instance, to judge the extent to which goals have been achieved or investments used wisely, etc. Benchmarks can be set, dashboards provided to capture and display information about employee or machine effectiveness, comparisons made to previous quarterly or annual performance, and so forth. It seems to be fundamental to human nature to see how one fares compared to others in a pecking order, particularly in realms such as sports and business. Thus, we measure.

Many aspects of business are easy to measure. For example, financial indicators are offered in very precise fractions and updated numerous times daily. In operations, managers strive for process improvements to yield zero defects, and if not zero, some small number, such as 3 or 4 parts per million, the standard set by the famed 6σ (being 99.999997% of high quality product). Evaluations need not be quantitative, but numbers are very attractive—they seem impressive, rigorous, and easy to understand.

Marketing managers care about some performance indicators that are easy to measure (ROI, brand share, profitability, etc.), but the ultimate concern in marketing, and the ultimate driver of indicators like ROI, is the customer. Customers' opinions are sought, usually in the form of surveys asking questions about perceptions of quality, experiences with a brand or purchase, likelihood to come back and buy again or tell friends about their experience, etc. That is, we're interested in the extent to which our customers are satisfied or dissatisfied.[13]

For example, customers might be asked to compare their perceptions of quality or satisfaction to what they had expected, rating "My experience with customer service at XYZ bank…" from 1 = "fell short of expectations" to 5 = "exceeded my expectations." That sort of question is informative if expectations are also measured or understood. Alternatively, we might ask, "My experience with customer service at XYZ bank…" was 1 = "bad" to 5 = "good."

It is also important to measure aspects of the product or service being evaluated. If customers of the afore-hypothesized bank were satisfied, then all is well, but if not, the overall evaluation wouldn't provide any diagnostic information regarding what in particular customers would like to see improved. Thus, to make surveys more useful and actionable, they should (and usually do) ask customers about several aspects of the purchase that they think might have caused their satisfaction (or dissatisfaction). For example, patients released from a hospital might be asked whether they had a good stay ("overall satisfaction"), and then the survey might drill down into sections of questions related to their daily care (helpfulness, sensitivity), nursing (skill, responsiveness, concern), doctors (attentiveness, availability, skill), living quarters (condition of room, visitor arrangements, food), etc. Such detailed information facilitates improvement

---

[13] Customer satisfaction surveys are big business and seem to be here to stay, so we'll use them as examples in this chapter. However, the technique of this chapter, factor analysis, is applicable to other surveys.

processes to enhance customer satisfaction. In the sections that follow, we'll see how to measure satisfaction and its contributing elements as best as possible.

Measurement Theory

Surveys are extremely valuable and fun—they're a great way to get really interesting data. People will answer questions on just about anything. It's true that customer opinions are subjective, so the marketer's task is more challenging than that of accounting, finance, or operations people, who deal with straightforward units of dollars, years, percentages, weight, speed, etc. That's okay—marketers are the superheroes in business.

Let's see why something like subjectivity matters. We begin with the notion of measurement error. Imagine measuring a friend's height, or the temperature of water for boiling pasta, or the speed of a runner going from point A to point B. In each case, there is an agreed upon convention for measurement scales: a ruler, a thermometer, a stopwatch. There are also agreed upon transformations among measures that result from using slightly different measuring instruments, e.g., inches to centimeters, Celsius to Fahrenheit, etc.

Yet even with standard scales and clear constructs of height, heat, and speed, there will almost certainly be measurement error—as with all statistical models, we'll assume that the observed data are a function of the truth and some error component: $X = T + \varepsilon$. Specifically, if everyone in class measured the height, temperature, or speed, the recorded data would have a distribution. We hope the mean of the data was at T (the true height, heat, or speed), and we acknowledge some noise plus or minus from that point.

We usually assume the error is random, such as when some people snap the stopwatch too quickly and others too slowly, rather than there being a systematic bias in the measurement instrument or in the measurer. If the errors are random (and the distribution pretty symmetric, perhaps normal), then the amount of overestimation should be roughly the same as the underestimation. If we average all the data points (X_1 through X_N), the positive errors will cancel out the negative errors ($\bar{\varepsilon} = 0$), and we will obtain a decent estimate of the truth, T.

If there is measurement error for scales of height and speed and such, imagine how much more complicated it is to measure a person's intelligence, a customer's attitude about a brand, a voter's inclination to go red or blue, and so forth. There are not agreed upon scales to measure these concepts…in fact, unlike height, a person's attitudes and opinions are not directly observable, so there aren't even agreed upon definitions of the concepts. So we rely on the beauty of averages again.

The average height (or heat or speed) that we computed a moment ago was from multiple measures that came from different people. Here, we'll average over multiple measures that come from the same person. For each concept we wish to measure, we design a survey asking a customer to respond to several items that triangulate around that concept. In asking several questions on each topic, we'll trust that the measurement errors cancel out across the items so that the scale reflects the basic nature of the concept. For example, if we wanted to know customers' opinions about Dell, we might ask questions like "Do you like Dell products?," "What brands of computers do you currently own?," "How likely are you to buy Dell products in the future?," "Do you think Dell provides good value?," and so forth. Each of those items might tap somewhat different aspects of customer opinion, but together they should reflect customer attitudes about Dell.

Reliability

To get specific, let's work with a survey we'll use in this chapter and in the next. Figure 4.1 shows a 15-item survey tapping customers' satisfaction with their recently purchased brand AZ printers. The 15 survey questions are listed in 5 groups of 3, reflecting customer perceptions of quality, price, value, satisfaction, and likelihood to purchase another AZ printer. The survey was given to 100 customers. The data are stored in a spreadsheet with 100 rows (one per customer) and 15 columns (one per variable, each of these survey items).

Measurement theory tells us that each of the 15 variables consists of a true score and some random measurement error. For example, the first three items may be written:

$$X_{quality1} = T_{quality} + \varepsilon_1, \qquad X_{quality2} = T_{quality} + \varepsilon_2, \qquad X_{quality3} = T_{quality} + \varepsilon_3.$$

The observed scores are X's, and the true scores are T's. If we have designed a good survey and written three questions that each tap a facet about quality, then the correlations among these three survey items, $r_{X1,X2}$, $r_{X1,X3}$, and $r_{X2,X3}$, should be high, and we'd say the scale was unidimensional (that's a good thing). We'd then examine the correlations among the next three items, those designed to capture customer reactions to price:

$$X_{price1} = T_{price} + \varepsilon_4, \qquad X_{price2} = T_{price} + \varepsilon_5, \qquad X_{price3} = T_{price} + \varepsilon_6$$

and similarly inspect the correlations, $r_{X4,X5}$, $r_{X4,X6}$, and $r_{X5,X6}$, expecting they would be high. We'd continue to do this for all five constructs in the survey, hoping to verify that we have the workings of 5 good scales, each with 3 items, for quality, price, value, satisfaction, and repeat.

Figure 4.1
Customer Satisfaction Survey for AZ Printers

	Strongly Disagree						Strongly Agree
The quality of the AZ printer I bought is excellent.	1	2	3	4	5	6	7
AZ printers are known to be highly reliable.	1	2	3	4	5	6	7
I'm sure my AZ printer will last a long time.	1	2	3	4	5	6	7
The AZ printer was reasonably priced.	1	2	3	4	5	6	7
AZ sets fair prices for its products.	1	2	3	4	5	6	7
The AZ printers are no more expensive than others.	1	2	3	4	5	6	7
I feel like I got good value for this purchase.	1	2	3	4	5	6	7
The quality of the printer is worth its cost.	1	2	3	4	5	6	7
I could tell my boss this purchase was good value.	1	2	3	4	5	6	7
I am very satisfied with my newly purchase AZ printer.	1	2	3	4	5	6	7
My printer is better than I expected it would be.	1	2	3	4	5	6	7
I have no regrets about having bought this printer.	1	2	3	4	5	6	7
I would buy another AZ if I had to buy another printer.	1	2	3	4	5	6	7
I would buy other AZ products.	1	2	3	4	5	6	7
I would tell my friends and coworkers to buy AZs.	1	2	3	4	5	6	7

When we say we hope we've created a "good" scale, what do we mean by good? Scale assessment is conducted along two criteria: reliability and validity. Reliability means that if we use the same scale again and again, the items will measure the same thing again. Validity means that items measure what we say they measure or what they were designed to measure. Measurement theorists speak of needing reliability in order to have validity—you can't really know what you're measuring (validity) unless what you're measuring is at least consistent (reliability). Let's look at each of these concepts in more detail.

Regarding reliability, it is good if the inter-correlations among the three items purported to tap the same construct are high. As one goes up, the others go up—that and how we designed the survey suggest the items measure the same thing (if you have an item that is reverse-coded, reverse its scoring before proceeding). A frequently used index to capture reliability is called "coefficient alpha." For our quality items, the standardized coefficient alpha is calculated using the quality correlations: $= \frac{3}{2}\left[1 - \frac{3}{3+(r_{X1,X2}+r_{X1,X3}+r_{X2,X3}+r_{X2,X1}+r_{X3,X1}+r_{X3,X2})}\right]$. We then calculate an α for the other four scales as well. In general, the standardized coefficient alpha is: $= \frac{p}{p-1}\left(1 - \frac{p}{p+\sum_{i\neq}^{p}\sum_{j}^{p} r_{ij}}\right)$, where p is the number of items in the scale (we have 15 variables, but we're taking them 3 at a time, so p = 3). It's easy to see how α works—for a given p, as the correlations get larger, the denominator of the fraction inside the parentheses gets larger. If the items are not correlated, the fraction would be p/(p plus a little something), whereas if the items are correlated, the fraction would be p/(p plus something much bigger). With high correlations, it means the fraction overall would become smaller, so the 1-fraction would become bigger. That would give us what we want—a large coefficient alpha.

For the purposes of understanding reliability, the next few paragraphs may be considered a technical aside, so feel free to skip to *** if you wish. The α above is called standardized because it is computed on the item correlations. The more general form of coefficient alpha is computed on the item variances and covariances: $\alpha = \frac{p}{p-1}\left(1 - \frac{\sum_{i=1}^{p}\sigma_i^2}{\sigma_T^2}\right)$, where σ_i^2 is the variance of each item i, and σ_T^2 is the variance of the total scale with all p items, $\sigma_T^2 = \sum_{i=1}^{p}\sigma_i^2 + \sum_{i\neq}^{p}\sum_{j}^{p}\sigma_{ij}$, and σ_{ij} is the covariance between items i and j.

Covariance, hmm. If the reader is anything like my typical student, you might be thinking that I'm talking gibberish. That's not how my students express it, of course. They say things like, "Er, I know what a covariance is, but could you remind us?"

Here's a refresher on covariance (or, using my own double-speak: here's for those of you who blew off learning what a covariance is because you thought you'd never need to know it). A correlation between two variables and a covariance between those variables both capture the essence of whether the two variables are positively or negatively related. A covariance between variables X and Y is just like a correlation r_{XY} in that it is negative when X goes up as Y goes down, zero when there is no particular relationship between the two variables, and positive when X goes up as Y goes up.

Here's why: in the equations for both, you'll see a term called "cross-products," $(x_i - \bar{x})(y_i - \bar{y})$. When a customer has a high (low) score x_i relative to the mean $\bar{x}$ and a high (low) score y_i relative to the sample mean $\bar{y}$, then that customer's cross-product will be positive, and if the data for many customers yield positive cross-products, we'll obtain a positive correlation or covariance. Conversely, when a customer has a high (low) score x_i relative to $\bar{x}$ and a low (high) score y_i relative to $\bar{y}$, then the cross-product will be negative, and many such customer data points would contribute to a negative correlation or covariance. When customers have a high (low) score x_i relative to $\bar{x}$ and then some customers have a high y_i and other customers have a low y_i, then there would be a mix of positive and negative cross-products, and they'd cancel each other out and the sum over the sample would be small (at the extreme, zero). Finally, don't forget that a correlation measures a linear relationship between X and Y, and so does a covariance, and we're okay with a linearity assumption because it's a pretty good approximation to much of our world.

A correlation r ranges from –1 to 1 and a covariance can range in theory from $-\infty$ to $+\infty$. That distinction arises because in computing a covariance, we retain the information regarding the standard deviations of X and Y. A correlation has that nice –1 to 1 standardized range because we've gotten rid of the standard deviations. Recall the equation for the correlation coefficient, r_{XY}: $r_{XY} = \frac{1}{N-1}\sum_{i=1}^{N}\left(\frac{x_i-\bar{x}}{s_x}\right)\left(\frac{y_i-\bar{y}}{s_y}\right)$. We have literally divided away s_x and s_y. Another way to think about "getting rid of" the standard deviations is to imagine taking our raw data, X and Y, and transforming them to z-scores, $z_X = \left(\frac{x_i-\bar{x}}{s_x}\right)$ and $z_Y = \left(\frac{y_i-\bar{y}}{s_y}\right)$. The means of z_X znd z_Y are 0, and their new standard deviations are 1.

Compare that equation for the correlation coefficient to this one for the covariance, cov(X,Y), or σ_{XY}: $cov(X,Y) = \frac{1}{N-1}\sum_{i=1}^{N}(x_i - \bar{x})(y_i - \bar{y})$. Regarding flipping back and forth, if you have a covariance, you may obtain r_{XY}: $r_{XY} = \frac{cov(X,Y)}{\sigma_X\sigma_Y}$, and if you have a correlation, you may obtain the covariance: cov(X,Y) = r_{XY} s_X s_Y.

***Okay, that concludes the primer on correlations and covariances. Meanwhile, back at the ranch, we were talking about coefficient alpha. In theory, it's supposed to range from 0 to 1, and when it exceeds 0.70, people concur that the scale of p items is reliable.[14]

If α is not particularly high, examine the item correlations. It is often the case that most of the items hang together but that one item is a "bad" item. The item might be ambiguously written in the survey, for example. If so, form the scale with all of the items except the bad one. The scale is shorter (p – 1) but the α should be higher, representing a scale that is more reliable. If that works, use that subset of good items going forward to represent the construct in any subsequent analyses.

Validity

Once we have reliable scales, we ponder the question of whether the scales are measuring the constructs we set out to measure. A cheap and easy form of "validation" (but one that isn't terribly scientific) is called "content validity" or "face validity." Essentially, the idea is whether we can affirm that the items look like they capture the content we were hoping to measure.

For example, in Figure 4.1, the first question asks whether the quality of the AZ printer is excellent. That looks as though it taps quality. The last question asks about recommending the printer to others. We are assuming that word-of-mouth is related to the construct we are calling repeat purchasing, but it's not quite. We are also assuming that customers who are happy with the AZ printers would recommend them, but it's possible that they bought an AZ printer that is too fancy and expensive to recommend to a friend and it isn't the brand sponsored at work, so there would be no

---

[14] If you'd like to test whether α is significant, with a null hypothesis H_0: $\alpha = c$, for some constant c, such as 0.50, use z = (α – c) / sqrt(Q/n), where $Q = \left[\frac{2p^2}{(p-1)^2(j'Vj)^3}\right][(j'Vj)(trV^r + tr^2V) - 2(trV)(j'V^2j)]$, j is a px1 vector of 1's, V is the variance-covariance matrix among the p items, and tr is the trace of a matrix. Similarly, a 95% confidence interval for α would be $\alpha \pm$ (1.96)(sqrt(Q/n)). See Duhachek, Coughlan, and Iacobucci, *Marketing Science*, vol.24 (2), 294-301 or Duhachek and Iacobucci, *Journal of Applied Psychology*, vol.89 (5), 792-808, for more.

point in recommending it to a coworker. That's okay. Remember, we hope that measurement errors cancel each other out, and that the common essence captured by the last three items is about repeat purchasing.

Content validity or face validity might serve as an initial marker. It would seem odd to proceed without it. If we purported to have a customer satisfaction survey, but all the items asked about belief in the existence of little green men on Mars, we'd be hard-pressed to convince others that the survey was indeed a valid measure of satisfaction.

Beyond establishing the basic benchmark of content or face validity, we're typically interested in examining our data for empirical evidence of what are called convergent and discriminant validity. Convergent validity asks the question, "Do the items correlate with other concepts they should be related to?" and discriminant validity asks, "Are the items uncorrelated with concepts they aren't related to?"

Let's use the data from the survey in Figure 4.1 to think about both, by simplifying the data a bit. We can pre-process the data such that in addition to the spreadsheet having columns for the items quality1, quality2, and quality3, and we'll add a column containing the mean over these three items, computed for each of the 100 survey respondents in the sample. Then we can do the same for the other sets of items—price, value, satisfaction, and repeat purchasing.

Next, we compute the correlations and covariances between the 5 concepts, over the $N = 100$ customers. Both matrices are presented in Figure 4.2. Note that the variances (in the diagonal of the second matrix) are on fairly comparable scales (all around 2), but probably due to the familiarity of correlation coefficients, it is easier to get a feel for the data by examining them (in the first matrix). The asterisks depict the significant correlations, $H_0: \rho = 0$, $p < 0.0001$.[15]

Figure 4.2
Correlations and Covariances

Correlations:

	quality	price	value	satisf.	repeat
quality	1.00				
price	-0.03	1.00		symmetric	
value	0.58*	-0.53*	1.00		
satisfaction	0.62*	-0.22	0.39*	1.00	
repeat	0.38*	-0.41*	0.19	0.58*	1.00

* $p < 0.0001$

Covariances:

	quality	price	value	satisf.	repeat
quality	2.0113				
price	-0.0719	2.5384		symmetric	
value	1.1926	-1.2155	2.0738		
satisfaction	1.2482	-0.4925	0.8035	2.0076	
repeat	0.7615	-0.9282	0.3866	1.1610	1.9957

We can conceptualize many forms of interrelationships among the five constructs of quality, price, etc., and we'll address precisely how to test such theorizations in the next chapter. For now, our purpose is to understand validity, so we will examine the correlations to see if they make sense with respect to convergent and discriminant validity.

Let's start with convergent validity. The correlations indicate relatively strong relationships (for real world data) between quality and value, quality and satisfaction, price and value, and satisfaction and repeat. We might have expected satisfaction to be correlated with everything. In the data, we find positive relationships with most, and an unexpected result that price was not significantly correlated with satisfaction. Perhaps price affects satisfaction only through perceptions of value. We might believe that quality and value are precursors to satisfaction, and that repeat is a consequence of satisfaction. We will test these formulations using the techniques in the next chapter. For now, we don't worry about whether value causes satisfaction, or the reverse.

We can examine the other constructs for convergent validity as well. Quality is related to value, satisfaction, and repeat, each of which makes sense, and not to price, which is interesting. There is a colloquial belief in a price-quality association; that's why we're willing to pay more for some purchases. Maybe the price-quality link doesn't hold for printers. Price itself is correlated with value and repeat purchasing, and both have negative signs, which makes sense. And so goes the subjective testing of convergent validity.

For discriminant validity, we're looking for two things. First, we're looking to verify that items measuring unrelated concepts shouldn't be correlated. In these data, almost everything is related to almost everything else. But if we were to bring in more variables from the survey, we would see, for example, that customers who bought printers in Florida were no more satisfied than those who bought them in California, or that satisfaction didn't vary by gender, etc.

---

[15] The $r = -.22$ is significant at $p < 0.05$, but we're using a more stringent criterion of 0.0001, because we've implicitly just conducted many hypothesis tests in this matrix, and also, the tests convey overlapping information because the items are correlated.

In addition, when people refer to discriminant validity, they're also hoping to demonstrate that any two concepts that are related have scales with items that are correlated but not completely redundant. For example, the correlation between value and quality is high, r = .58. However, it is significantly lower than 1. Usually when we test hypotheses about correlations, we posit H_0: $\rho = 0$. Here, we test H_0: $\rho = 1$, with the idea being that if we cannot reject the hypothesis, then we don't really have 2 scales measuring 2 concepts; we have 2 scales measuring the same concept. To test either H_0: $\rho = 0$ or H_0: $\rho = 1$, convert the r to a "Fisher z transform" (r's have squirrely distributions): $z' = \frac{1}{2}[\ell n(1 + r) - \ell n(1 - r)]$. Then pop this z' into the following equation for a z-test, using 0 or 1 (or whatever) for the constant c in the numerator: $= \frac{z' - c}{\sqrt{1/(N-3)}}$. If we test H_0: $\rho = 1$ for r = .62 (the largest r in Figure 4.2), we get 2.71; so we conclude that r = 0.62 is significantly less than 1, therefore quality and satisfaction are not measuring the same thing. Given that we tested the maximum r, we can further generalize and say that the concepts being measured by the 5 scales appear to be empirically distinct.

We can pose even more precise tests for convergent and discriminant validity in the context of the models we'll see in the next chapter. In the remainder of this chapter, we turn to factor analysis. We have been examining r's just by eyeballing them, and that's fine to get a feel for some concepts. Factor analysis provides an analytical model to examine the pattern of correlations among variables in a far more systematic manner.

Eigenvalues and Eigenvectors

Imagine a data matrix (like our spreadsheet), X, with N rows (one for each customer who answered our survey) and p columns (one for each variable in the data set). (Our data spreadsheet probably has many more variables, but we're focusing on the p in X for now.) Each element x_{ij} is the jth measure on the ith respondent. To simplify later computations, we'll subtract the mean for each variable from each data point, so that X is a "deviation" matrix, containing elements: $x_{ij} - \bar{x}_j$. For our purposes, we can continue with the p = 15 items measuring attitudes about AZ printers from Figure 4.1.

We might be interested in predicting customer satisfaction as a function of quality and value. The term "prediction" suggests a regression model. Yet we have 3 items that measure customer satisfaction—should we run a regression using each item in turn as the dependent variable, and if so, how do we combine the results of 3 regressions? In addition, if we enter the 3 quality items and the 3 value items as 6 predictors in such a regression, we can absolutely anticipate piles of multicollinearity, because each set of 3 variables are clearly by definition correlated within themselves (at least if they measure the same construct). So while having multiple items is generally a good thing—it helps with reducing measurement error and enhancing reliability—it nevertheless complicates other analyses.

One way to simplify our modeling challenges would be to continue with the 5 means we've been discussing. Then, instead of having p = 15 variables for subsequent models, we'd have only 5. Yet in the real world, it might not be so easy, for the patterns in the data might not be so clear. For example, what if one or two of the quality items were correlated not just with the other quality items, but also with some of the value or repeat items. But would we feel confident computing means; would we ignore the cross correlations? It would be nice to have a technique that systematically finds the underlying factors and helps us to reduce the number of items to a more manageable number. Factor analysis achieves these goals.

In a factor analysis, our goal is to find a way to combine the original p variables into a new score (just one for now) that captures as much of the information as possible contained in the original larger set of p variables. That is, we want to create a new variable, X_i^* (for customer i), as a simple linear combination of original variables, the X's: $X_i^* = b_1 X_{1i} + b_2 X_{2i} + \cdots + b_p X_{pi}$. A factor analysis model finds the b's to create an X* that will explain as much of the information contained in the original $X_1, X_2, \ldots, X_p$ as possible.

When we refer to the "information" contained in a set of p variables, we're talking about the variances and covariances of those variables. We've seen in a variance-covariance matrix like the one in the bottom of Figure 4.2 that there are variances along the diagonal and covariances in the cells on the off-diagonals. If p = 1, the variance-covariance matrix would be 1×1, and the only entry would be the variance of that single variable (there is no other variable with which it could co-vary). What factor analysis does is astounding—it begins with a $p \times p$ variance-covariance matrix, and tries to mash all of that information down into a 1×1 matrix—the variance captured by a single new factor. That factor will indeed explain as much of the original variance-covariance matrix as it can, and if there is leftover information to be explained, we'll extract a second factor. For now, we'll begin with just the one factor.

So, when creating a single new factor, what is the variance of X* that we're trying to maximize? For a simple linear transformation, y = bx, it is known that $\sigma_y^2 = b^2 \sigma_x^2$. The same relationship holds for multivariate transformations.

The equation, $X_i^* = b_1X_{1i} + b_2X_{2i} + \cdots + b_pX_{pi}$, can be written more succinctly in matrix algebra as X* = Xb, where X* has N rows (one for each respondent) and 1 column, X is our original N×p data set, and b has p rows (one to hold each weight in the equation) and 1 column. Then, we'll call S the p×p covariance matrix (like in Figure 4.2) with variances for the p variables along the diagonal, and the off-diagonal in row i and column j is the covariance between variables i and j. Given the weights in b, the covariance matrix for X* is S_{X*} = b'Sb. The apostrophe symbol means transpose—rows become columns and columns become rows (like one of the "paste special" options in Excel). If your neurons are producing steam, you might pause and find a matrix algebra primer (e.g., Namboodiri, *Matrix Algebra*, Sage).

Instead of working with S, let's continue with the more familiar p×p correlation matrix, R. A matrix like R may be factored or decomposed by several matrix algebra methods. It is particularly useful to us to decompose R into "eigenvalues" and "eigenvectors." The eigenvectors will form the columns of the matrix V (and the rows in the transpose, V'). The eigenvalues are placed along the diagonal of Λ. The factoring of R then looks like this: $R = V\Lambda V'$.

Why do we do this, and what do we get when we obtain an eigenvalue-eigenvector solution of R? First, let's look at the set of eigenvectors. Each eigenvector is p×1. The p values sitting in the eigenvector are the weights that create linear combinations of our original X's. In particular, the weights in the first vector, the v_1, combine the X's in such a way that X* captures the maximum possible amount of variance among the p X's. To form the weights in the second eigenvector, v_2, the factor analysis model looks at all of the remaining variance still to be explained, and derives the next set of weights that would combine the X's to explain the greatest amount of the remaining information in a way that is uncorrelated with the X* combination created by v_1. The constraint of making the new X* uncorrelated with the first one is to provide fresh information that has not already been explained.

The matrix decomposition also produces eigenvalues. It's fairly standard in factor analysis to call an eigenvalue lambda, λ, and they are ordered from largest to smallest: $\lambda_1 \geq \lambda_2 \geq \ldots \geq \lambda_p \geq 0$. They are stored along the diagonal of a matrix Λ. Each λ_i is associated with a particular eigenvector, v_i (eigenvalues and eigenvectors come in pairs, like in Noah's ark). What are eigenvalues? When we say v_1 contains the weights that will combine the X's to a new score that captures the most variance possible, λ_1 is the variance of that new composite. Of the variance left to be explained, the weights in v_2 explain the next largest amount of variance with the caveat that the new score is uncorrelated with the first composite, and that second variance is λ_2.

Figure 4.3 is a depiction of the concepts of eigenvalues and eigenvectors. In both graphs, we've plotted our original variables x_1 and x_2. For this illustration, p = 2, and of course, IRL that's too small to bother with doing a factor analysis. The large oval represents the scatterplot of all the data points in the sample—every customer is represented in that plot with coordinates x_1,x_2, their scores on the two variables. In 2-d, the scatterplot looks roughly like a smashed (American) football.

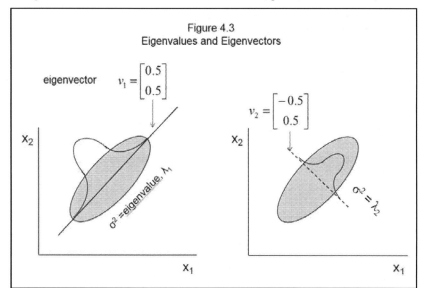

Figure 4.3
Eigenvalues and Eigenvectors

The plot to the left depicts the first eigenvector, which finds the direction of maximum variability in the data. In this plot, the direction of maximum variability runs southwest to northeast, or in the direction of the length of the football. The vector v_1 has elements 0.5 and 0.5 (you can see the vector runs along the 45° angle between x_1 and x_2). If we take any customer's data on x_1 and x_2, and use the weights in v_1, $0.5x_1 + 0.5x_2$, we'd obtain a new score that no longer lives in the 2-d x_1-x_2 space, but rather lives along the orientation of the eigenvector v_1. That is, we've simplified our world from our vast p variables (okay, 2) to only a single new composite, and that new composite has a variance, and that variance is λ_1.

Next, in the graph to the right, we see the same p = 2 variables plotted. We've already explained the maximum amount of variance using v_1, along what is called the "principal axis" in the data ellipse (hence factor analysis is often called "principal factors" or even "principal axis factoring"). What's left, and what would be uncorrelated with v_1, would be to set v_2 orthogonally to (uncorrelated with) the first vector, running across the width of the smashed football. That vector contains weights $-0.5, 0.5$, thus, to project all the customer data points onto this new axis, we'd create the new composite variable, $-0.5x_1 + 0.5x_2$. The new composite scores would have a distribution, and that variance is λ_2.

Now let's return to the typical situation in which we have p variables—far more than 2. We run an eigenvalue-eigenvector decomposition and obtain matrices V, Λ, and V'. The model will extract p eigenvalues and their corresponding p eigenvectors. That would give us p sets of weights to apply to our data X's, which would mean that we'd take our original p variables and transform them into p X*'s. But that seems silly, given that one of our goals was to simplify our world, from p variables down to a smaller number. Instead, we've gone from p original variables (X's) to p eigenvector-weighted transformed variables (X*'s). We'd like to go from p X's to some smaller number of factors—perhaps 1, but if not 1, then r $\ll$ p. So, we take the first r eigenvalues and vectors, and we'll probably recapture a decent approximation to our correlation matrix: $\approx V_r \Lambda_r V_r{}'$. (We'll address more specifically how to determine a good value for "r" shortly.)

Factor Analysis

The model $R = V\Lambda V'$ is an eigenvalue-eigenvector decomposition, and the equation $R \approx V_r \Lambda_r V_r{}'$ is an approximation to the data, R, that we believe captures much of the information, and does so parsimoniously given that r $\ll$ p. We can rearrange the matrices a bit. The matrix Λ is diagonal with λ's on the diagonal and 0's on the off-diagonals. If we take the square roots of the eigenvalues on that diagonal, $\sqrt(\lambda)$, then we can factor the $V\Lambda V'$ equation. Specifically, define $B_r = V_r \Lambda_r{}^{.5}$ and then $R \approx B_r B_r{}'$. This reformulation is known as "principal components analysis." The p×r matrix B_r contains the "loadings" of the p variables on the r components. For now, we can take a "loading" to mean the correlation between the row variable and the column principal component.

Principal components is a perfectly nice model, but it's basically just crunch, crunch, crunch—we have p variables, let's mash them and rearrange them into fewer components. By comparison, factor analysis is derived from richer measurement theory. In factor analysis, we posit unobservable constructs that give rise to, or are reflected in, the manifest observed variables. For example, a consumer carries an attitude about AZ printers in his/her head, and we're trying to discern it. We do so by measuring slightly different aspects of the attitude so as to see the overlapping or covarying essences of the survey items that we hope together reflect the otherwise unobservable or latent attitude. Given the underlying theory, factor analysis is more elegant, so we'll almost always prefer a factor analysis model to a principal components analysis. Let's compare the models a bit more.

We've just seen that in principal components, we factor R to get $V\Lambda V'$ and then rearrange the terms to get an approximation, $R \approx B_r B_r{}'$. What this means is that we're modeling each of our original p variables, $X_1, X_2, \ldots X_p$ as a function of the first r underlying principal components. Here's what that equation looks like for the jth variable:
$$x_j = b_{j1}P_1 + b_{j2}P_2 + \cdots + b_{jr}P_r.$$
The factor analytical model appears only slightly different:
$$x_j = b_{j1}F_1 + b_{j2}F_2 + \cdots + b_{jr}F_r + d_jU_j$$
$$= b_{j1}F_1 + b_{j2}F_2 + \cdots + b_{jr}F_r + c_jS_j + e_jE_j.$$
The values for the b's and r are not necessarily the same in principal components and factor analysis, but the structures of the models are written with the same terms to make the comparison easier. In the factor model, the F's are the "factors" or the "common factors" (to reflect the goal of factor analysis capturing the common variability, i.e., the co-variability across a set of items).

The factor analysis model also contains additional terms. The equation adds a weight (d) associated with a factor that is unique U to variable j. Recall the survey questions—while we hope the 3 items measuring value share the common thread about value, we want to be sure to acknowledge and model the slight idiosyncrasies of the variables. The factor "U" is called a uniqueness factor. Factor 4.4 illustrates conceptually what a factor analysis model looks like for 6 items measuring value and satisfaction. The observed measured variables are depicted in the boxes, the 2 common factors, F_1 and F_2, are in the ovals to the left, and there are arrows from the factors to the variables to represent that the factors are reflected in or give rise to the observed variables. Also contributing to the variables are the uniqueness factors to the right. The strengths of the reflections of the common factors are the b coefficients, and the uniqueness factors have the d coefficients. As noted in the second line depicting the factor analysis model above, we could decompose the uniqueness factors further into pieces that represent a systematic "specific" factor, S (something systematic and unique about the item), and a random measurement error, "E" (just noise).

Whereas the objective in principal components is data simplification, attempting to explain as much variance in the p original variables by the components as possible, in factor analysis, we explain the variances for each of the p variables fully (via those U terms), so that we may focus the model on extracting and understanding as much of the covarying information among the p variables as possible—we want to explain as much covariance as possible.

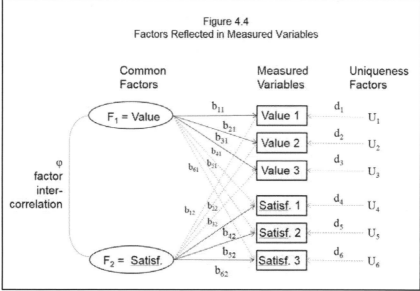

Figure 4.4
Factors Reflected in Measured Variables

So in factor analysis, we don't actually factor R. In factor analysis, the first thing the model or computer does is to adjust R for those uniqueness factors. We don't have a good estimate of uniqueness per se, but we can get an estimate of its obverse, the communality, or the extent to which a variable j shares a lot in common with the other variables. The model or computer will compute $R^2_{1 \bullet 2,3,...,p}$, $R^2_{2 \bullet 1,3,...,p}$, ..., and $R^2_{p \bullet 1,2,3,...,p-1}$, where each squared multiple correlation (SMC) tries to predict each variable in turn from all the others. (Then the uniqueness of a variable is 1 minus its communality.) We (the computer) pop those SMCs into the diagonal of R, and then obtain the eigenvalues and vectors of that adjusted R matrix: $R_{adjusted} = R_{SMC} = V \Lambda V'$. Once again, we can break the eigensolution in two, defined $B = V \Lambda^{.5}$ so $R_{SMC} = BB'$ or $R_{SMC} \approx B_r B_r'$. Just like déjà vu all over again.

Figure 4.5 illustrates these steps: the model begins with the correlation matrix among the 6 items measuring value and satisfaction. The squared multiple correlations for each of the 6 variables appear beneath the matrix R, and they are inserted into the diagonal of R to obtain R_{SMC}. That adjusted matrix is factored into eigenvalues and eigenvectors.

Figure 4.5
Matrix Multiplication of Eigenvector to Factor

$$R \longrightarrow R_{SMC} \longrightarrow V\Lambda V' \longrightarrow BB'$$

R

1.000	0.971	0.944	0.402	0.371	0.382
0.971	1.000	0.957	0.404	0.369	0.386
0.944	0.957	1.000	0.387	0.355	0.379
0.402	0.404	0.387	1.000	0.964	0.948
0.371	0.369	0.355	0.964	1.000	0.967
0.382	0.386	0.379	0.948	0.967	1.000

SMC's ($R^2_{1-2,3,4,5,6}$; $R^2_{2-1,3,4,5,6}$; ...):

| value1 | value2 | value3 | satisf1 | satisf2 | satisf3 |
| 0.946 | 0.958 | 0.921 | 0.935 | 0.958 | 0.940 |

R_{SMC}

0.946	0.971	0.944	0.402	0.371	0.382
0.971	0.958	0.957	0.404	0.369	0.386
0.944	0.957	0.922	0.387	0.355	0.379
0.402	0.404	0.387	0.935	0.964	0.948
0.371	0.369	0.355	0.964	0.958	0.967
0.382	0.386	0.379	0.948	0.967	0.940

To keep things simple, we've extracted only r = 2 vectors, and they comprise the columns of V in the figure. Matrix multiplication works off the rows of the first matrix and columns of the second, so if we compute 0.409*2.00115 + 0.407*0 = 0.819, we obtain the loading b_{11} in B. A second example appears in the dashed circles: using the 5th row and the 2nd column to get the (5th, 2nd) element in B, b_{52}: 0.406*0 − 0.425*1.30979 = −0.557.

The columns in B are the factors. The first factor explains the most covariance among the p variables (remember, in factor analysis the variances are already covered and explained), the second factor explains the next most covariance that remains among the p variables such that the second factor is orthogonal to or uncorrelated with the first factor, and so on, through r factors. Let us turn to the question of "What is r?"

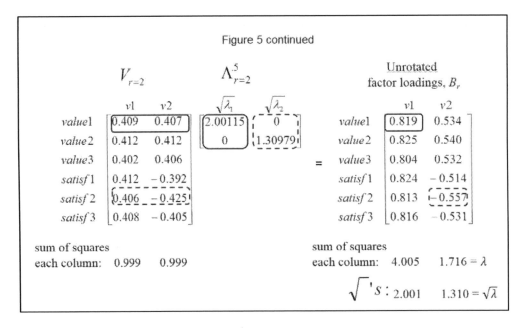

Figure 5 continued

$V_{r=2}$ $\Lambda^5_{r=2}$ Unrotated factor loadings, B_r

	v1	v2
*value*1	0.409	0.407
*value*2	0.412	0.412
*value*3	0.402	0.406
*satisf*1	0.412	−0.392
*satisf*2	0.406	−0.425
*satisf*3	0.408	−0.405

$\sqrt{\lambda_1}$ $\sqrt{\lambda_2}$

2.00115	0
0	1.30979

=

	v1	v2
*value*1	0.819	0.534
*value*2	0.825	0.540
*value*3	0.804	0.532
*satisf*1	0.824	−0.514
*satisf*2	0.813	−0.557
*satisf*3	0.816	−0.531

sum of squares each column: 0.999   0.999

sum of squares each column: 4.005   1.716 = λ

$\sqrt{}$'s : 2.001   1.310 = $\sqrt{\lambda}$

Selecting "r," the Number of Factors

If we took all p eigenvalues and their corresponding eigenvectors, then we would have p sets of weights to take our original data X's and transform them into factors. But that would be silly, given that one of our goals was to simplify our world, from p down to a smaller number, if not 1, then say, r << p. So, we take the first r eigenvalues and vectors, and probably recapture our correlation matrix pretty well: $\approx V_r \Lambda_r V_r'$.

We've seen this trade-off in statistics before—in multiple regression, an R^2 will increase as we add variables, but at some point, the model will have become ridiculously complex. In the factor analytic model, if we take many eigenvalues and vectors, that is, if r is large and approaching p, then we'll capture R really well. If we take very few eigenvalues and vectors, that is, r is small, then we won't capture R as well as one might hope, but we'd gain in simplicity

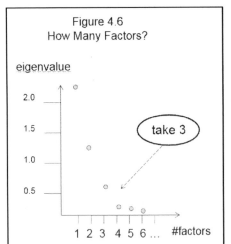

Figure 4.6
How Many Factors?

eigenvalue

take 3

1 2 3 4 5 6 ...   #factors

and parsimony. Thus the determination of "what is r; how many factors do we need" will be one of diminishing returns—we'll take one factor, assess how much it explains, then take two factors and see whether it explains a sufficient additional amount that it's worth taking it and making the picture more complicated with two factors instead of one. We'll solve this dilemma fairly easily.

Figure 4.6 shows a plot of eigenvalues, and we're going to look for a break, or an elbow in the curve. The break appears between the 3rd and 4th eigenvalue, so we'll take the number of factors, r, to be the number to the left or above the break, hence, 3 in the figure. The idea is that the first three values are large enough that each factor explains a decent amount of (co)variance, but the 4th and 5th and onward are probably not worth retaining because they explain so little of the data.

This heuristic has been systematized into a program. When we factor analyze some data, on p variables and a sample size of N, we'll get certain eigenvalues to plot. The program will generate a data set with the same p and N, but all the "data" are random. In random data, the variables shouldn't be correlated, so when the program extracts eigenvalues from the random correlation matrix, they too are essentially random, or noise. We'll then plot our real eigenvalues against the random ones, and where the curves cross each other, we'll know which part of our data is real—so they're the factors—vs. which part looks like random and residual error.

Orthogonal Rotations (But Use an Oblique Rotation Instead)

There is one final issue in factor analysis that is very important. In factor analyses, we'll rotate the factor axes to enhance interpretability. While the factor matrix B has the nice math property of the first factor explaining the greatest amount of covariability (known as the principal-axis elliptical orientation), there may be some other orientation of the r factors in space that is more desirable.

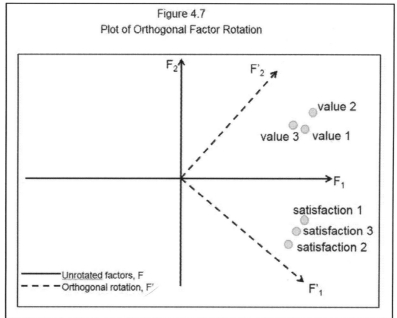

To understand the issue, consider Figure 4.7. The 6 survey items for value and satisfaction are plotted along the horizontal and vertical axes, which are the factors derived right from the R_{SMC}, eigenvectors to B computations we just finished. Note that if we projected the variables onto these initial factors, the coordinates would say that factor 1 is a combination of all 6 variables, and factor 2 contrasts the value and satisfaction variables. That's okay, but it doesn't make for a very parsimonious interpretation of factor 1.

If we take the original factors and rotate the axes, by spinning them together just slightly clockwise, in this plot by approximately an angle of $\theta = 45°$, the new axes would appear where the dashed lines are. Those axes would be the factors after an orthogonal rotation. Orthogonal means the factors are still uncorrelated, and the axes are perpendicular to each other. Now project the variables onto the orthogonally rotated factors, F'_1 and F'_2. The factors are simpler to interpret and characterize—factor 1 is satisfaction and factor 2 is value.

Wait, can we just do that? Why yes. Yes we can.

Here's assurance that we can conduct such rotations. Recall the factor model is: $R_{SMC} = BB'$. Say we wish to rotate the factors using a transformation matrix, T, and we'd do so via $A = BT$ (or note $B = AT^{-1}$. We could write our model like this: $R_{SMC} = BIIB'$, where the I's are two innocuous identity matrices (like multiplying a number by 1). Any matrix times its inverse equals 1; e.g., $TT^{-1} = T^{-1}T = I$ (and for these orthonormal transformation matrices, T' also equals T^{-1}). Thus we can substitute: $R_{SMC} = BIIB' = B(T'T^{-1})(T'^{-1}T')B' = (BT)(T^{-1}T'^{-1})(T'B') = AIA' = AA'$. How about that. We had one set of original factors in B, and when we transformed them, the newly rotated factors in A, formed an alternate factor analysis solution.

Now we know that a transformation is permissible, so next the question is how to do it. If we sought the graphical rotation of 45°, we could use the sine and cosine of that angle in a matrix to transform the raw, original, unrotated factors, F_1 and F_2, to their new location as the orthogonally rotated factors, F'_1 and F'_2. This orthogonal rotation is depicted in Figure 4.8. The matrix at the right contains the new factor loadings.

Computers aren't very handy at estimating angles or using protractors, so naturally there are algorithms for factor rotations. The most popular and best algorithm for an orthogonal rotation is called "varimax" for variance maximization. The logic is that if the factors were simple and clean, there would be a few high loadings (large coordinates in the factor loadings matrix, e.g., the one at the right in Figure 4.8) and many very small loadings depicting variables that do not define that factor axis. If we had a few large loadings and many small loadings, the distribution of loadings would be bimodal. A bimodal distribution has the maximum variance of any distributional form (e.g., compared to a normal distribution), so what we'll do is to turn these principles inside out, and maximize the variance of the loadings on each factor. Then we'll end up with a few large loadings and many small ones. The variance of the p (squared) loadings on factor j is: $\sigma_j^2 = \frac{1}{p}\sum_{i=1}^{p}\left(b_{ij}^2 - \overline{b_{ij}^2}\right)^2$, so over all r factors, the variance that the computer is maximizing is: $\sigma = \frac{1}{p}\sum_{i=1}^{p}\sum_{j=1}^{r}\left(b_{ij}^2 - \overline{b_{ij}^2}\right)^2$.

Figure 4.8
Matrices for Orthogonal Factor Rotation

	Unrotated factors, B_r		transformation		Orthogonally rotated factors	
	F_1	F_2			F'_1	F'_2
value1	0.819	0.534	0.708	.706	0.203	0.956
value2	0.825	0.540	$-.706$	0.708	0.202	0.965
value3	0.804	0.532			0.193	0.945
satisf1	0.824	-0.514			0.946	0.219
satisf2	0.813	-0.557			0.969	0.180
satisf3	0.816	-0.531			0.953	0.201

$$\begin{bmatrix} \cos\theta & -\sin\theta \\ \sin\theta & \cos\theta \end{bmatrix}$$
$$\theta \approx 45°$$

Oblique Rotations

We could do an even better job of finding clean, clear, simple, interpretable factors if we did a rotation where we were willing to forgo the usual property of axes being orthogonal (i.e., perpendicular). A so-called oblique rotation allows factors to be correlated, as depicted by the factors F''₁ and F''₂ in Figure 4.9, drawn with the dotted lines.

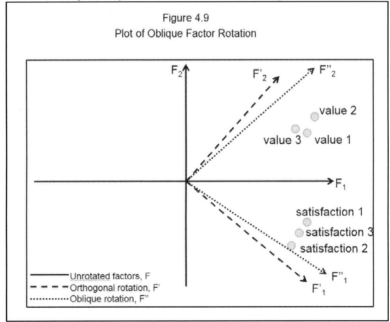

Figure 4.9
Plot of Oblique Factor Rotation

The best-performing oblique rotation is called "promax." The easiest way to describe this algorithm is that we begin with a varimax rotation. So let's start with the unrotated factor loadings matrix B, and use the orthogonal transformation matrix T, to obtain the new orthogonally rotated factor loadings matrix A: A = BT'. Then the promax model essentially raises every loading to a power. For example, imagine taking the loadings in A and squaring them. Then a large loading in A gets smaller (e.g., 0.7→0.49), but the small loadings get really small (e.g., 0.3→0.09) (that's a good thing). In truth, the power used in promax is often cubic, in part to retain the positive or negative signs of the loadings in A, if there are any. Figure 4.10 shows the factor loadings from A transformed by cubing them to obtain the oblique factor loadings matrix, A*, in the right of Figure 4.10.

An oblique rotation means the factors may be correlated. The matrix Φ contains the inter-correlations among the factors. For these data, the correlation is moderate, but greater than zero, suggesting we should work with the oblique factors. If φ had been very low, e.g., 0.1, then we might find it simpler to stick with the orthogonal rotation. If φ had been very high, e.g., 0.7 or higher, we might worry that we've extracted too many factors, because the very high correlation suggests that one of the factors is rather redundant with another. We should probably return to the first stages of factor extraction and reduce our r (take one fewer factor).

In nearly any application we'll see, dealing with consumers or business customers (who are ultimately run by human agents), we'll probably be dealing with constructs that we expect will be somewhat related to each other. If that's the case, we should work with factors that have been rotated to an oblique solution. When factors are correlated, then an orthogonal rotation will only be a rough representation. Oblique rotations can never do worse than orthogonal rotations, and at "worst" will simply equal the orthogonal rotation (when all the factor inter-correlations: φ's = 0). Thus: go for an oblique rotation.

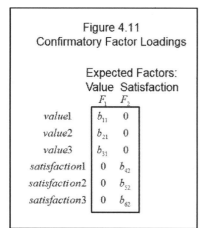

Figure 4.10
Matrices for Oblique Factor Rotation

Orthogonally rotated factors

F'_1	F'_2
0.203	0.956
0.202	0.965
0.193	0.945
0.946	0.219
0.969	0.180
0.953	0.201

^3 →

Oblique factor loadings

	F''_1	F''_2
value1	0.008	0.874
value2	0.008	0.898
value3	0.007	0.843
satisf1	0.848	0.010
satisf2	0.910	0.006
satisf3	0.865	0.008

$\phi = 0.385$

In the factor loadings matrix (at the right in Figure 4.10), we interpret the factors by using the loadings that exceed 0.3. Thus, F''_1 is defined by the last 3 variables—so we would likely label that factor as reflecting "satisfaction," and similarly, F''_2 would be labeled "value." Going forward, we would be confident that our 2 sets of 3 variables hung together and covaried in the right patterns. We can use all 6 items, or we can compute 2 means (one for value and one for satisfaction), in either case confident that the measurement is clean.[16] See Table 4.1 for a quick summary of factor analysis.

Figure 4.11
Confirmatory Factor Loadings

Expected Factors:
Value Satisfaction

	F_1	F_2
value1	b_{11}	0
value2	b_{21}	0
value3	b_{31}	0
satisfaction1	0	b_{42}
satisfaction2	0	b_{52}
satisfaction3	0	b_{62}

Confirmatory Factor Analysis

Before we close, it's important to note that there is yet another class of factor analysis. We have been conducting what is called "exploratory factor analysis." The idea is that we have a handful of variables, and we want to get a better sense of the pattern of correlations underlying those variables. In contrast, a technique called "confirmatory factor analysis" assumes we have a pretty good idea about which variables should load on (and help define) each factor.

To illustrate, we have a factor loadings matrix in Figure 4.11 with a block of loadings in the first factor (that will be estimated), and some in the second column as well. In each factor column, there are also blocks of 0's. A zero in a confirmatory factor analysis means we don't believe that the row variable should load on the column factor. So if that column factor represents a construct that should not be reflected in that row-measured variable, we won't even estimate a loading for that element in the matrix.

When we're in confirmatory mode, we're looking to see whether the factor loadings matrix estimated on our data fits this pattern. The b's may still be estimated to be any value, but if one of the 0 elements corresponds to a loading in our data that is small but still nonzero, that difference will contribute to a lack of fit. Hence, confirmatory factor analysis is a rigorous measurement model.

IRL, most factor analyses are of the exploratory variety we've seen throughout the chapter. However, one of

---

[16] You might hear it suggested that you create "factor scores," but research continues to show superior empirical performance for computations of simple unit-weighted means of variables.

the places where we will see confirmatory factor analyses is in conjunction with path models, in what are called structural equations models, all of which are the topics of the next chapter.

Summary

Good marketers and good companies care about their customers. We want to know whether they're satisfied or not, and it's important to know what drives those assessments so that we can continue to do well, or improve and do better. Satisfaction and many other types of marketing metrics are measured with some subjectivity. Factor analysis helps both to assess and assure that we're measuring those customer attitudes and perceptions as cleanly as possible.

Table 4.1: Helpful Tips for Factor Analysis

What does factor analysis do?

- ☐ Analyzes interrelationships among a large number of variables
- ☐ Explains the correlations in terms of what the variables have in common, i.e., the underlying factors
- ☐ Helps simplify, via data reduction, from p variables to r common factors, helps with survey refinement
- ☐ Recognizes measurement error, can estimate reliability
- ☐ Allows you to choose factor analysis over principal components

What decisions to make?
- ☐ Which questions to include in the data collection survey, what variables to draw from an existing database, be thoughtful, otherwise: gigo (garbage in, garbage out)
- ☐ Sample size: bigger is better (but small can be sufficient if the measurement is clean, i.e., the loadings are large on the correct factors and negligible on the other factors).
- ☐ Use factor analysis (a.k.a. principal factors, works with R_{SMC}), not principal components analysis (works with R), and be precise with the terms—they're not the same model
- ☐ To select the appropriate number of factors, use a plot of eigenvalues, or program systematizing cross-over with eigenvalues of random R
- ☐ Factor rotation—do oblique (promax) first. If all $|\varphi|$'s ≤ 0.3, you can use the orthogonal (varimax) rotation (because it's simpler to understand as a model and to communicate in plots). If any $|\varphi| > 0.3$, use the oblique solution (because the assumption of uncorrelated factors needed for varimax is evidently not true). If any $|\varphi| > 0.7$, you might have extracted too many factors—reduce r and rotate again.
- ☐ Interpret the factor pattern matrix, not the factor structure matrix (for orthogonal factors, these are identical). A variable is useful in understanding, defining, and labeling a factor if its factor loading is ≥ 0.3 or ≤ -0.3.
- ☐ Yay, you are now a bonafide factor analyst!

References

Intro texts on factor analysis:
- Cliff, Norman (1987), *Analyzing Multivariate Data,* San Diego: Harcourt Brace Jovanovich.
- Comrey, Andrew L. and Howard B. Lee (1992), *A First Course in Factor Analysis, 2nd* ed., Hillsdale. NJ: Erlbaum.
- Cooper, John C. B. (1983), "Factor Analysis: An Overview," *The American Statistician,* 37 (2), 141-147.
- Iacobucci, Dawn (1994). "Classic Factor Analysis," in Richard Bagozzi (ed.), *Principles of Marketing Research,* Cambridge, MA: Blackwell, 279-316.
- Gorsuch, Richard L. (1983), *Factor Analysis* 2nd ed., Hillsdale, NJ: Erlbaum.
- Kim, Jae-On, and Charles W. Mueller (1978), *Introduction to Factor Analysis: What It Is and How to Do it,* Beverly Hills, CA: Sage.
- Kim, Jae-On, and Charles W. Mueller (1978), *Factor Analysis: Statistical Methods and Practical Issues,* Beverly Hills, CA: Sage.

Info on measurement theory:

- Allen Mary J. and Wendy M. Yen (1979; 2002), *Introduction to Measurement Theory*, Prospect Heights, IL: Waveland Press.
- Anastasi, Anne (1982), *Psychological Testing* 5th ed., NY: Macmillan.
- Cronbach, Lee J. (1984), *Essentials of Psychological Testing* 4th ed., NY: Harper & Row.
- Ghiselli, Edwin E., John P. Campbell, and Sheldon Zedeck (1981), *Measurement Theory for the Behavioral Sciences*, San Francisco: Freeman.
- Nunnally, Jum C. and Ira H. Bernstein (1995), *Psychometric Theory* 3rd ed., NY: McGraw-Hill.
- Duhachek, Adam, Anne T. Coughlan and Dawn Iacobucci (2005), "Results on the Standard Error of the Coefficient Alpha Index of Reliability," *Marketing Science*, 24 (2), 294-301.
- Duhachek, Adam and Dawn Iacobucci (2004), "Alpha's Standard Error (ASE): An Accurate and Precise Confidence Interval Estimate," *Journal of Applied Psychology*, 89 (5), 792-808.

Confirmatory factor analysis and maximum likelihood estimation:

- Joreskog, K. G. (1967), "Some Contributions to Maximum Likelihood Factor Analysis," *Psychometrika*, 32, 443-82.
- Joreskog, K. G. (1969), "A General Approach to Confirmatory Maximum Likelihood Factor Analysis," *Psychometrika*, 34, 183-202.
- Long, J. Scott (1983), *Confirmatory Factor Analysis*, Newbury Park, CA: Sage.

Thumbnail sketch regarding software:

- SAS: Proc factor, method=ml for maximum likelihood or method=principal, priors=smc (default is priors=one for principal components), nfactors=3 (start with a large number to get scree), rotate=promax (includes varimax orthogonal as part of it).. For help: support.sas.com/documentation/
- SPSS: go to analyze, data reduction, factor, select your variables, choose extraction (principal factor or maximum likelihood) and rotation (promax). For help: search "IBM SPSS documentation," and open the "statistics base" manual.
- XLStat: choose menu dropdown of modeling data, choose logistic regression, response variable is your dep var, then select qualitiative predictors for logit, and if you want, add quantitative predictors for logistic regression. For help: www.xlstat.com, click on "support" and then "tutorials."

Chapter 5: Drivers of Customer Satisfaction and Path Models

Marketing Concept: Drivers of Customer Satisfaction and Other Marketing Metrics
Modeling Concept: Path Models, Structural Equations Models, CLV

Chapter Outline
5. Introduction
6. Path Models—Like Regression on Steroids
7. How to Fit Path Models
8. Structural Equations Models
9. Customer Lifetime Value (CLV)

Introduction

In Chapter 4, we discussed the measurement of some concepts like customer satisfaction that marketing managers care about that are a bit more challenging to capture than variables like ROI, brand share, profitability, etc. (not that these don't have their own issues!). Yet of course the measurement in and of itself is not the end goal. The ultimate concern in marketing is to understand those customers' opinions and the drivers of their evaluations, to give us a sense of how we might improve our customers' experiences, and perhaps also our profitability.

For convenience, Figure 5.1 recalls the 15-item customer satisfaction survey from Chapter 4, with its groups of 5 constructs: customer perceptions of quality, price, value, satisfaction, and likelihood to repeat their purchase. In this context, our mission is not simply to measure satisfaction, rather, we seek to understand which attributes are the strongest drivers, or predictors, of repeat purchases, or the aspects of the purchase that contribute the most to customers' feelings that they might purchase this brand again.

Figure 5.1
Customer Satisfaction Survey for AZ Printers

	Strongly Disagree					Strongly Agree
The quality of the AZ printer I bought is excellent.	1 2 3 4 5 6 7
AZ printers are known to be highly reliable.	1 2 3 4 5 6 7
I'm sure my AZ printer will last a long time.	1 2 3 4 5 6 7
The AZ printer was reasonably priced.	1 2 3 4 5 6 7
AZ sets fair prices for its products.	1 2 3 4 5 6 7
The AZ printers are no more expensive than others.	1 2 3 4 5 6 7
I feel like I got good value for this purchase.	1 2 3 4 5 6 7
The quality of the printer is worth its cost.	1 2 3 4 5 6 7
I could tell my boss this purchase was good value.	1 2 3 4 5 6 7
I am very satisfied with my newly purchase AZ printer.	1 2 3 4 5 6 7
My printer is better than I expected it would be.	1 2 3 4 5 6 7
I have no regrets about having bought this printer.	1 2 3 4 5 6 7
I would buy another AZ if I had to buy another printer.	1 2 3 4 5 6 7
I would buy other AZ products.	1 2 3 4 5 6 7
I would tell my friends and coworkers to buy AZs.	1 2 3 4 5 6 7

To assess these drivers, we might begin simply, with a regression model in which we try to predict repeat purchasing as a function of the other 4 constructs: quality, price, value, and satisfaction. With those 12 predictors, we'd expect multicollinearity, because the 3 variables that measure quality are surely correlated amongst themselves, as would be the 3 that measure price, and so on. We can simplify our world by verifying the measurement pattern via factor analysis, and then computing 5 means, so as to have 1 score each on the dependent and 4 independent variables.

Even with the simplification of taking 15 variables to 5 scales, we might still worry a bit about lingering multicollinearity—it seems likely that these predictors would be correlated. Nevertheless, we would proceed as usual in a regression. Regressions are easy to do, and most people we'll be dealing with either understand them or at least have heard of them, so communication of the results is enhanced, etc.

Regression is a simple and powerful approach and indeed it serves us very well. But we can do even better—path path models will make you forget that you ever heard about regression.

Path Models—Like Regression on Steroids

As great as regression is, it is still a bit simplistic. For example, we might suspect that repeat purchasing is the end result of a chain reaction from, say, value to satisfaction to repeat. This chain is a conceptual model that is slightly more complicated, but therefore it is probably also more realistic of customers' perceptions and evaluations of brands in purchasing decisions. Yet a regression wouldn't allow us to examine that model. To test the chain, we might run two regressions, in the first using value to predict satisfaction: value→satisfaction, and in the second, using satisfaction to predict repeat: satisfaction→repeat. When these analyses were complete, we would have the results of two regressions, but no way to integrate their results.

Figure 5.2 depicts a model that contains the chain we just described, along with a few other hypothetical causal relationships. The model doesn't look terribly complex conceptually, but it would prove puzzling to fit via regression. Path models to the rescue!

Each relationship hypothesized by an arrow can be estimated and tested (for significance), all in a single model. Each arrow will have a path coefficient, analogous to a regression coefficient, and they're all estimated simultaneously, which is important so that each path coefficient is as pure an estimate as possible, having partialled out, or statistically controlled for, all the other relationships. If the path coefficient estimates look odd, or the model doesn't fit, we can insert additional paths (or variables), extract some of these paths (or variables), or both, just as we might in regression.

Figure 5.2
Path Model

How to Fit Path Models

Given that path models allow for more complex forms of models, we need a few new pieces of jargon and notation. In regression, we use X_1, X_2, X_3, etc., as predictors or independent variables, and Y as a dependent variable. In a path model, we might posit paths from A to B to C, and if we were to fit the model in pieces, variable B would serve as a dependent variable in the A→B piece, but B would serve as a predictor in the B→C piece. So we'll use slightly different terms.

Just as in regression there is a distinction in terminology that we use independent variables to predict the dependent variable, in path models, we distinguish exogenous (predictors) and endogenous (dependent) variables. Specifically, in path models, if a variable has any precursor, i.e., any arrow coming into it, it is called an endogenous variable, and is denoted η ("eta"). Variables that are not posited to be the effects of any predictors are called exogenous variables ξ ("ksi"). Thus, in the A→B→C string, variable A is exogenous and variables B and C are both endogenous.

In Figure 5.2, quality and cost are exogenous, and value, satisfaction, and repeat are endogenous variables. There is nothing magic in this distinction; if we were to remove the links from quality and price to value, then value would be another exogenous variable. Further, we can

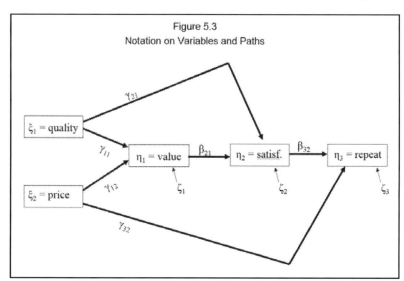

Figure 5.3
Notation on Variables and Paths

acknowledge that IRL, quality probably has precursors, but we don't have any in our data and for our current purposes, we don't really care what they are.

In Figure 5.3, we see the exogenous variables labeled with ξ, and the endogenous variables are called η's. In addition, the path coefficients between the variables are labeled. The coefficients that reflect the strength of relationship between one endogenous variable (η) and another endogenous variable (η) are called β, and the coefficients that reflect relationships that link an exogenous variable (ξ) to an endogenous variable (η) are called γ. Those two sets of path coefficients are called different things, β and γ, but they're both interpreted just like regression coefficients in regression.

In addition, Figure 5.3 displays 3 ζ terms that are errors, like ε in regressions. In the path model, we're trying to predict each of those η's, and we realize there will be some prediction error. The error variances (σ_{ψ}^2) capture lack of fit, just like $1 - R^2$ in regression.

The path model depicted in Figure 5.3 implies the following relationships—note that there is one equation per endogenous variable (η):

$$\text{value} = \gamma_{11} \text{ quality} + \gamma_{12} \text{ price} + \zeta_1,$$
$$\text{satisfaction} = \gamma_{21} \text{ quality} + \beta_{21} \text{ value} + \zeta_2,$$
$$\text{repeat} = \gamma_{32} \text{ price} + \beta_{32} \text{ satisfaction} + \zeta_3.$$

Figures 5.4 and 5.5 contain all these path coefficients compiled neatly into two matrices, Γ and B. Both matrices are formatted such that the column variable affects the row variable; e.g., γ_{21} extends from quality to satisfaction.

Figure 5.4
Effects of Exogenous on Endogenous

$$\Gamma = \begin{array}{c} \eta_1 = value \\ \eta_2 = satisf \\ \eta_3 = repeat \end{array} \begin{array}{|cc|} \hline \xi_1 = quality & \xi_2 = price \\ \gamma_{11} & \gamma_{12} \\ \gamma_{21} & 0 \\ 0 & \gamma_{32} \\ \hline \end{array}$$

Figure 5.5
Effects of Endogenous on Endogenous

$$B = \begin{array}{c} \eta_1 = value \\ \eta_2 = satisf \\ \eta_3 = repeat \end{array} \begin{array}{|ccc|} \hline \eta_1 = value & \eta_2 = satisf & \eta_3 = repeat \\ 0. & 0 & 0 \\ \beta_{21} & 0. & 0 \\ 0 & \beta_{32} & 0. \\ \hline \end{array}$$

Figure 5.6 contains the covariance and correlation matrices from Chapter 4, computed over a sample of 100 customers. Statistical theory for path models was developed on covariance matrices, so we need to use covariance matrices if we want to be sure that the statistical tests of the path coefficients and the fit statistics for the overall model are valid. Recall $cov(X, Y) = r_{XY}\sigma_X\sigma_Y$ and $r_{XY} = \dfrac{cov(X,Y)}{\sigma_X\sigma_Y}$.

Figure 5.6
Covariances and Correlations

Covariances:

	quality	price	value	satisf.	repeat
quality	2.0113				
price	-0.0719	2.5384			
value	1.1926	-1.2155	2.0738		
satisfaction	1.2482	-0.4925	0.8035	2.0076	
repeat	0.7615	-0.9282	0.3866	1.1610	1.9957

Correlations:

	quality	price	value	satisf.	repeat
quality	1.00				
price	-0.03	1.00			
value	0.58	-0.53	1.00		
satisfaction	0.62	-0.22	0.39	1.00	
repeat	0.38	-0.41	0.19	0.58	1.00

When the model in Figure 5.3 is fit to the covariance data in Figure 5.6, the path coefficients that are estimated are found in Figure 5.7. Most of the anticipated paths are significant ($p < .05$, noted by the asterisk). Altogether, the estimated model in Figure 5.7 tells us that value seems to be a trade-off between quality and price, satisfaction appears to be a function of quality but not value (at least for this product purchase). And the big prize is what we wanted to know about what drives repeat purchasing—it seems to be a function of satisfaction and price.

The path coefficient from value→satisfaction was not significant. That result might have been a surprise, e.g., we could have anticipated it to be significant so we included it in our model, and now we want to think about deleting it or moving it around in the model. Or the result might not have been a surprise—maybe we didn't care that much about whether it would be significant, but we included it in the model as a statistical control because others would expect the link to be represented.

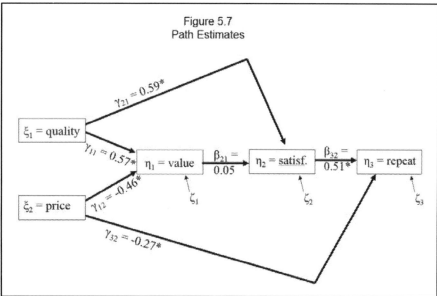

Figure 5.7
Path Estimates

Path model programs produce several kinds of fit indices. There are fits for the individual endogenous equations. The R^2 for the value equation is 0.603, R^2 for satisfaction is 0.387, and R^2 for repeat is 0.389. These are all decent R^2s for real data, and they tell us that we have done a better job of predicting value than satisfaction and repeat. The difference might be due to our conceptualizing value better, in which case we might play with moving paths or adding predictors for satisfaction and repeat. Alternatively, we might have measured the variables relevant to value more cleanly than those for satisfaction and repeat, in which case we might want to review the survey to see if it was perhaps a bit ambiguous (measurement error) or too broad in scope in its questions about satisfaction and repeat (model is poorly specified).

There are many indices that capture the extent of fit for the entire path model as a whole. One index is called the standardized root mean residual (SRMR). The residuals are simply the difference between each of the covariances in our data (from Figure 5.6) and the corresponding predicted covariance using the path model coefficients. The average of these residuals is computed, and the square root of that is taken. The index is standardized by scaling the residuals by the standard deviations. In the equation that follows, p is the number of endogenous variables (like Y's), q is the number of exogenous variables (like X's), and k = p + q, then $= \sqrt{\left\{\sum_{i=1}^{k} \sum_{j=i+1}^{k} \left[(s_{ij} - \hat{\sigma}_{ij})/(s_{ii}s_{jj})\right]^2\right\}/[k(k+1)/2]}$.

Residuals reflect lack of fit, since they compare the data, s_{ij}, to the model's prediction for the covariances, σ_{ij}. Thus, while we seek large values for R^2, we look for small values in SRMR. If the model predicted the data perfectly, SRMR would equal 0; ideally we'd like a value smaller than 0.09. For the data in Figure 5.6, the Standardized RMR = 0.073, a fit that isn't bad, but could probably be improved if we reconceptualized some of the relationships, variables, and links.

As a final note regarding fit, keep in mind that these fit indices are intended to provide guidance, yet they shouldn't be taken as hyper-reality. For example, in regression, a model may have a fairly low R^2 yet be very useful— real world data tend to be very noisy, the dependent variables may be complex (e.g., consumer behavior!), samples tend to be rather heterogeneous (e.g., adding even more variance), etc. In many scenarios, R^2s of 0.3 could be impressive, and the model may explicate the relative importance of different predictors and directions for the brand manager to take. Conversely, sometimes a very high R^2 is associated with a model that isn't that helpful, perhaps because some predictor variable is very similar to the dependent variable, thus yielding a strong fit yet providing little more "explanation" than a tautology. In path models also, if the fit is poor, consider whether some variables have been left out of the model and it could be improved, and if the fit is suspiciously high, consider whether the model could be made more parsimonious (such as by removing a path or two or a variable or two).

Before leaving discussions of path models and how they're fit, we note 3 points. First, like most of the techniques described in this book, path models are applicable to many settings and many kinds of data. Thus, while we have focused on customer satisfaction judgments, these models can be used in just about any context. For example, Figure 5.8 depicts a path model for a B2B purchase decision, in which reliability and service helped reduce risk, and risk and price affected repeat (note that we would expect all path coefficients to be negative in this example). In the B2C path model, we have incorporated the classic effects of advertising affecting awareness, which in turn enhances attitudes about the ad, attitudes about the brand, etc. Conceptually, this model is fundamental to marketers, and while it would be clumsy to fit via regressions, it is easy to fit via a path model.

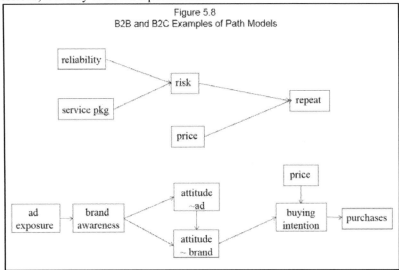

Figure 5.8
B2B and B2C Examples of Path Models

Second, the path model for one sample can be compared to the path model on another sample. One arena in which this comparison is useful is in comparing customer judgments across offices, particularly for global multinational firms. It is well known that customers in Japan fill out surveys predictably differently from customers in Brazil, England, or the U.S.. Those differences are reflected in means (e.g., scoring higher or lower on a 7-point scale) and variances (e.g., using 1s and 7s vs. using 3s and 5s), but path models and structural equations models can control for these differences. The path model focus is on the structure of associations between the constructs, and would allow a global brand manager to conclude that, rating styles aside, the Brazilians seem to appreciate qualities A, B, and C whereas customer satisfaction in Singapore is more driven by qualities C, D, and E.

Third, there are always ways to increase the complexity of path models themselves, to fit even more sophisticated (and therefore probably more realistic) models. One extension is to allow for multi-item scales measuring each of the constructs. For example, instead of taking the mean of the 3 quality items, as we did on our survey from the beginning, we could represent each of the 3 items rather than their aggregate. That representation of how the constructs are measured is done in a factor analysis, and when that factor analytic measurement model is combined with the structure of a path model, the overall fuller model is called a structural equations model.

Structural Equations Models (SEMs)

Structural equations models (SEMs) are a combination of the measurement model of factor analysis (from Chapter 4) and a path model (as just described). The factor analysis part of the model relates the variables to the constructs, and the path model captures the structural links relating constructs to other constructs.

We're bringing in the factors, so we need a few more touches of notation. The exogenous variables have been labeled x, their constructs or factors are ξ's, and the factor loadings (like the B matrices in Chapter 4) that relate the x's to the ξ's are in a matrix called Λ_x. Similarly, we've been calling the endogenous variables y, their constructs or factors are η's, and the factor loadings that relate the y's to the η's are in the matrix Λ_y.

The factor analysis in an SEM model is a confirmatory factor analysis (as described briefly at the end of Chapter 4). We have a pretty good idea that the "value" survey items should load on one factor that we'll call value, the same for the repeat purchasing items, etc. Thus, we formulate factor loadings matrices like those in Figure 5.9. (There is a 1.0 in each column to normalize each factor.)

While the factors are the new part in SEMs, the path model terms relating the constructs or factors to other constructs or factors remain the same. In contrast to the factor analysis part of an SEM being referred to as the measurement model, the path model is often referred to as the structural model. The path model of structural coefficients is unchanged:

$$\eta = B\eta + \Gamma\xi + \zeta$$

where η and ξ are the endogenous and exogenous factors, B relates the η's to other η's, Γ reflects the effects of the ξ's on the η's, and the ζ's are the lack of fits per η. An encyclopedia of terms is listed in Figure 5.10.

Figure 5.9
Confirmatory Factor Loadings (arrow goes from column j to row i)

factor loadings for exogenous constructs:

	quality ξ_1	price ξ_2
$x1 = q1$	$\lambda_{11} = 1$	0
$x2 = q2$	λ_{21}	0
$\Lambda_x = x3 = q3$	λ_{31}	0
$x4 = p1$	0	$\lambda_{42} = 1$
$x5 = p2$	0	λ_{52}
$x6 = p3$	0	λ_{62}

factor loadings for endogenous constructs:

	value η_1	satisf. η_2	repeat η_3
$y1 = v1$	$\lambda_{11} = 1$	0	0
$y2 = v2$	λ_{21}	0	0
$y3 = v3$	λ_{31}	0	0
$\Lambda_Y = y4 = cs1$	0	$\lambda_{42} = 1$	0
$y5 = cs2$	0	λ_{52}	0
$y6 = cs3$	0	λ_{62}	0
$y7 = r1$	0	0	$\lambda_{73} = 1$
$y8 = r2$	0	0	λ_{83}
$y9 = r3$	0	0	λ_{93}

Figure 5.10
The Structural Equation Model and Notation

The factor analytical measurement models for the exogenous and endogenous variables:

$$x = \Lambda_x \xi + \delta \qquad y = \Lambda_y \eta + \varepsilon$$

The path model of structural coefficients:

$$\eta = B\eta + \Gamma\xi + \zeta$$

with terms defined as follows:

- x is a vector of independent, or exogenous, variables
- Λ_x is the matrix of exogenous factor loadings of x on ξ
- ξ is a vector of the independent latent variables, exogenous constructs or factors
- δ is vector of measurement errors in x
- y is a vector of observed variable indicators that are dependent or endogenous
- Λ_y is the matrix of endogenous factor loadings of y on η
- η is a vector of latent dependent, or endogenous constructs or factors
- ε is vector of measurement errors in y
- Φ is not shown above, but it will contain the correlations among the ξs
- Γ is a matrix of coefficients of the ξs on the η's (the structural relationships)
- B is a matrix of coefficients of the η's on η's (also part of the structural relationships)
- ζ is a vector of equation errors (random disturbances) trying to predict the endogenous constructs η (these are the lack-of-model-fit errors).

The fit of the overall SEM model is assessed like a path model. There are many fit indices, but there is fair agreement to report the three that follow. First, as we've seen for path models, we'll report the "standardized root mean square residual." Once again quickly: we compute the residuals (differences between data and model predictions), and take the average and then the square root. SRMR ranges from 0.0 to 1.0, where larger numbers mean a worse fit (so it's a "badness-of-fit" index). The hope is that our SRMR is 0.09 or lower. SRMR is zero when the model predictions match the data perfectly. The index is a good one to use in part because it is fairly robust—relatively insensitive to violations of various assumptions.

Second, we'll also report the X^2 (and its degrees of freedom and p-value). Ideally, for a model that fits the data, the X^2 would not be significant ($p > 0.05$), but it often is because the X^2 is sensitive to sample size. As a result, we consider a model to fit reasonably well if the statistic adjusted by the degrees of freedom does not exceed 3.0; that is, we want $X^2/df \leq 3$.

Third, we'll report the "comparative fit index" (CFI), which should be 0.95 or higher. Whereas the X^2 compares a model to data, the CFI takes the fit of one model and compares it to the fit of another model (i.e., the model of independence in which no paths are estimated), hence, capturing relative goodness of fit. It also attempts to adjust for model complexity or parsimony, by including the model's degrees of freedom directly in the computation. CFI ranges from 0.0 to 1.0, where larger numbers are better.

Finally, while it's not necessarily expected that we report additional statistics, for our own knowledge we might view the R^2's for the η's, as we did in the path model example. If the overall model fit isn't great, the R^2's can be diagnostic to see where we could strengthen the model.

Customer Lifetime Value (CLV)

In the final section of this chapter, we're going to disconnect regarding path models and SEMs, but continue with the marketing content of customer satisfaction. A consideration of customer satisfaction data would be remiss if we didn't also consider Customer Lifetime Value (CLV). CLV is completely different from path models. It's simpler in many ways—it just relies on spreadsheet crunching—and yet it is also very valuable for understanding customers.

One of the reasons brand managers want their customers to be satisfied is because satisfied customers are more likely to return, buy again, become loyal, perhaps generate word of mouth, etc. The value of keeping current customers has been shown in countless studies and industries. Here is a simple thought exercise. Imagine a company that currently has 10,000 customers. Say they add 1000 customers each year, and say they lose (or churn) 10% of their customers (no brand or industry enjoys 100% repeat). In year 1, they'd have 10,000 customers + 1000 new – 1100 churn, for a yield of 9900 customers. Even at the end of just 1 year, we can see the company's customer base is heading in the wrong direction, demonstrating attrition rather than growth. Each subsequent year brings worse news: year 2 begins with 9900, adds 1000 new, loses 1090 yielding 9810; etc., until, at the end of 5 years, they have 9590.5 customers. In contrast, imagine the company made improvements resulting in happier customers such that its churn was reduced to 5%. Year 1 would end with 10,450 customers (woohoo, growth!), and year 5 would end with 12,036, a much better trajectory.

The comparison we've just examined is only a head count—things can look even worse when you consider profitability. For example, while efforts at customer acquisition (like advertising) can be expensive, they constitute necessary business practice, for growing the customer base or even just replacement and maintenance; e.g., imagine how inefficiently advertising money is spent until more is known about the target customers. There are retention costs as well, such as issuing coupons to members who use their premium cards at purchase, but in many industries, retention costs tend to pale in comparison to acquisition costs.

In CLV spreadsheet models, these costs are estimated by brand managers, and compared against the customer contributions. Different customer segments might be differentially costly (e.g., some are more difficult to locate, harder to sell, or require higher maintenance), and different segments buy different SKUs, some of which are more profitable than others. Thumbnail sketches of CLV begin with averages, then drill down to segments, and ultimately could be calculated at the level of individual customers. Then the brand manager knows how much a particular customer is worth—if a customer is upset, how much effort should go into placating them?

Figure 5.11 shows a simple spreadsheet model that yields an estimate of CLV for a customer, customer segment, or entire customer database, depending on what values are inserted into the table—the individual customer's purchases or averages computed on the database. Say the brand managers estimate that it costs about $40 to find a new customer.

	year 1	year 2	year 3	year 4	year 5…
acquisition costs	($40)				
retention costs		($10)	($10)	($10)	($10)
customer pays	$100	$200	$300	$400	$400
net contribution	$60	$190	$290	$390	$390

Figure 5.11
Customer Lifetime Value (CLV)

→sum = $1,320

This estimate is derived from knowing budgets of spending on marketing efforts like advertising, and then dividing it by the number of new customers to purchase or sign up during the year.

That figure is rough, of course, because marketing efforts should provide synergies, and unpaid testimonials via word of mouth can bring in new customers as well. The sweet advantage of spreadsheets is that such guesstimates can be varied to find upper- and lower-bounds to get a feel for a reasonable range of inputs. The final results (in this case, the CLV estimates) can be compared for the high vs. low estimates of the input acquisition costs, and if the CLV estimates vary a lot, then it's clear that the acquisition costs are important to that outcome and the brand manager might wish to ascertain an even more precise estimate of the acquisition costs. If the CLV estimates vary only a little, then it's clear that the role of acquisition costs is minor, and a rougher estimate will suffice.

Next in the figure, subsequent years incur retention costs, such as coupons or deals issued to card-carrying members. The third row shows incomes from the customer, and finally, margins are taken into account to reflect the kind of purchases the customer makes—basic or higher end, more or less profitable. The table conveys this information out to 5 years, but here too, different brands experience different life spans—the L in CLV, from 1.5–2 years for baby diapers to 4–5 years for a car, etc. Summing all the net contributions over all years we expect the customer to be ours, from $60 through $390, yields $1,320. That number might not seem huge, so now you know why many businesses require volume. Furthermore, that number is likely an overestimate. Here's why.

Given the desire to understand a customer's value over time, it is worth introducing into the spreadsheet modeling an additional twist or two. First, retention rates can be estimated and protracted, as in the 2nd and 3rd rows of Figure 5.12. Second, financial discounting can bring forward estimates of the customer's valuation, as in the last 2 rows of Figure 5.12. The retention rates adjust the CLV from $1,320 to a mere $654. If that isn't depressing enough, the financial tweaking brings today's estimate down a little further, to $612 (a discount rate of only .03 was used because for some time now, the standard .07 has seemed too high and a little silly).

Figure 5.12
CLV with Retention and Financing Tweaks

	year 1	year 2	year 3	year 4	year 5...	
net contribution	$60	$190	$290	$390	$390	
avg. retention rates	100%	75%	75%	75%	75%	
cumulative retention	100%	75%	56.25%	42.19%	31.64%	
expected contribution	$60	$142.50	$163.12	$164.54	123.40	→sum = $653.56
discount rate .03	1	1.03	1.0609	1.0927	1.1255	
today's value	$60	$138.35	$153.76	$150.58	$109.64	→sum = $612.33

Whether the numbers are high or low, they at least begin to offer a means of assessing customer value, customer by customer, or segment by segment. This knowledge helps the marketing manager prioritize customer relationship resources.

Summary

Good marketers and good companies care about their customers. We want to know whether they're satisfied or not, and it's important to know what drives those assessments so that we can continue to do well, or improve and do better. Path models are extremely useful in understanding what goes into customers' considerations of purchases and brands and such. Path models are like regression but they're far more versatile. While we've focused on customer satisfaction, it should be obvious that path models may be applied to modeling any marketing or financial metric, to find the drivers of any performance measure. Next, if customers are satisfied, marketers hope they are loyal and purchase repeatedly. With very few benign assumptions, a simple spreadsheet approach can be used to estimate customers' value to the firm over their "lifetime" (CLV). The spreadsheet aspect contributes to the usefulness of the CLV approach IRL, in part because the elements are so easy to modify as one's business needs require.

References

Intro texts:
- Bollen, Kenneth A. (1989) *Structural Equation Models with Latent Variables*, NY: Wiley.
- Iacobucci, Dawn (2010), "Structural Equations Modeling: Fit Indices, Sample Size, and Advanced Issues," *Journal of Consumer Psychology*, 20 (1), 90-98.

- Iacobucci, Dawn (2009), "Everything You Always Wanted to Know about S.E.M. (Structural Equations Modeling) But Were Afraid to Ask," *Journal of Consumer Psychology*, 19 (4), 673-680.
- Kline, Rex B. (2004) *Principles and Practice of Structural Equation Modeling 2nd ed.*, New York: Guildford.
- Raykov, Tenko and George A. Marcoulides (2000) *A First Course in Structural Equation Modeling*, Mahwah, NJ: Erlbaum.
- Tenko and George A. Marcoulides (2000) *A First Course in Structural Equation Modeling*, Mahwah, NJ: Erlbaum.
- Schumacker, Randall E. and Richard G. Lomax (2004) *A Beginner's Guide to Structural Equation Modeling* (2nd ed.), Mahwah, NJ: Erlbaum.

Help with software, Lisrel, Eqs, Amos:

- Byrne, Barbara M. (2006) *Structural Equation Modeling with Eqs: Basic Concepts, Applications, and Programming*, Mahwah, NJ: Erlbaum.
- Byrne, Barbara M. (2001) *Structural Equation Modeling with Amos: Basic Concepts, Applications, and Programming*, Mahwah, NJ: Erlbaum.
- Byrne, Barbara M. (1998) *Structural Equation Modeling with Lisrel, Prelis, and Simplis: Basic Concepts, Applications, and Programming*, Mahwah, NJ: Erlbaum.
- Hayduk, Leslie A. (1987), *Structural Equation Modeling with Lisrel*, Baltimore, MD: Johns Hopkins U Press.
- Kelloway, E. Kevin (1998), *Using LISREL for Structural Equation Modeling: A Researcher's Guide*, Sage.
- Long, J. Scott (1983), *Covariance Structure Models: An Introduction to LISREL*, Newbury Park, CA: Sage.Raykov,

To run LISREL, go to http://www.ssicentral.com, and at the welcome screen, click on "Lisrel," then on the left bar, click free downloads. Here is simple syntax (the "<<" and text to the right are comments):

```
path example.                        <<title ends with a period.
da ni=5 no=100 ma=cm                 << "da"=data, ni=#input vars, no=sample size, ma=cm (analyze cov matrix)
cm sy
 2.0113
-0.0719  2.5384
 1.1926 -1.2155  2.0738
 1.2482 -0.4925  0.8035  2.0076
 0.7615 -0.9282  0.3866  1.1610  1.9957
la                                   << "la"=labels or variable names, next line (ni of them)
q c v cs r
se                                   << "se"=select, endogenous first, then exogenous
v cs r q c /
mo ny=3 ne=3 nx=2 nk=2 lx=id,fi td=di,fr ly=id,fi te=di,fr ph=st,fr be=fu,fr ga=fu,fr
pa be                                <<above, "mo"=model statement, ny=#y vars, ne=#etas (endogenous constructs),
0 0 0                                <<nx=#x vars, nk=#ksis (exogenous factors), td=theta delta, te=theta epsilon, both
1 0 0                                <<are diagonal and free (to be estimated), lx=lambda on the x's (pattern of 1s to be
0 1 0                                <<estimated and 0s fixed at zero; "id" says identity matrix, "fi" says fix it (don't
pa ga                                <<estimate), ly=lambda y (confirmatory factor loadings matrix for y vars), ph=phi
1 1                                  <<matrix correlations among ksis, be beta matrix is "full" and "free" (to be
1 0                                  <<estimated), ga gamma matrix also full and free. Be and Ga fu,fr then modified
0 1                                  <<by pa statements, 0's means don't estimate (fix at zero) and 1's mean estimate.
pd                                   <<draw a path diagram
ou                                   <<produce outputs
```

Chapter 6: Perceptual Maps and Multidimensional Scaling

Marketing Concepts: Perceptual Maps, Positioning, Preferences,
Market Structure, Brand Associations
Modeling Concepts: Multidimensional Scaling, Attribute Vectors,
Ideal Points, Correspondence Analysis

Chapter Outline

Introduction

Positioning is at the heart of marketing—we want to create a consumption experience for our customers that matches their needs and desires, and communicate to them that we offer a unique value proposition. A positioning statement includes information about what our brand is, and that information is frequently conveyed with respect to how it is distinct from our competitors. Pictorial representations of such market structures are often rendered as "perceptual maps."

A picture is worth a megabyte of words, and most businesspeople react with, "Cool!" when they see a perceptual map. Instantly, at a glance, it is clear which brands are similar to ours (the ones closest to ours in the map), and are therefore most substitutable in the eyes of our customers, and therefore are the brands of the competitors we should worry about the most. Competitors and brands that are farther away on the map are like Antarctica on a geographical map—we know it's there, but we don't give it much thought.

Where do perceptual maps come from? How do we create them? We'll talk about perceptions and preferences. We'll interpret the perceptual map for its configuration—where the groups of brands and competitors are, where the empty spaces are that portend opportunities, and so on. In addition, people who see perceptual maps always want to know, "what are the axes"—what are the labels equivalent to the directions on a real map: North, South, East, and West—so we'll see how to interpret the dimensions, and back up our interpretations as well. We'll then overlay the map of perceptions with consumer preference data, because in addition to "How do customers see our brand?," we want to know "Which brands do they like best?"

Sit back for a most excellent time.

Perceptual Maps

There are three ways to create a perceptual map: 1) make it up, 2) use simple data, and 3) use multidimensional scaling. The first option is lame and leads to a result that has no credibility, yet it is used remarkably frequently. The second option is better because it's empirical, so we will look briefly at what is required regarding data collection and analysis. However, ideally, a perceptual map is derived via the third option, using a multidimensional scaling (MDS) model, so it is the topic of the rest of this chapter.

With regard to the second, simple (non-MDS) approach, we can extract secondary data or we can create a short survey where we ask questions like, "How does our brand rate on attribute X?," and "How important is attribute X to you?" Figure 6.1 shows how these questions might be used to assess an online news source. A sample of consumers is asked these questions, the data are entered into a spreadsheet such as Excel, and the means computed over all respondents, for each of the 6 performance questions and the 6 importance questions.

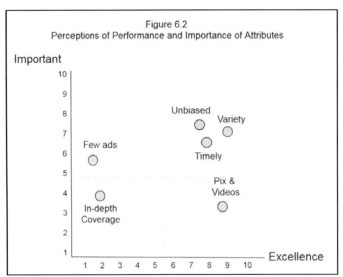

Figure 6.1
Survey Questions to Generate Means for a Simple Perceptual Map

Performance	strongly disagree									strongly agree
MSN.com delivers unbiased news.	1	2	3	4	5	6	7	8	9	10
MSN.com is always very up-to-date.	1	2	3	4	5	6	7	8	9	10
MSN.com covers a great variety of stories.	1	2	3	4	5	6	7	8	9	10
MSN.com has great pictures and videos.	1	2	3	4	5	6	7	8	9	10
MSN.com offers in-depth coverage.	1	2	3	4	5	6	7	8	9	10
Ads on MSN.com are not too intrusive.	1	2	3	4	5	6	7	8	9	10

Importance	not at all important									extremely important
Objectivity in reporting is important to me.	1	2	3	4	5	6	7	8	9	10
The timeliness of stories is important to me.	1	2	3	4	5	6	7	8	9	10
Variety in story coverage is important to me.	1	2	3	4	5	6	7	8	9	10
Pictures and videos are important to me.	1	2	3	4	5	6	7	8	9	10
Depth of information is important to me.	1	2	3	4	5	6	7	8	9	10
Minimal online advertising is important to me.	1	2	3	4	5	6	7	8	9	10

Figure 6.2
Perceptions of Performance and Importance of Attributes

The 12 means are then plotted in 6 pairs; the horizontal axis reflects the brand's performance, and the vertical axis represents the importance of each of the attributes, for all 6 attributes. Figure 6.2 is the resulting perceptual map. It shows customers' perceptions of a single company or brand. The brand's relative strengths and weaknesses (at least among those attributes the survey measured) are relatively clear. While the axes consist of the 1 to 10 scale, mirroring the survey, the dashed lines mark the midpoint of the scale, which breaks the plot into quadrants.

In the upper right of the plot are the attributes that are strengths, and attributes that are important to customers. The brand wants to maintain those strengths. The upper left contains attributes that are also important to customers, but those for which the brand doesn't succeed as well—these attributes are priorities to be fixed. The lower portion of the plot contains attributes that customers don't care about as much, so the fact that there are some attributes on which the brand does not perform well (lower left) is not much cause for concern, and the attributes for which the brand excels (lower right) are not much cause for celebration—indeed, they may give us pause to consider whether we are devoting too many resources to do well on an attribute that customers don't value.

Many variations of these simple perceptual maps can be created. For example, on the performance questions, the survey might ask, "Is Brand X 'worse than competitors,' 'at parity with competitors,' or 'better than competitors'?" Then the x-axis in Figure 6.2 would be divided into thirds, and we would interpret the results vis-à-vis the competitive status.

Alternatively, competitive analysis may be represented by collecting data, computing means, and inserting points to represent a larger set of brands. Figure 6.3 selects two of the attributes that customers said were important: lack of bias in reporting and in-depth, detailed coverage. We plot the means on performance for these attributes for multiple brands, and we see that our focal brand dominates a few others in this space with respect to perceptions of unbiased reporting, but it is dominated by a few other brands by their greater depths of reporting.

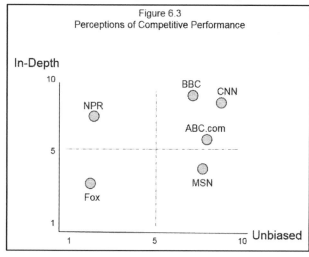

Figure 6.3
Perceptions of Competitive Performance

Perceptual maps are helpful to understand brand similarities and differences. MSN might wish to chase ABC.com by increasing its depth of coverage, but going after BBC and CNN would prove a much larger challenge (they're farther away). These maps show us customers' perceptions with regard to brands that are similar and those that are different. The maps represent market structure—they show spaces where there is perhaps too much competition and it is difficult to distinguish a brand, as well as spaces where there is too little or no competition, which offer an opportunity for a new entrant or a repositioning of a current brand.

This approach to creating perceptual maps is simple—simple in the kind of data that must be collected, simple in the analyses required to yield the map, and simple to interpret. There is an intuition when looking at the map that most viewers quickly and readily understand. Yet a potential shortcoming of this approach is that it depends on the attributes selected. If customers cared more about different attributes than those included in the survey, we wouldn't know it because we'd have no relevant data. Mapping is cool but it doesn't perform miracles.

When we use multidimensional scaling (MDS) to create a perceptual map, the survey questions are different. The perceptual question is, "How similar are brands X and Y?" asked for all pairs of brands. No specific attributes are stated, so presumably customers would compare brands X and Y along whatever attributes matter to them. It's up to us to infer what the attributes are. The similarities judgments are gathered and modeled.

The essence of the MDS model is the analogy between similarity and closeness, or dissimilarity and distance. Brands are placed in a perceptual map such that brands that are similar are represented as points close in space, and brands that are seen as pretty different are represented as points farther away in space. The model will provide a plot of the map, and the coordinates of the brands in the map, and it is up to us to interpret the map. There are several elements of interpretation—the first being the configuration, e.g., what brands are closest and therefore likely toughest competitors, are there any empty spaces in the map that may indicate an opportunity for brand development, etc. The second part of interpreting the space is labeling the axes, that is, we usually wish to infer the perceptual equivalent to "North, South, East, and West" in the map.

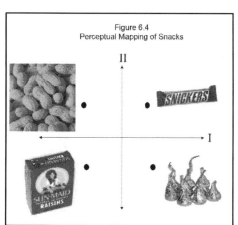

Figure 6.4
Perceptual Mapping of Snacks

For example, Figure 6.4 shows a 2-dimensional (2-d) MDS plot for similarity judgments among four snack foods. To interpret dimension I, we consider what Snickers and Hershey Kisses have in common that make them distinct from peanuts and raisins. Perhaps dimension I is "chocolate vs. healthier snacks." Dimension II is interpreted as whatever peanuts and Snickers have in common that distinguishes them from raisins and Hershey Kisses—thus, the "North" seems to be the snacks with peanuts, and the "South" seems to be the snacks with …peanuts-envy. Some maps are easily, indisputably interpreted. Others are trickier, so later in this chapter, we'll conduct an analysis to help us interpret the results, or verify our interpretations of the results.

Unidimensional Scaling

It helps to know where MDS came from. Before we go all "multi," let's start with unidimensional scaling.

Early psychometricians sought a way to capture the fact that we would like to have measures of many things that are subjective and not directly observable, such as intelligence or attitudes. If we want to understand a customer's attitude toward an ad or brand, we don't have the luxury of objective measures like height or weight. Furthermore, the psychological experience of something objective can still be subjective, and we deal with people's perceptions—indeed, "perception is reality."

For example, a physicist might say, 1 gram is less than 2 grams is less than 3 grams, and 1 gram is half of 2, 2 is half of 4, etc. But a subjective perception isn't the same as an objective reality. Here's how we could replicate an early psycho-physics experiment: we blindfold our participant and put a 1 gram weight in the participant's left hand, and a 2 gram weight in the right. We ask, "Which weight is heavier?" and the respondent will probably say that both weights are the same. We remove the 1 and 2 gram weights and replace them with 1 and 3 gram weights, and we get the same response. That is, thus far we have learned that the psychological experience of 2 or 3 grams is indistinguishable from the experience of 1 gram, in terms of perceived "heaviness." At some point, say when comparing 1 vs. 5 grams, the respondent says the latter is heavier.

This increment is called a "just noticeable difference" (j.n.d.). If the j.n.d. data came out at 1 gram, 5 grams, 9 grams, 14 grams, etc., then while the scale of objective weight is 1, 2, 3, 4, …, 14 grams, the scale of psychological weight would be 1 (at 1 gram), 2 (at 5 grams), 3 (at 9 grams), etc.

Rating weights may seem like a yawn, but we can apply the same logic to just about anything. Figure 6.5 shows the data from a sample of 100 people who were asked the simple question, "Which Stooge do you think is funnier, Larry or Moe?" The pairs of Stooges were rotated, resulting in 6 total questions, to represent all possible combinations. The table shows the number of people who thought the column Stooge was funnier than the row Stooge.

Figure 6.5
Number of People (of Sample Size = 100) Who Said
Column Stooge is Funnier than Row Stooge

	Larry	Moe	Curly	Shemp
Larry	-	47	59	35
Moe	53	-	64	45
Curly	41	36	-	12
Shemp	65	55	88	-

Let's look at the examples that are underlined. When comparing Moe and Larry, 47 people said Moe was funnier than Larry, but 53 said Larry was funnier than Moe. These numbers are nearly 50:50, which means Larry and Moe are about as funny as each other—we'd say they are close, or similar in their funniness. When comparing Curly to Shemp, 88 people said Curly was funnier whereas only 12 said Shemp was. These numbers show a greater dominance, meaning many more people think that Curly is funnier than Shemp then vice versa. Imagine translating this information to some kind of ruler measuring funniness—Larry and Moe should get scores pretty near each other, and Curly's score ought to be much higher than Shemp's.

To proceed and actually create such a ruler, or a unidimensional scale of funniness, we'll make a fairly benign assumption that there will be some individual differences. Specifically, whatever Curly's score of funniness is, not everyone would agree precisely; some people will think he's funnier, others will think he's not as funny, and we'll assume those differences cancel each other out. Picture a symmetric (specifically, normal) distribution of funniness judgments around any Stooge—each will have a mean and a variance. If two Stooges are equally funny, their scores should be the same, and their normal distributions and means would be sitting on top of each other. If one Stooge is a lot funnier, his score (mean) would be higher, and his whole normal distribution would be further up the scale, with less overlap between his distribution and the less funny Stooge's distribution. As Figure 6.6 indicates, the distribution for Larry is only slightly above Moe's, but Curly's is quite a

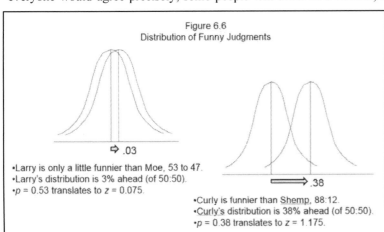

Figure 6.6
Distribution of Funny Judgments

⇨ .03

- Larry is only a little funnier than Moe, 53 to 47.
- Larry's distribution is 3% ahead (of 50:50).
- $p = 0.53$ translates to $z = 0.075$.

⇨ .38

- Curly is funnier than Shemp, 88:12.
- Curly's distribution is 38% ahead (of 50:50).
- $p = 0.38$ translates to $z = 1.175$.

bit ahead of Shemp's. We're going to use this intuition of overlap to get the scores. We'll translate the 47:53 and 88:12 to proportions of funny dominance, and use the proportions to represent the areas under the curves.

Usually when we use z-statistics tables, we have a z-score and we want to find the probability under the curve (the probability that we would obtain a z-score as high as ours or higher, given the assumption that our working null hypothesis is true). In this case, we have a proportion (of overlap between curves), so we want to look up the z-score. The easiest way to do this these days is to use the "norm.inv" function in Excel. Enter 0.47, a mean of 0.0 and a standard deviation of 1.0 (the latter two are for standard normal curves, i.e., z-scores). When we enter 0.47, we obtain –0.075. When we enter 0.53, 0.88, and 0.12, the function returns the values 0.075, 1.175, and –1.175. These z-scores are entered in the matrix in Figure 6.7 (the scores and their negative counterpart scores are mirrored in what's known as an "anti-symmetric" matrix… just another service from geeks-r-us).

The final unidimensional scaling steps are easy—we take the column averages, and adjust all scores so that the scale starts at zero (in this case, we add 0.422 to all scale scores). The resulting scale of funniness, and the scores of the famous Stooges, appear in Figure 6.8. These numbers convey rank order, but also interval order—Curly is quite a bit funnier than Larry, Larry and Moe are similarly funny, but both are a lot funnier than Shemp, by almost the same margin as Curly dominates Larry. Recall that for interval scales, differences between points may be compared, so for example, Moe is funnier than Shemp (.34) almost as much as Curly is funnier than Larry (.38), and the difference between Curly and Larry (.38) is almost 3 times the difference between Larry and Moe (3 ×.14 = .42).

Cool, right? You can create a solid unidimensional scale for anything—the hotness of your classmates, the desirability of different job offers, the sophistication of world cities, the lust you feel for different exotic sports cars, the entertainment value of very different genres of movies or music or books, and on and on. You can also take an athletic season for any sport, put the teams in as rows and columns of a matrix like that in Figure 6.5, entering the wins and losses in the heart of the table, and follow the unidimensional procedure just described to get a scaling of the teams. (We'll see such an example at the end of this chapter.) The applications are endless. But wait, there's more!

With the unidimensional scaling under our belts, we're ready to proceed to multidimensional scaling. We will first talk about the kinds of data that can be used. We'll see how a MDS model extracts dimensions for a solution. We'll interpret the dimensions by inserting "attribute vectors" and we'll overlay the whole plot with ideal points representing respondents' preferences.

Figure 6.7
z-Scores for Funny Stooges

Stooges in original order
(from Figure 6.5)

	Larry	Moe	Curly	Shemp
Larry	0	-.075	.228	-.385
Moe	.075	0	.075	-.126
Curly	-.228	-.358	0	-1.175
Shemp	.385	.126	1.175	0

Stooges rearranged to
show anti-symmetry

	Shemp	Moe	Larry	Curly
Shemp	0	.126	.385	1.175
Moe	-.126	0	.075	.358
Larry	-.385	-.075	0	.228
Curly	-1.175	-.358	-.228	0
Means:	-.422	-.077	.058	.440

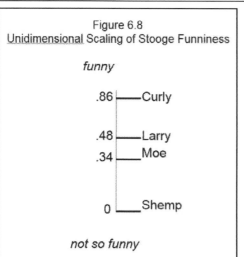

Figure 6.8
Unidimensional Scaling of Stooge Funniness

funny

.86 ——Curly

.48 ——Larry
.34 ——Moe

0 ——Shemp

not so funny

Kinds of Data

In this section, we will look at the kinds of data that are required to conduct an MDS analysis. We will see: 1) the overall instructions to the survey, 2) familiarity ratings, 3) proximities judgments (and their instructions), 4) attribute ratings for each stimulus, 5) preference ratings, and 6) demographics and attitudinal respondent data. We will consider these issues in the context of movies.

Instructions

It is important to give the survey participant an overall sense of what to expect. If you just jump right into "Rate the similarity between these two movies: *Bambi* and *Snow White*," one might think, oh, *Bambi* was sad, the doe dies, how tragic. But if the next pair of movies includes one from the *Saw* series, *Bambi* looks infinitely gentler by comparison. Don't surprise your respondents—give them the whole context, the whole decision set that will be relevant.

Instructions should look like this: *"Read over the following list of movies. As you read the list, try to imagine each movie. Think about how much you enjoyed it, and what you liked or disliked about it. Think about how these movies are different and how they are similar."* Then proceed to list all the movies, or show clips or their advertising posters, or a story synopsis from imdb.com, etc.

Familiarity Ratings

Next, get some kind of indication as to the respondent's knowledge of each of the stimuli. If a person has not seen a movie, his or her data about that movie will likely be errorful, or at least not based on personal knowledge or experience. You may wish to toss that person's data, or at least any judgment involving that movie, but you cannot delete data without others thinking you are doing something suspicious. You'd have to have a defensible reason, and lack of familiarity would persuade most people.

The rating can be simple. For example, *"Please rate each movie with respect to your familiarity. Circle the appropriate response."* The choices may be, *"1 = never heard of it," "2 = haven't seen it," "3 = have seen it."*

Proximities Data

Recall that the basic metaphor underlying the MDS model is that similarities are like closeness on a map and dissimilarities are like distances on a map. We wish to represent stimuli, such as brands, as points in space so that brands perceived to be quite different are points distant in space, and brands perceived to be similar are closer in space. As a result, all we need are data that are real distances or perceived differences, defined pretty broadly, as we shall see. Also, a technical piece of jargon: instead of continuing to refer to similarities and dissimilarities, these types of data are generically referred to as "proximities" data. If a larger number means "more different" (i.e., represented with more distance), we could call the data dissimilarities. If a larger number means "more similar" (i.e., represented closer together), we could call the data similarities.

(Dis)similarities ratings. A standard means of collecting proximity data is to simply ask on a survey, "How similar are these two things?" Imagine we have a list of some established, commercially successful movies, such as *Star Wars, Toy Story, Spider-Man*, etc. In the survey, we cycle through all possible pairs of movies, asking, "How similar are these two movies: *Star Wars* and *Toy Story*," and provide a scale, where 1 is "very similar" and 9 is "very different." (Traditionally, the 1 in the rating scale is used to reflect "similar" and the larger number is used to express "different"; hence, these ratings are referred to as dissimilarities, as opposed to, say, correlations, where higher positive numbers represent similarities.)

When asking respondents to make all pairwise judgments from a set of "p" stimuli, it is important to note that the number of ratings rises quickly, on the order of p^2; specifically, the number of all pairwise judgments would be: $\binom{p}{2} = \frac{p(p-1)}{2}$. Thus, if you're a brand manager in a large product category like cereal, cars, or indeed movies, you're going to have to preselect a subset of brands you are interested in to make the ratings task less tedious for your survey respondents.

When asking respondents to make proximities judgments, it is important to urge them to keep their consideration as broad and as personally relevant as they can. Thus, special instructions usually precede the ratings. For example,

> *Please rate each of the following pairs of movies in terms of how similar they seem to you. Use any criteria you wish on which to base your similarity judgments. If you think two movies are very similar, circle the rating of 1; if you think two movies are very different, circle a 9. (If you are not familiar with one or both of the movies in a pair, skip that pair, and go on to the next pair.)*

It usually surprises people that the instructions explicitly encourage the raters to "use any criteria you wish." How will we know what criteria they use? We will deduce the dimensions—MDS modelers are master sleuths. As a teaser, here's an example. A McDonald's *Happy Meal* box (hey, my research for my students knows no bounds!) contained the riddle, "Which of these is different?" and it had pictures of: a lion, a tiger, a zebra, and a striped domestic cat. If you think the lion is different, I can deduce that you used the criterion of "stripes." If you think the zebra is different, I know you paid attention to a "cat" vs. "not cat" dimension. If you think the domestic cat is different, for you the attribute of "wildness" was most important. (If you think the tiger is different, you're a goober.) This kind of inference is what we do in MDS.

Some marketing researchers try to help speed up the pairwise judgments by cycling through the ratings in a "do-loop" rotation. They ask respondents to think about brand A, and judge how different it is from B, then C, then D. When the brands are depleted, the respondents think about brand B and how it differs from C, then D., etc. This task moves more quickly, but given that MDS is based on a history of being concerned with psychometrics and perception, there is a concern that the focus on one brand at a time introduces some kind of biases in the psychological processing. The alternative they offer is to draw a random order of pairs—the randomness would seem to be pure in reducing bias. Nevertheless, a random draw can also be "weird," as in: "Please rate pairs B&C, then B&A, then B&D, then A&D, then D&C, then A&C." The first three ratings are subject to the same criticism.

A smarter solution is called a "Ross ordering." The pairs are balanced top to bottom, e.g., brand A appears as frequently at the top of the list, in the center of the list, and at the end of the list. No one could argue that there is any bias or that some brand enjoys a favorable rating position if the survey is completely balanced.

Dominance data. In dominance data, pairs of entities are pitted against each other, and we record how frequently one wins over the other. The Stooges data are an example—we learned how often Stooge A was deemed funnier than B, and by how many people B was thought funnier than A. Marketers collect dominance data when they ask, "Which of these brands do you prefer: A or B, A or C," etc.

A huge source of dominance data is the results of sports teams' games after their seasons conclude. We can collect data expressing the number of wins and losses for all teams in a set (e.g., a conference or division), aggregated over every time each pair of teams, A and B, met. The pairwise wins are truly a measure of the frequency with which one team dominated another. (For teams that don't meet as frequently in a given season, as in football, historical data can be accumulated and then the teams scaled.) We can then model the teams using either the unidimensional approach we used on the Stooges data, or the MDS models we'll see shortly.

Dominance data are usually expected to (even assumed to) demonstrate transitivity, which means that if Stooge A is funnier than B (or team A beats B), and B dominates C, then A would likely dominate C. However, a great example of a non-transitive triad is the children's game of rock, paper, scissors: rock (A) dominates scissors (B), scissors (B) dominates paper (C), so transitivity would dictate that A beat C; but of course, if this were true, all kids would always form their hands into the shape of a rock, since it would beat all. That is, the rules are non-transitive—paper (C) dominates rock (A)—which evens the game's odds.[17]

Confusions data. Another class of proximities data is called "confusions data." These too have historical (and current) interest. There is a paradigm, both substantive and methodological, called "signal detection theory." It mostly means figuring out what's a signal vs. what's noise. But it can also mean "which" signal has been detected. This consideration occurred often in the human engineering applications in the military. For example, on a ship, when we're listening for Morse code, is the letter we just heard a "- - ." or was it a "- . ."? Or, in a plane, when we're reading radar and trying to figure out whether that blip is friend or foe (i.e., shoot or don't shoot), there isn't a lot of time to figure out, yes, that's our machine, vs. no, those wings are pitched differently. In training, a sound ("- - .") or a blip (friendly plane) is presented, and the trainee is asked to identify the letter or plane. The question is, what is the proportion of times that a sound or visual blip is confused with, and misidentified as, another sound or blip.

Marketers create confusions data when we conduct blind taste tests. Pepsi used them to establish itself against Coke. Coca-Cola used them to position Coke Zero against its own Coke Classic. Most people claimed they could identify a sip of Pepsi or Coke, or Diet Coke or Dr. Pepper, etc. if blindfolded. Remarkably, most people cannot. Run the study yourself (or see if people can discern which wine costs more, which water is bottled vs. tap, which beer is regular vs. lite, etc.).

Co-ownership data. In Chapter 2, we saw some "co-ownership" data of consumer household vehicles. These data were an example of a class of proximity data known as "joint probabilities." We'd ask a sample of households, "Which of these soft drinks do you buy (check all that apply): Coke, Pepsi, 7Up, Sprite, etc.?" We'd compute the proportion of households in the sample that bought both brands i and j and proceed to model these similarities data. Alternatively, we could extract co-purchasing information from scanner data, say, over the period of a quarter or a year. The survey data, "check all that apply," would give us binary data for each household; i.e., for each pair of brands, yes

---

[17] Go to YouTube and search "*Big Bang Theory*" and "rock, paper, scissors" to see the new entities: Spock and Lizard (e.g., Spock vaporizes rock, Lizard eats paper).

or no, whether they were both bought. The scanner data aggregated across the year would count the number of co-purchases.

Sociometric data. Social network ties are data that can help marketers with brands in social media. Your class's social network can be mapped if the tie data are gathered. The survey is the class roster, and each class member checks (or rates) the classmates he or she likes, respects, studies with, etc. Observational data can also be obtained that reflect social ties, such as the amount of time spent together, numbers of emails exchanged, etc. With sociometric data, a higher score means "likes a lot" or "communicates frequently." Thus, while the data are not similarities per se, higher numbers indicate closer links. The most tightly linked friends in the network would be represented as points close together in the map, with more distal friends represented farther apart. Sociometric data were modeled frequently using MDS when MDS first appeared. The application is becoming popular again with the plethora of social networks servers and social media data they capture.

Derived dissimilarities. Recall our discussion of profile data and measures of association in Chapter 2. There, we were profiling customers and using clusters to find segments. Now let's switch to the idea of creating brand profiles. We'd ask customers to rate several brands on a number of attributes (such as profiling MSN, BBC, etc. per Figure 6.3). We'd then compute a correlation or distance score between each pair of brands. We'd input the correlations (similarities) or distance scores (dissimilarities) into the MDS. The MDS would map the brands according to these proximities (similarities or dissimilarities) data. The extent to which any pair of brands are thought to be proximal was not a direct judgment (e.g., "How similar do you think A and B are?") but was indirect, derived from the attribute variables.

Derived dissimilarities are a very popular way to obtain data for MDS. This approach does not require the sometimes lengthy section of the survey of the $p(p-1)/2$ pairwise judgments, so that is a time savings for the respondents. Paired comparisons also get a little boring after making about 10 or 20 such judgments. By comparison, attribute ratings are familiar to respondents and can go rather quickly.

However, remember the Happy Meal example? The astounding quality of MDS is not that it will give you a map—although that is obviously great. Rather, the astounding thing about MDS is the claim that we can let customers use any criteria they wish to make their paired comparisons, and we can infer the attributes or dimensions along which the customers had been comparing the brands. If we run MDS models on derived dissimilarities, we have negated this amazing quality—we would have given the customers a list of the attributes we think are important, and the customers would dutifully judge the brands. This approach would never allow us to learn something unexpected from customers, whose perceptions obviously might be different from our own.

Still, sometimes the practicalities of data collection override the quest for new knowledge, and a perceptual map is desired even when the data are "only" a matrix of brands by ratings. When these data are the main source, a strict MDS might not be the optimal way to go. Instead, consider the technique called Correspondence Analysis, described later in the chapter.

So, there are many ways to obtain proximities data in a variety of formats and meanings. We are almost ready to examine the MDS model, but we have a few more sections to the survey.

Attribute Ratings for each Stimulus

The next section of ratings will help us create and defend a relatively objective interpretation of the MDS solution—the configuration and the labeling of the dimensions. In this section, we ask respondents to rate each stimulus (e.g., brand, movie, etc.) on a number of attributes that we suspect will be the criteria that they're thinking about. For example, for the films, we might ask about the genre, story line, actors, music, etc. For brands of soft drinks, we might ask questions about sweetness, energy-inducing, celebrity imagery, etc.

Note that these attributes are the very ones we just referred to if we were going to compute derived dissimilarities. We collect these attribute judgments to help us interpret the map.

Preferences Ratings

The proximities data are the data we need to construct an MDS perceptual map. That result is fun and informative, but it isn't the whole story, at least for marketers. Marketers want to know customers' perceptions about brands, their relative strengths and weaknesses, similarities and differences, of course. However, it's also very important to understand customers' preferences. We'll collect data on what customers like, and we'll model those data as ideal points, overlaid onto the MDS map.

To be able to insert an ideal point into the MDS space to represent a person's preferences, we have to know which brands they like the most. This rating can be done via a ranking or rating on each brand. The scale can be 7-point, 15-point, 100-point, or whatever, and the higher numbers are the most preferred.

Demographics and Psychographics

In the final portion of the survey, it would be very helpful to capture information about the respondents themselves. We can ask demographic questions: gender, age, household income, etc. We can also ask attitudinal and behavioral questions, such as their behavior in the purchase category (preferred brands, frequency of purchase in the product category), purchase occasions, or competitive behaviors. We are likely to find that perceptions and MDS spaces differ across customer segments, and it would be nice to know if the perceptual differences are correlated in some systematic way with customers' demographics or psychographics.

Multidimensional Scaling Models

Suppose we have proximities data of some sort. What does the MDS model do with them? We will start with an intuition before proceeding to the math of the model.

Figure 6.9 Data on 3 Brands			
	A	B	C
A	-		
B	1	-	
C	3	2	-

Figure 6.9 contains a small data set of dissimilarities among 3 brands. Brands A and B are very similar, and brands A and C are the most different. If we were to represent these brands as points in space, we could plot them along a line. A would be 1 unit from B, C would be 2 units farther down, and the linear arrangement would also yield that A and C would be 3 units apart. Our 1 dimensional representation would fit the data perfectly.

Imagine, however, that the data in Figure 6.9 were $d_{AB} = 1$, $d_{BC} = 2$, $d_{AC} = 2.24$. These data reflect the same rank order from the smallest pair (A and B) to the largest pair (A and C), but obviously 2.24 in this example is not the same as 3 in the previous example. If we align brands A and B 1 unit apart, and put brand C 2 units farther down the line, then the linear model fits for the data points d_{AB} and d_{BC} but now the model predicts that the distance between A and C is 3, when in fact it is 2.24.

The contrast between these 2 examples raises a number of issues. First, there are different classes of MDS models—some are called "metric," which basically means that we take the numbers at face value as having been measured rather precisely. Alternatively, there are "nonmetric" MDS models, which acknowledge the likely errors of measurement that occur and creep into the data set when we gather perceptual data such as dissimilarity ratings. Nonmetric models do away with the seeming precision of 1, 2, 2.24, and transform all input data to ranks (hence 1, 2, 3) before proceeding to the heart of the modeling. In this case, the nonmetric modeling of 1, 2, 2.24 would be as good as the metric modeling had been for the data in Figure 6.9: 1, 2, 3.

Second, we may wish to defend the rigorous and precise measurement of our data, and not desire the transformation of 1, 2, and 2.24 to their ranks. In this case, we stick with the metric MDS model, but increase the dimensionality of the solution space. If we allow the result to be depicted in 2 dimensions, then we can again place these 3 brands in space so as to fit the data perfectly. We would place brand A on some arbitrary point and brand B on a point 1 unit to the east of A; then, if we place brand C 2 units south of B, we would satisfy $d_{AB} = 1$ and $d_{BC} = 2$. Then, recall the Pythagorean theorem: for our data, $1^2 + 2^2 = 2.24^2 = 5$, and thus $d_{AC} = \sqrt{5} = 2.24$. By the way, instead of going "east" for A and "south" for B, we could have gone slightly northwest for A and farther northeast for C, say. These differences are known as reflections (flipped, like in a mirror) and rotations (turned like a spinner). Neither of these kinds of changes would alter the configuration, which is the set of interpoint distances.

Third, it is geometrically true that if we have p brands, we can fit them perfectly to our data (i.e., with no error) if we go up to $p - 1$ dimensions. (Remember, in geometry a line (1-d) is defined by 2 points, a plane (2-d) is defined by 3, etc.) For this example, $p = 3$, so 2 dimensions provides a perfect fit, and a 2-d plot is very understandable. But if we have data on $p = 15$ cereals, say, we are not likely to retain a 14-dimensional model—it may fit perfectly but it would be difficult to comprehend (for oneself) or communicate (to others). The point here is that we will always consider the tension between fitting the data very well and yet having a solution that is parsimonious. Recall the analogous tension in regression—there, if we continue to add predictor variables, such that their number approaches the sample size, it's true that the R^2 will approach 1, however, it's also true that the model is likely to be overly complicated, weird and uninterpretable. In the MDS world, we'll see shortly that we actually make this tension work for us—we'll determine how many dimensions seem reasonable for our data, in part as a function of how well our data are fit in 3, 4, or 5 dimensions, and so on.

Let's take our example one step further. In Figure 6.10, we have added data for a fourth brand. To get a sense of what the computer or model is doing, let's begin with brands A, B, and C in the 2-d triangle formation, as in the left panel in Figure 6.11. The question now is where to put brand D. The data say that A and D are as similar as A and B, so in the middle panel of Figure 6.11, we depict a circle around A with radius 1; D could be anywhere on that circle, including, for the moment, coincident with B. In the third panel of Figure 6.11, we use the information that B and D are 1.41 units apart—D is more different (more distant) from B than A. We have narrowed the sensible locations for D to just two potential places.

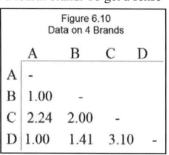

Figure 6.10
Data on 4 Brands

	A	B	C	D
A	-			
B	1.00	-		
C	2.24	2.00	-	
D	1.00	1.41	3.10	-

In Figure 6.12, we use the last new data point, that C and D are the most different brands, to select the location for D to be the top of the two remaining choices (the lower option would have been too close to C). Note, consistent with the previous discussion, that D is not precisely 3.10 units from C; we would have to raise D into a third dimension, go to nonmetric MDS models, or withstand a small amount of lack of fit to our data. The plot at the right in Figure 6.12 shows what a computer output would give us.

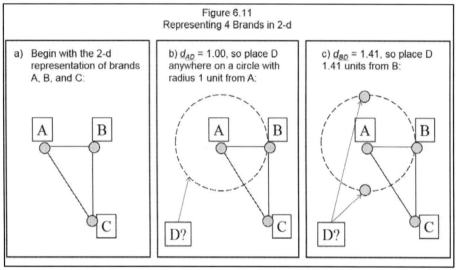

Figure 6.11
Representing 4 Brands in 2-d

a) Begin with the 2-d representation of brands A, B, and C:

b) d_{AD} = 1.00, so place D anywhere on a circle with radius 1 unit from A:

c) d_{BD} = 1.41, so place D 1.41 units from B:

Obviously the model is fitting all the brands and their interpoint distances simultaneously, and then the computer spits out the answer. We traced the process as if the model were developed sequentially to understand how the data create enough constraints so that the ultimate locations are rather precise.

It's easy to see that while the placement of the first point on the map is arbitrary, additional data points assert constraints on the locations of the other points such that they are fairly precisely mapped (again, up to a reflection or rotation). We began with the number of possible locations for D as ∞^2; an infinite number of locations east to west, and an infinite number of locations north to south. With the constraint about D needing to be 1 unit from A, we have reduced the number greatly, to a mere ∞; any point on the circle with 1 unit radius from A. Incorporating more data told us that either of 2 points in space could be D's location. The final data complete the perceptual map by indicating the more likely location for D. *Et voilà*. Note, of course, that the actual plot wouldn't have the circle and other working symbols we used—it would contain just the 4 points for A-D, as in the right-hand panel of Figure 6.12.

We can also acknowledge that stepping through this mapping example was a bit disingenuous because the computer fits the estimates of all the points simultaneously, but the methodology for doing so is a bit technical.

We have two more discussions before we see the first actual MDS models. We need a refresher on distances and geometry.

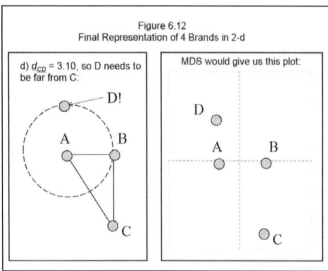

Figure 6.12
Final Representation of 4 Brands in 2-d

d) d_{CD} = 3.10, so D needs to be far from C:

D!

MDS would give us this plot:

Distance Metrics

Let's begin with some notation. Distances are defined as relations between points in space. For marketers, those points are usually brands, but they may also be companies, countries, customers, or any such "stimuli," to use the generic label.

Point (or brand) A has coordinates (X_{A1}, X_{A2}), and point B has coordinates (X_{B1}, X_{B2}). The first subscript represents the stimulus (e.g., brand A or B), and the second subscript represents the dimension (e.g., 1 or 2).

In 2-d, we use the Euclidean distance: $d_{AB} = \sqrt{(X_{A1} - X_{B1})^2 + (X_{A2} - X_{B2})^2}$. For maps in 3 or 4 or 5 or more dimensions, we'll call the number of dimensions r, and the distance formula generalizes to: $d_{AB} = \sqrt{(X_{A1} - X_{B1})^2 + (X_{A2} - X_{B2})^2 + \cdots + (X_{Ar} - X_{Br})^2}$, which can be written more succinctly as: $d_{AB} = \sqrt{\sum_{k=1}^{r}(X_{Ak} - X_{Bk})^2}$. With these definitions, let's see how distances behave.

There are three basic rules that govern whether a metric can be called a distance. First, "non-negativity and equivalence" states that: a) $d_{ij} \geq 0$, that is, the distance between points i and j can be zero, or greater, but distances cannot be negative, b) $d_{ii} = d_{jj} = 0$, the distance between a point and itself is zero, and c) $d_{ij} = 0$ only if points i and j coincide on all r dimensions.

The rule of "symmetry" says $d_{ij} = d_{ji}$, meaning that the distance from i to j, is the same as the distance from j to i. That rule sounds reasonable for geometry, but will it hold for data? If we model the distance between cities, then the distance between New York and London, say, is indeed symmetric, but if we were to model flight times, it takes longer to fly east than west.

The wonderful primer on MDS by Kruskal and Wish also pointed to asymmetries that would likely arise in people's judgments—their example was that it sounded more sensible to ask, "How similar is Cuba to Russia?" than to ask, "How similar is Russia to Cuba?" For marketers, the analogy is that it sounds more appropriate to ask, "How similar is the store brand to Coke?" vs. asking, "How similar is Coke to the store brand?" We can avoid the issue by phrasing the question itself symmetrically, as in "How similar are Coke and Pepsi?"

The third rule for distance metrics is that they satisfy the "triangle inequality." This rule states that for any 3 points i, j, and k, $d_{ik} \leq d_{ij} + d_{jk}$. The equality will hold, $d_{ik} = d_{ij} + d_{jk}$, when i, j, and k fall along a line, and the inequality will hold, $d_{ik} < d_{ij} + d_{jk}$, when the 3 points form a triangle in 2-d. The relationship of d_{ik} exceeding the sum of d_{ij} and d_{jk} is not possible (try it for yourself).

Once again, while this definition necessarily holds in geometry, psycho-perceptually it might not hold for data (even without considering measurement errors). Imagine the following: a consumer might say that Pepsi and Coke are fairly similar and rate them a "2." They might also say that Pepsi is pretty similar to Diet Pepsi, and rate them a "2." Then, when asked to rate Coke against Diet Pepsi, the consumer might think, "way different," and give a rating of "5." The largest of the ratings exceeds the sum of the other two. Yet the data seem sensible.

While the assumption of the triangle inequality can be violated frequently in our data, we don't care, because it's easily resolved by using the "additive constant," which the MDS programs do automatically to prepare the data for subsequent modeling. The solution is simple. We have denoted the distances d, so we'll call the data δ, for distinction. If the data, δ_{ij}'s, don't satisfy the triangle inequality, the δ^*_{ij}'s will, where $\delta^*_{ij} = \delta_{ij} + c$, and $c = \max_{ijk}(\delta_{ij} - \delta_{ik} - \delta_{jk})$. In our Pepsi and Coke example, we take $5 - 2 - 2 = 1$ to be c. (If we had more brands, there would be more triples, and if there were a bigger number than 1, that number would be c.) Add c to all the data, so $\delta_{ij}, \delta_{ik}, \delta_{jk}$ (2, 2, 5) becomes $\delta^*_{ij}, \delta^*_{ik}, \delta^*_{jk}$ (3, 3, 6), and then the triangle inequality holds. See, no biggie. Plus the computer will automatically do that for you, so you've got that going for you...

Geometry for MDS

MDS takes advantage of other geometric properties, in addition to interpoint distances. We will represent brands as points in space, but it is worth remembering that the configuration, or the full set of geometric relationships, could be just as well rendered as vectors emanating from the origin. We're going off on this seeming tangent not just because we're geeks, but to see some more properties that assist MDS models.

To emphasize the configuration among the points in space and not just their coordinates, let's look at Figure 6.13. Panel "a" shows what the computer might produce for us for 3 brands. The matrix of coordinates of brands A, B, and C on dimensions I and II is found beneath the plot. (The mean of the coordinates on dimension I is 1.0, and the mean on dimension II is 2.0.)

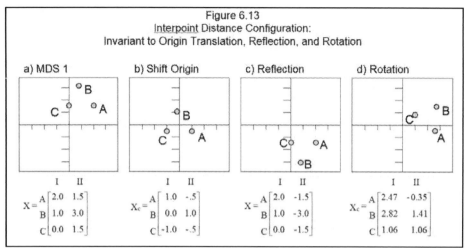

Figure 6.13
Interpoint Distance Configuration:
Invariant to Origin Translation, Reflection, and Rotation

In panel "b," we see that the origin is arbitrary, or at least does not affect the interpoint distances. Accordingly, it is standard for MDS programs to set the origin to the centroid of the stimulus coordinates. To do so, we simply recenter dimensions I and II, that is, subtract the mean on dimension I from all the dimension I coordinates, and subtract the mean on dimension II from all the dimension II coordinates. That adjustment is plotted in panel "b," and the new matrix shows the new coordinates, wherein the mean in each column is now 0. You can see in the plot that centering has no effect on interpoint distances. As an illustration, the distance between A and B in terms of the original coordinates was $d_{AB} = \sqrt{[(2-1)^2 + (1.5-3)^2]} = \sqrt{1^2 + (-1.5)^2} = \sqrt{(1+2.25)} = 1.803$, and the distance between A and B in terms of the newly recentered coordinates is $d_{AB} = \sqrt{[(1-0)^2 + (-.5-1)^2]} = \sqrt{1^2 + (-1.5)^2} = \sqrt{(1+2.25)} = 1.803$, of course. The concept of a mirror-like reflection and a rotation like the spinner in a board game is depicted in panels "c" and "d." Note that the coordinates change, but the interpoint distances are maintained.

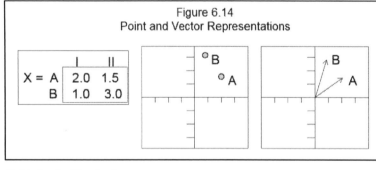

Figure 6.14
Point and Vector Representations

In Figure 6.14, brands A and B are plotted as both points and vectors. Recall that the Law of Cosines defines the (squared) distance between two points A and B vis-à-vis their length, the distances (lengths) of those points from a third, and the angle θ between them: $d_{AB}^2 = d_{AC}^2 + d_{BC}^2 - 2d_{AC}d_{BC}\cos\theta_{AB}$. For convenience, we'll take point "C" to be the origin. Let's rearrange terms, taking the d_{AB}^2 to the right, the negative product term to the left, and divide both sides by 2:

$$d_{AC}d_{BC}\cos\theta_{AB} = (d_{AC}^2 + d_{BC}^2 - d_{AB}^2)/2,$$

and recall $d_{AB} = \sqrt{(X_{A1} - X_{B1})^2 + (X_{A2} - X_{B2})^2}$,
(and of course similarly for d_{AC} and d_{BC}), thus, plugging in coordinates for distances:

$$d_{AC}d_{BC}\cos\theta_{AB} = \frac{1}{2}[(X_{A1}^2 + X_{A2}^2) + (X_{B1}^2 + X_{B2}^2) - ((X_{B1} - X_{A1})^2 + (X_{B2} - X_{A2})^2)],$$

The right two pieces arise from the properties of vectors, proceeding from the head of the vector of A to that of B. We can expand all the terms:

$$= \frac{1}{2} [X_{A1}^2 + X_{A2}^2 + X_{B1}^2 + X_{B2}^2 - (X_{B1}^2 + X_{A1}^2 - 2X_{B1}X_{A1}) - (X_{B2}^2 + X_{A2}^2 - 2X_{B2}X_{A2})]$$

The negative signs allow some terms to cancel:

$$= \frac{1}{2} [-(-2X_{B1}X_{A1}) - (-2X_{B2}X_{A2})] = X_{B1}X_{A1} + X_{B2}X_{A2}$$

which, in matrix algebra, can be written in vector form:

$$= [X_{A1} \ X_{A2}] \begin{bmatrix} X_{B1} \\ X_{B2} \end{bmatrix}.$$

This result goes by many names—the scalar product, dot product, or inner product between vectors A and B. It is the sum of the cross products of the coordinates for A and B, and it tells us about the relationship in space between A and B.

If we standardize our variables, in this case to make the lengths of the vectors for A and B both be length 1, then the equation:

$$d_{AB}^2 = d_{AC}^2 + d_{BC}^2 - 2d_{AC}d_{BC}\cos\theta_{AB}$$

simplifies to:

$$d_{AB}^2 = 1 + 1 - 2(1)(1)\cos\theta_{AB} = 2 - 2\cos\theta_{AB}.$$

Take the square root to obtain the distance:

$d_{AB} = \sqrt{2(1 - \cos\theta_{AB})} = \sqrt{2(1 - r_{AB})}$. That is, the correlation coefficient r, familiar to us in its algebraic form, has a geometric counterpart of the cosine of the angle between two vectors/variables. We are geeks, let us count the ways.

For more regarding the algebraic and geometric relationship, consider some special cases. The Law of Cosines simplifies to the Pythagorean Theorem when the angle between the vectors A and B is a right angle: $d_{AB}^2 = d_{AC}^2 + d_{BC}^2$. For example, the angle between dimension I and dimension II is $\theta = 90°$, and $\cos 90 = 0$. For such vectors—or variables represented by such vectors—we say they are orthogonal (perpendicular) or uncorrelated. If a vector "E" sat right along dimension I, the angle would be $\theta = 0°$, with $\cos\theta = \cos 0 = 1$, and we would say the two vectors (the variables they represent) are colinear (as in multicollinearity), that is, they are perfectly correlated. If a vector "F" fell along dimension I, but it pointed west instead of east, the angle $\theta = 180°$, $\cos 180 = -1$, and we would say the two vectors/variables are perfectly negatively correlated (as scores on dimension I get higher, those on F get smaller, and vice versa).

Classic Metric MDS

We'll now put the geometric relations to use and study the classic metric MDS model. In Figure 6.15, we have the dissimilarities data from 1 person comparing 4 brands, A, B, C, and D. The middle panel shows the triangle inequality test, which results in an additive constant of 2, which is then added to all values in the matrix at the right.

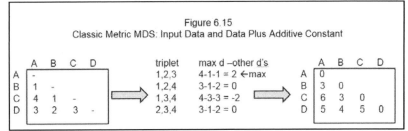

Figure 6.15
Classic Metric MDS: Input Data and Data Plus Additive Constant

	A	B	C	D		triplet	max d –other d's		A	B	C	D
A	-					1,2,3	4-1-1 = 2 ←max	A	0			
B	1	-				1,2,4	3-1-2 = 0	B	3	0		
C	4	1	-			1,3,4	4-3-3 = -2	C	6	3	0	
D	3	2	3	-		2,3,4	3-1-2 = 0	D	5	4	5	0

We'll call those values δ_{ij}, the data being the dissimilarity judgment for brands i and j. These values are squared, and centered by removing the effects of the row means, column means, and the grand mean (see Figure 6.16):

$$\delta_{ij}^* = -.5[\delta_{ij}^2 - (\bar{\delta}_{i.}^2 - \bar{\delta}_{..}^2) - (\bar{\delta}_{.j}^2 - \bar{\delta}_{..}^2) - \bar{\delta}_{..}^2]$$
$$= -.5[\delta_{ij}^2 - \bar{\delta}_{i.}^2 - \bar{\delta}_{.j}^2 + \bar{\delta}_{..}^2]$$

The matrix Δ^* with elements δ_{ij}^* is basically our data with a little pre-processing. The matrix Δ^* contains the scalar products of vectors representing brands i and j, which may be expressed as the sum of squares and cross-products of the coordinates for the brands i and j in r-dimensional space in X. It is factored into $\Delta^* = XX'$, where the matrix X contains the coordinates for p points (brands) in r-dimensional space (thus making it of dimensionality p × r, read "p by r," meaning p rows and r columns. This problem is solved as $\Delta^* = V\Lambda V'$ (an eigensolution with V being the matrix of eigenvectors and Λ the diagonal matrix with eigenvalues of Δ^*), so if we define $X = V\Lambda^{1/2}$, then we obtain the desired result, the product of the matrix of coordinates X, and its transpose X': $\Delta^* = XX'$.

The equation $\Delta^* = XX'$ is perfect (i.e., we reproduce our data perfectly) if we extract p dimensions (like p = 15 cereals would mean extracting 15 dimensions). For reasons of parsimony, we usually select r dimensions, where r $\ll$ p (often r is 2 or 3), and thus the relationship is an approximation: $\Delta^* \sim X_r X_r'$:

$$\Delta^* = \{\delta_{ij}^*\} = \begin{bmatrix} x_{11} & \cdots & x_{1r} \\ & \cdots & \\ x_{i1} & \cdots & x_{ir} \\ x_{j1} & \cdots & x_{jr} \\ & \cdots & \\ x_{p1} & \cdots & x_{pr} \end{bmatrix} \begin{bmatrix} x_{11} & x_{i1} & x_{j1} & x_{p1} \\ \cdots & & & \\ x_{1r} & x_{ir} & x_{jr} & x_{pr} \end{bmatrix} = XX'.$$

Figure 6.17 contains the 2-d solution, both plotted and in the form of **X**. For this simple example, the fit is perfect even in just 2 dimensions, e.g., the distances in the right triangle formed by points A, B, and D are $= 5^2 = 3^2 + 4^2$. Note that this configuration of distances would be maintained even if the current "T" appearance were reflected vertically or horizontally, or rotated through any angle degree.

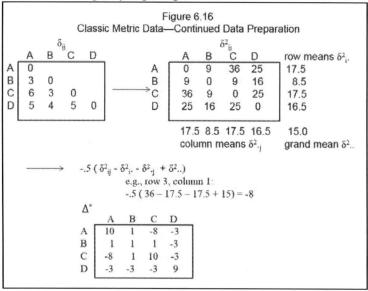

Figure 6.16
Classic Metric Data—Continued Data Preparation

We next look at 2 alternative MDS models, nonmetric MDS and individual differences scaling. After we have 3 MDS models in our tool belts, we will return to address the questions of: 1) how many dimensions are there in my data?, and 2) what do they mean?

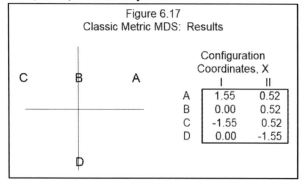

Figure 6.17
Classic Metric MDS: Results

	Configuration Coordinates, X	
	I	II
A	1.55	0.52
B	0.00	0.52
C	-1.55	0.52
D	0.00	-1.55

Nonmetric MDS

Recall that metric MDS models treat data such as 1, 2, 4 at face value, whereas "nonmetric" models look only at the rank information in the data, essentially 1, 2, 3. The dissimilarities data are ranked from the most similar pair to the most different. The data themselves might be rank judgments from customers, or they could be ratings data (e.g., 1 to 9, where 9 means "very different"), where we aren't comfortable assuming an interval level property of the data. Note that as cool as metric MDS is, nonmetric MDS is actually astounding! It begins with data that are only ranks or ordinal-level, and they will result in a model of distances, which are ratio-level.[18]

Like metric MDS, in nonmetric MDS, we seek to estimate coordinates **X** that result in model-fitted distances to match our dissimilarity data as well as possible. For metric MDS, the model-derived distances d_{ij} are a linear function

---

[18] The X matrix of coordinates seems to be ratio-level also, but recall that we can move the origin, so really, it's interval.

of the dissimilarities data, δ_{ij}. For nonmetric MDS, the model-derived distances d_{ij} are a monotonic function of the data δ_{ij}. A monotonically increasing function is one that always rises or stays level, but never goes down.[19]

To understand the monotonic relationship, which is the essence of the difference between metric and nonmetric MDS, consider Figure 6.18. The data for 5 brands are translated to their rank order. In Figure 6.19, the ranks appear from 1 to 10 (column 3), along with the pairs they represent (column 1), and the original data points, δ's, for reference (column 2). At this point, the model works with the ranks and the original δ's are essentially forgotten.[20]

Figure 6.18
Nonmetric MDS Data Preparation

data δ_{ij} → translate to ranks

$$
\begin{array}{c|ccccc}
 & 1 & 2 & 3 & 4 & 5 \\
\hline
1 & - & & & & \\
2 & .34 & - & & & \\
3 & .47 & .39 & - & & \\
4 & .92 & .45 & .50 & - & \\
5 & .25 & .56 & .72 & .23 & -
\end{array}
\qquad
\begin{array}{c|ccccc}
 & 1 & 2 & 3 & 4 & 5 \\
\hline
1 & - & & & & \\
2 & 3 & - & & & \\
3 & 6 & 4 & - & & \\
4 & 10 & 5 & 7 & - & \\
5 & 2 & 8 & 9 & 1 & -
\end{array}
$$

Figure 6.19
Nonmetric MDS and Monotonic Regression

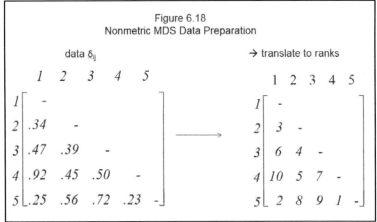

stimulus pair ordered max to min i,j	δ_{ij}	rank of δ_{ij}	estimates disparities form at current monotonic function iteration d_{ij}		$\hat{d}_{ij}$
5,4	.23	1	3		3
5,1	.25	2	6	→	4.5
2,1	.34	3	3˙	→	4.5
3,2	.39	4	5		5
4,2	.45	5	8		8
3,1	.47	6	10		10
4,3	.50	7	13	→	11
5,2	.56	8	11˙	→	11
5,3	.72	9	9˙	→	11
4,1	.92	10	15		15

We know MDS tries to place the 5 brands in space such that their distances approximate the data. Say we catch this nonmetric MDS computer model midstream. At whatever iteration it's in, it would have tentative coordinates for the 5 brands, which could be used to calculate the current distances to see which brands need to be farther apart or closer together (via the "steepest descent algorithm"). The column labeled d_{ij} gives the distances that the model predicts at this point in the iterations.

---

[19] There are 2 model choices for defining monotonicity: 1) strong monotonicity states that whenever in the data $\delta_{ij} < \delta_{kl}$, then in the model it should also be the case that $d_{ij} < d_{kl}$. The alternative is 2) weak monotonicity, where, if in the data $\delta_{ij} < \delta_{kl}$, then in the model $d_{ij} \leq d_{kl}$. We will almost always choose the second alternative because it is less restrictive and makes a less demanding assumption about the data, which are likely to be somewhat errorful.

[20] Another model choice concerns how to treat ties. If the data for 3 brands were $\{\delta_{AB} = .2, \delta_{AC} = .5, \delta_{BC} = .4\}$, the data would be ranked: 1, 3, 2. If instead the data were $\{\delta_{AB} = .2, \delta_{AC} = .5, \delta_{BC} = .5\}$, the question would be how to align the 2nd and 3rd ranks. The choices are: 1) the primary approach to ties, which states that if $\delta_{ij} = \delta_{kl}$ in the ranked data, then d_{ij} may or may not equal d_{kl}. The alternative is 2) the secondary approach to ties, which states that if in the data $\delta_{ij} = \delta_{kl}$, then the model should represent that relation faithfully, with $d_{ij} \equiv d_{kl}$. We will almost always go with the first choice because it is more flexible and less restrictive for data we know are likely to be errorful.

If you run down that column, you'll notice that it is not monotonically increasing—there are several spots indicated by * where the relative sizes reverse. We begin with 3, proceed to 6, and thus far, those 2 distances convey monotonicity. As we proceed to the next value, 3, monotonicity is broken—that is, 3, 6, 3 doesn't work. We can restore it if we average the 6 and the second 3, to 4.5. Now the series is 3, 4.5, 4.5, 5, 8, 10, 13—so far, so good. Then we hit another reversal, so we correct it by averaging 11 and 13 to get 12. The next value is another bump, so we average the 13, 11, and 9 to get three values of 11, and then the final value is fine. These adjusted values are called "disparities" (fixing the distances when they're disparate from the monotonic function) and they're denoted $\hat{d}$. These values are plotted against the rank data to show the monotonic function.

Thus a monotonic regression (sometimes called an isotonic regression) has three values to watch for each pair of stimuli (brands) i and j:

- The initial data point, the dissimilarity δ_{ij}, which is immediately translated to ranks.
- The distances d_{ij} computed at each iteration in the model, from which, in turn, we'll obtain estimates of the coordinates.
- And the disparities, the $\hat{d}_{ij}$, which are values needed to make the monotonic regression machinery run, but are not otherwise used (or reported). They are close to d_{ij} values, but they are not distances (i.e., they will not necessarily satisfy the distance axioms).

In regression, there is a measure of how well the model predicted estimates ($\hat{y}$) match the data (y), namely, R^2. Naturally there is a comparable question here: how well do the disparities values (which roughly follow the rank of our data) fit the model-derived distances at this iteration? A plot of $\hat{d}$ vs. δ_{ij} is called a Shepard diagram, and a measure of badness of fit called Stress compares the $\hat{d}$ and d values:[21]

$$\text{Stress} = \sqrt{\sum_{i<j}\left(d_{ij} - \hat{d}_{ij}\right)^2 / \sum_{i<j} d_{ij}^2}.$$

The summation notation of "$i < j$" means to sum over all pairs. (A badness of fit measure means larger numbers are worse, unlike goodness of fit measures such as R^2 where larger numbers are better.) In the next iteration, we wiggle the X_{ij} coordinates, compute new distances d_{ij}'s and an updated value of stress, and we continue to iterate in such a manner, trying to improve the locations of the points, doing so until stress doesn't move more than some value, e.g., 0.0001.

The solution to which the computer model converged is presented in Figure 6.20. The output contains both the matrix X of coordinates, and a plot of the configuration. (FYI: metric and nonmetric solutions often look rather similar in real data.)

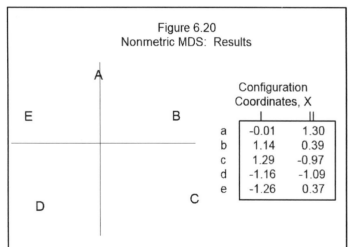

Figure 6.20
Nonmetric MDS: Results

Configuration Coordinates, X		
	I	II
a	-0.01	1.30
b	1.14	0.39
c	1.29	-0.97
d	-1.16	-1.09
e	-1.26	0.37

Individual Differences MDS

Classic metric MDS and nonmetric MDS models are applicable to only one data matrix at a time. The data from each study participant may be modeled separately, or, as is usually the case, the lower triangle matrices of data are averaged across respondents, and that matrix of mean dissimilarity judgments is modeled.

Averages don't always tell the whole story, so there is a class of MDS models that allow for individual differences in perceptions. When people are asked to make comparative judgments between stimuli, different people may focus on different features, or, we'll say that different people discriminate between the stimuli along different dimensions.

---

[21] Named for and by Roger Shepard and Joseph Kruskal, pioneers and giants in the MDS world.

We have data δ_{ijk}, where $i, j = 1 \ldots p$ stimuli (brands), and the last subscript represents sources of data, $k = 1 \ldots N$. Usually the multiple sources are a sample of people, but k has been used to represent time points, different ad

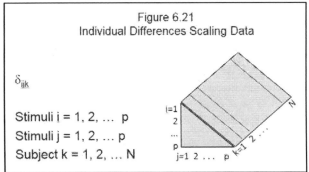

Figure 6.21
Individual Differences Scaling Data

δ_{ijk}

Stimuli i = 1, 2, ... p

Stimuli j = 1, 2, ... p

Subject k = 1, 2, ... N

campaigns, or experimental conditions, etc. This matrix is 3-dimensional and is said to be "2-mode" (stimuli by stimuli by subjects). An example appears in Figure 6.21. We would likely have had such data for the classic metric and nonmetric MDS models as well, but we would have averaged over the data to obtain a single triangle. Here, we'll use all the data, including the variance and idiosyncrasies of all the respondents.

The Individual Differences Scaling model, INDSCAL, is a metric model that takes these $\{\delta_{ijk}\}$s and outputs two matrices (see Figure 6.22). One is the usual p x r matrix **X**, containing the coordinates of the configuration of the p points in r-dimensional space. The second matrix **W** is N by r, and it contains the "subject weights." These weights w_{kt} represent the weight that person k puts on the tth dimension, or the degree to which that dimension is more or less salient to them in their judgments comparing the pairs of stimuli.

The coordinates in matrix X are said to represent the "group stimulus space," and the weights essentially adjust that aggregate view to suit each individual's data better. While we have been defining distances using the familiar Euclidean formulation, $d_{ij} = \sqrt{\sum_{t=1}^{r} (x_{it} - x_{jt})^2}$, we now turn to the weighted Euclidean distance model, $d_{ijk} = \sqrt{\sum_{t=1}^{r} w_{kt} (x_{it} - x_{jt})^2}$, defined for i = stimulus, t = dimension, and k = subject. The models are not so different—if we rewrite the weighted model to appear as

$$d_{ijk} = \sqrt{\sum_{t=1}^{r} (\sqrt{w_{kt}} \, x_{it} - \sqrt{w_{kt}} \, x_{jt})^2},$$

and define new coordinates (one set for each respondent) as $y_{itk} = (\sqrt{w_{kt}}) \, x_{it}$, then the distance formula looks more familiar:

$$\sqrt{\sum_{t=1}^{r} (y_{itk} - y_{jtk})^2}.$$

If we sought to understand how a particular person's (or a segment of customers') view of a set of brands differed from that of the group overall, we'd look at the weights, w_{kt}'s. For example, if w_{1t} were very large, and w_{2t} were very small, it is as if person (or segment) t emphasized dimension 1 in their judgments and nearly ignored how the

Figure 6.22
The Two Matrices Output by INDSCAL

1 2 ... r

X

p

X contains the group stimulus space. x_{jt} is the coordinate of stimulus j on dimension t.

1 2 ... r

W

N

W is the matrix of "subject weights." w_{kt} is the weight or salience of dimension t for subject k.

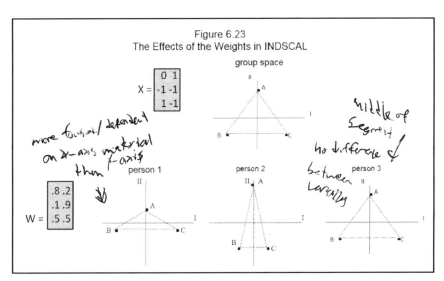

Figure 6.23
The Effects of the Weights in INDSCAL

$X = \begin{bmatrix} 0 & 1 \\ -1 & -1 \\ 1 & -1 \end{bmatrix}$

group space

$W = \begin{bmatrix} .8 & .2 \\ .1 & .9 \\ .5 & .5 \end{bmatrix}$

person 1

person 2

person 3

brands differed on dimension 2. Imagine taking any of the perceptual maps we've seen thus far and stretching it along the first axis and simultaneously mashing it down from top to bottom (see Figure 6.23, lower left).

There will likely be another group of respondents who weight dimension 2 more heavily than 1, and perhaps still another group who weight the dimensions roughly equally. Not surprisingly, subject weights have been used to identify customer segments.

If we had gathered additional information on the respondents, such as demographics or attitudinal ratings, we could correlate the subject weights with those indicators to get a better picture of the people who view the map in a particular manner. Note, to do so, it is recommended that the weights be adjusted slightly. The size of w_{kt} for person k is not directly comparable to $w_{k't}$ for person k' because the MDS model might fit better for one person than for the other. For each person k in the sample, take the sum of their squared weights (going across in their row k): $SS_k = \sum_t w_{kt}^2$. Then in subsequent analyses, use the relative subject weights, $w_{kt}^* = w_{kt}/\sqrt{SS_k}$ where the w*'s have been normed per each individual. Then you'll be "comparing apples to apples."

How to Determine Dimensionality

We know that the goal for MDS is not just fitting points into space in such a way as to be consistent with data—it's to do so in minimal dimensionality. Here is how we make that trade-off between fit and parsimony.

In nonmetric MDS, we discussed the badness of fit measure, Stress. Classic metric MDS and INDSCAL also produce fit statistics (an eigenvalue in classic, and R^2 in INDSCAL). They are both goodness of fit measures because they are essentially indices of variance accounted for (VAF). We will run several MDS models, for 1-d, 2-d, 3-d, and so forth, and with each analysis, we will note what the fit measure was. We'll plot these, as in Figure 6.24. The x-axis depicts when we ran 1-d, 2-d, etc., and the vertical axis depicts the measure of fit (or lack of fit). Each measure of fit comes from a different model run (e.g., a different output). We're looking for a break in the curve that we just plotted—the break is called an elbow.

If the measure of fit is a "badness of fit" index such as Stress in nonmetric MDS, then we take the likely number of dimensions for an optimal solution to be the number below (or to the right of) the break in the curve. The reasoning is as follows: if we take just 1 dimension, the Stress value is pretty high. If we extract 2 dimensions, Stress improves, but it's still kind of high. If we extract 3 dimensions, the same thing happens—Stress is improving but we wonder if we can't do better. If we model the data with 4 dimensions, Stress is reduced a lot, to the point that taking additional dimensions does not help much more. The trade-off we are looking for is diminishing returns. If we take 4 dimensions, the improvement of fit is worth the fact that we have to explain 4 dimensions. If we took 5 dimensions, the improvement would be negligible, and not worth the need to explain still another dimension. Thus, in the plot to the left in Figure 6.24, we see a break between 3 and 4, so we settle on 4 dimensions.

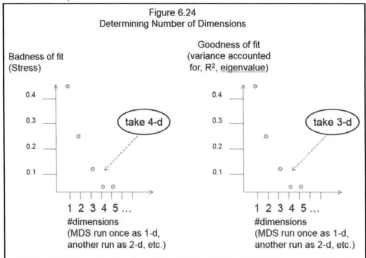

Figure 6.24
Determining Number of Dimensions

On the other hand, if your favorite computer program produces a measure of fit that is a "goodness of fit" index, such as eigenvalues (in classic MDS) or R^2 (typical in INDSCAL models), then we'll take the number of dimensions to be the number above (or to the left of) the break. Here, the logic is that if we take 1 dimension, we have explained some of the data. If we take 2 dimensions, we've explained a bit more. Taking 3 dimensions explains still more, but the amount of variance explained by the 4th (or 5th etc.) dimensions is miniscule, and not worth including in the model, which we're trying to keep as simple and clean as possible.

Two last thoughts about dimensionality. Sometimes people seem to be making claims about the "true" number of dimensions for some map. There is no such thing. The "truth" depends on your stimulus set. For example, if customers compared the soft drinks Pepsi, Coke, Diet Pepsi, and Diet Coke, you might get a single dimension (diet vs. regular). If you ran another study and included 7Up and Sprite, probably a second dimension would pop (cola vs. uncola). If you ran a third study, and included Cherry 7Up and Cherry Pepsi, etc., no doubt a third dimension would reflect this new distinctive taste. The bottom line is that it is important to be thoughtful when designing the study regarding which brands to include and which are acceptable to exclude.

Why would we exclude any brands? Recall that as the number of brands included, p, grows, the number of pairs to compare grows by the factor p(p – 1)/2 (essentially at the rate of p^2). With 15 brands, there are 105 comparisons, and that task can take about an hour. Have pity on your study participants. If you work in an industry with many brands (e.g., soft drinks, cereals, or cars, etc.), there are techniques to have people rate subsets of pairs, and compile the data together.

Lastly, recall from the previous basic geometry review that dimensionality depends in part on the number of points in that r-dimensional space. MDS experts advise that if you wish to clearly define "r" dimensions, you'll need at least 4r + 1 stimuli. That comes from the rule of thumb that the number of comparisons (p(p – 1)/2) should equal or exceed twice the number of coordinates the MDS model has to estimate. That is, $(p(p-1)/2) \geq 2pr$. Turning that inequality inside out and solving for p, you get p $\geq$ 4r + 1.

Attribute Vector Fitting

In Figure 6.25, we see a simple MDS plot. The computer model produces a plot (or the coordinates for us to plot), and it is up to us to interpret the perceptual map. We look to interpret maps in two different ways: first, we want to understand the configuration as a whole, and second, people can't resist wanting to label the axes.

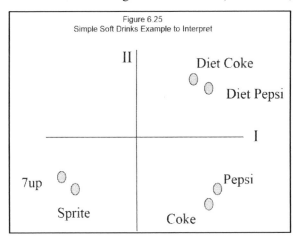

Figure 6.25
Simple Soft Drinks Example to Interpret

Regarding the configuration, we see that some pairs of soft drinks are perceived to be more similar to each other— Coke and Pepsi, Diet Coke and Diet Pepsi, and 7Up and Sprite. That closeness information tells us about who our toughest competitors are, or what brands are seen as substitutes for our own. Brands that are far from ours are ones we don't have to worry about. If we do not like our location, or the company of the other brands we keep, we may wish to work on marketing to reposition the brand. We also see empty spaces in the map. If it were not for the fact that we already know there are diet versions of 7Up and Sprite, we might think to concoct such drinks because there is a market opportunity there.

In terms of labeling the axes, the first dimension seems to be the difference between colas and uncolas. The second dimension seems to be the diet vs. non-diet distinction. Of all the ways these brands differ, it's apparently these two dimensions that are the characteristics that consumers primarily use to discriminate among the brands.

This map is simple, so this interpretation of the axes, while subjective, would be one on which there would be a great deal of consensus. However, most real perceptual maps are more complicated, so it would be handy to have a more objective means of interpreting the dimensions than our ocular app. Happily there is an easy method to do so. We'll first apply it to the soft drinks map, so we can be convinced it works, and then we'll see it applied to a more complicated map.

The technique is called "vector fitting" (or sometimes even "profit" for property attribute vector fitting). Recall that when we gathered the proximities data that we have modeled via MDS, we also obtained respondents' ratings of each brand on each of a number of attributes. We take these data and compute the means over all respondents, to produce a p×r matrix of means, one row for each brand, and one column for each attribute. These means reflect, on average, how customers see each brand on each of the attributes.

To fit the vectors, and help us interpret the map, we run a series of multiple regressions, one for each attribute. The attribute serves as the dependent variable, and the coordinates of the brands in the perceptual map serve as the independent variables. Our data are represented in Figure 6.26. We have the coordinates on dimensions I and II (plotted in Figure 6.25), and 3 variables that represent various properties or attributes of these drinks: diet vs. regular, cola vs. uncola, and the mean over our sample of customers' ratings on the sweetness of each brand.

Figure 6.26
Vector Fitting to Interpret MDS

	Coordinates on Dimensions:		0=nondiet 1=diet	0=uncola 1=cola	sweetness mean 1-7	Standardized Coordinates	
	I	II				I	II
Coke	0.5	-0.5	0	1	3.2	0.641	-0.862
Pepsi	0.6	-0.4	0	1	6.3	0.808	-0.637
Diet Coke	0.4	0.5	1	1	2.7	0.474	1.387
Diet Pepsi	0.5	0.4	1	1	5.4	0.641	1.162
7Up	-0.7	-0.3	0	0	3.5	-1.366	-0.412
Sprite	-0.6	-0.4	0	0	4.8	-1.198	-0.637
					mean:	0.000	0.000
					standard deviation:	1.000	1.000

Before running the regressions, we must first pre-process the data (don't skip this step!): we standardize the dimension coordinates such that each dimension in the MDS has a mean of zero and a standard deviation of 1. That is, we transform the dimension coordinates into z-scores (some programs produce coordinates that are already standardized, but if not, any statistical package can help you do this transformation easily). The standardized coordinates appear in the last 2 columns of Figure 6.26. A plot of standardized coordinates will look similar to a plot of the raw dimension coordinates, except that the raw configuration is likely to look more oval and the standardized coordinates will look more like a circle (transforming the dimension to z-scores divides out their unequal standard deviation, thereby equating the lengths of the axes). Thus for each brand or stimulus, we plot the standardized coordinates (to means = 0 and standard deviations = 1), and use the new values (we'll call them zdim) in the following regressions.

Figure 6.27
Attribute Vector Fitting via Regression

	R^2	b1	b2	β1	β2	$\sqrt{(b1^2 + b2^2)}$	normed b1	b2
diet	0.987	0.060	0.490	0.117	0.949	0.494	0.122	0.992
cola	0.993	0.498	0.044	0.964	0.086	0.500	0.996	0.088
sweetness	0.103	0.398	-0.383	0.283	-0.273	0.552	0.720	-0.690

For the first regression, we use the diet/non-diet attribute as the dependent variable, and the standardized coordinates on the dimensions as the predictors:

$$\hat{diet} = b_0 + b_1 zdimI + b_2 zdimII$$
$$\text{or } \hat{diet} = \beta_1 zdimI + \beta_2 zdimII.$$

The regression equations will produce both raw regression coefficients (the b's) and standardized regression coefficients (the β's), and we can work with either.[22] The first row in Figure 6.27 shows the results for the diet attribute. The R^2 is large, which means the 2-d space captures most of the diet/non-diet variance. In MDS, we would say that the diet vector helps us interpret the 2-d map. The raw and standardized regression coefficients are in the next columns, and the square root of the sum of squared raw regression coefficients is the next column (i.e., $\sqrt{(b_1)^2 + (b_2)^2 + \cdots + (b_r)^2}$). The last 2 columns are the result of taking b_1 and b_2 and norming them (e.g., $normed\ b_1 = (b_1)/\left(\sqrt{(b_1)^2 + (b_2)^2}\right)$). That square root value is the length of the vector in geo-land, so in dividing it out, all of the vector lengths are now equated to each other, and specifically to 1.0.

Similarly, for cola vs. uncola, we fit the next regression:
$$\hat{cola} = .964\ zdimI + .086\ zdimII, \quad R^2 = .99.$$
For the data reflecting the sweetness of the drinks, rated 1 to 7 (7 = "very sweet"):
$$\hat{sweetness} = .283\ zdimI - .273\ zdimII, \quad R^2 = .10.$$

---

[22] If we choose to work with the raw regression coefficients (the b's), we don't need b_0 (but do not fit a regression forcing the intercept to be zero). A nonzero b_0 would merely move the origin around or up and down, but the vector we'll plot would be parallel; hence, we can essentially ignore b_0 (alternatively, of course, you can subtract the attribute mean x_i- and then b_0 will be 0 anyway).

What do these regressions tell us? The regression coefficients tell us where to put the head of an attribute vector emanating from the origin. If a vector points to the "east," then that's the direction in which the attribute is maximized—brands that are farther and farther east are those thought to have the most of that attribute. When we plot our 3 vectors in Figure 6.28, we see that the diet property points almost due north, the cola vector points almost straight east, and the sweetness vector points southeast. These vector orientations mean that the brands farthest north are the diet drinks, and by implication, through the origin heading in the opposite direction, south, are the non-diet drinks; brands farthest east are the colas, those farthest west are the uncolas. We will talk about sweetness (and its very small R^2) shortly.

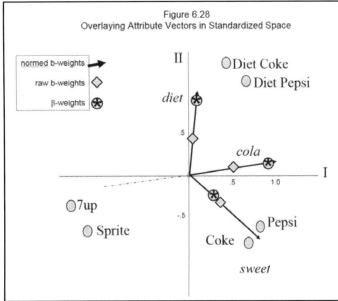

Figure 6.28
Overlaying Attribute Vectors in Standardized Space

Recall that one part of the interpretation of a MDS space is the configuration itself—to examine what brands are close, what holes or opportunities exist, etc. It is also important to try to label the dimensions, because everyone you show a perceptual map will want to know what it is. In this example, we're lucky to have a vector aligned with each dimension (or at least closer than you're ever likely to see in real data). If no vectors sit atop a dimension, it's not a problem. You'll see in another example shortly that the configuration is still ultimately the most important thing.

To use the attribute vectors, we project (i.e., draw the brand back onto the vector in such a way that it meets the vector at an orthogonal, or 90°, angle). Then, compare the brands as they have been projected along the vector—the brands that project closest to the head of the vector are those that are perceived to have the most of that attribute.[23] For example, on the diet vector, Diet Coke and Diet Pepsi would project onto the vector with the highest scores, eventually followed by 7Up, Pepsi, Sprite and Coke.

In Figure 6.28, there are 3 marks along each vector—one is the vector head itself, another is a diamond shape, and another is a circle with an asterisk inside it. These reflect different choices of plotting the normed b-weights (the vector head), the raw b-weights (the diamonds), or the betas (the stars). Note that they all fall along the same directionality from the origin, so any could assist in interpretation.[24]

- The point of norming the attribute b-values is to put all the vectors on an equal footing—here the idea is that all the attributes will fall around on a unit circle, and all you are interested in is direction. (These vectors correspond to the "direction cosines.")

---

[23] Note that it is not the case that the brands that are closest to the vector, or even closest to the head of the vector, are those with the most of that attribute. The interpretations require you to extend the vector in the direction it is pointing, extend it backward through the origin in the other direction, and then project (meet the vector orthogonally) each brand onto the vector (indeed perhaps past the head itself). Once they are all sitting on that vector, then the brands farthest in the direction in which the vector is pointing are those seen as having the most of that attribute. The projection, in geometry, equals the $\hat{y}$ in the regression. I know. It's all awesome.

[24] One way to be convinced is to see that the angles are the same, e.g., for the diet attribute, b1/b2 = 0.060/0.490 = 0.1229, β1/β2 = 0.117/0.949 = 0.1229, and normed b1/ normed b2 = 0.122/0.992 = 0.1229. The angles are important, because they capture information about the configuration, or relative positions. The only differences between the pairs of b, β, and normed-b values are the lengths of the vectors they produce.

- Drawing vectors that stop at the diamonds (using the raw b-weights) would indicate the same directionality, but the lengths reflect the variances of the attributes, as well as the R^2 or how well the vector fits the space.
- Drawing vectors that stop at the stars (using beta weights) maintains the directionality, and the R^2 or the fits in the space, but the lengths are corrected for the attribute variances.

For the b-vectors or β-vectors, it's not a coincidence that the vectors that are longer are also associated with the regressions with the highest R^2s. The regression is algebra, and the vector is geometry—the R^2 tells us about the fit of a regression, and its geometric manifestation is the length of the vector (or its distance from the origin).

Thus, we can look at the β's and know that large R^2s and long vectors indicate that the attribute is important in interpreting the plot. Small R^2s or short vectors indicate that the attribute is not useful in interpreting the plot. Note that if the MDS has more than 2 dimensions, the length of a vector is interpretable only with respect to a particular plot. A short vector in a I-II plot may be longer in the overall MDS space or in a plot depicting a different view like the I-III plane.

With that in mind, we can revisit the sweetness vector. Looking at the data that the regression has to work with—the means in Figure 6.26—we can see why the little vector struggles. It's pulled first in the direction of Pepsi and then Diet Pepsi (the 2 highest means), and looking at the configuration of where these two brands exist (Pepsi in the "southeast" of the map and Diet Pepsi in the "northeast"), it's difficult to head toward both brands simultaneously. The next means continue to confuse the possible directionality; e.g., Sprite is in the "southwest," etc. These results don't necessarily mean that sweetness isn't a relevant or helpful attribute. What is likely the case is that if we were to go back and extract a 3-d solution (instead of 2-d), the third dimension may well be sweetness. If that were the case, we would probably see the brands in their current locations, except that Pepsi, Diet Pepsi, and Sprite would rise above the surface of the 2-d map, and the less sweet drinks would recede beneath it. In that map, sweetness would point to the top of the 3-d representation, and the R^2 would be much higher. We'd have to think about whether we wanted to include sweetness or maintain the 2-d solution for parsimony.

It is analytically legitimate to interpret (for yourself) and communicate (to others) any set of the b-weights, β-weights, or b-weights normed to the unit circle. One set might be easier to plot, one set might strike you as more intuitive, etc. Be consistent, of course, in that if the diet vector is represented by the b-weights, don't put the cola vector in using β-weights. A final tip—sometimes, depending on the variance of the attributes and the R^2, the vectors resulting from the b's or the β's will be very short, and the map simply becomes difficult to read. In that case, multiply all b's (or β's) by some (the same) constant, so as to extend them or shrink them and make it possible to see them more clearly.

To give you a real appreciation of the helpfulness of this attribute vector fitting, let's look at a slightly more complicated example. Figure 6.29 features the plot of an MDS solution for 6 cereals. Customers rated the similarity among these brands: Cheerios, Frosted Flakes, Lucky Charms, Mini-Wheats, Raisin Bran, and Rice Krispies. They also rated each cereal on 7 attributes: is the cereal cute, expensive, good, healthy, for kids, often on sale, and trustworthy.

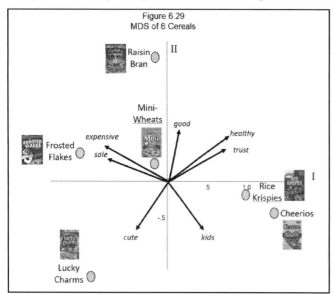

Figure 6.29
MDS of 6 Cereals

Unlike with the soft drinks in Figure 6.28, even a clever marketer would be hard-pressed to interpret these figures without the assistance of the attribute vectors. With the attributes superimposed on the MDS, we can venture interpretations as (roughly): I) healthy and trustworthy (to the right) vs. more expensive yet often on promotion (to the left), II) good (at the top) vs. cute and for kids (at the bottom). There are many other observations we can detect in this plot: 1) we see that Rice Krispies and Cheerios are near substitutes so they are likely to be fierce competitors, 2) Frosted Flakes is seen as expensive, a positioning they might question or verify and then reconsider—perhaps they like offering the promotional activities rather than staying stable at an everyday low (or high) price, and 3) cereals for children still struggle with the perception that they are not necessarily good or healthy.

Ideal Point Preference Models

Perceptions are powerful and fundamental, but marketers are also interested in what brands people like and want. Preference data can be collected in a number of ways, such as, "What kinds of movies do you like to watch? (rank the genre)," "What brand of soft drink do you buy most often?," "Approximately how many of each of the following candy bars do you buy each month?," and so forth. Preference can be treated like another attribute, i.e., such that each customer's data are represented by a vector in the space. However, you'll more frequently encounter the "ideal point" preference model.

Ideal points work a lot like the original points representing the brands. Each respondent will be represented by his or her own point in the same space as the brands. While the inter-point distances between brands represent similarities and differences, the distance between an ideal point representing a customer and any brand represents how much the customer likes that brand. The customer's ideal point will be located closest to the brands that the customer likes the most.

In fact, the concept of an ideal point is that if there were a brand right where the customer's ideal point is, that would be the customer's ideal brand—that location in the MDS space has just the right mixture of all the dimensions and attributes which that customer would like the most. If there is no such ideal product on the market, then, first, marketers have an opportunity to create such a thing, and second, we'd predict that the customer most often chooses the brand that is closest to the ideal point. If that real brand were stocked out (e.g., soft drinks in a vending machine) or otherwise inaccessible (as in priced too high for the customer), then we'd predict the customer would choose the brand that was next closest to the ideal point, and so on.

An ideal point model of preferences is often called an "Unfolding Model." It gets this name from the idea depicted in Figure 6.30, in which a consumer is represented as a point along the same continuum as the brands. Figure

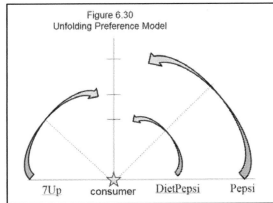

Figure 6.30
Unfolding Preference Model

6.30 is only 1-dimensional, to keep things simple. The consumer is noted at the star on the dimension, with 7Up noted at a point to the consumer's left, and Diet Pepsi and Pepsi to the consumer's right. You can probably eyeball that line and see that the Diet Pepsi is closest to the consumer, and Pepsi is the farthest. Those distances would be made clearer if we were to fold up the dimension at the point where the consumer star is. Then, the consumer would form the base of a vertical axis, and Diet Pepsi would have some score above the consumer, 7Up above that, and Pepsi up higher still. A preference model then predicts that the consumer likes the brands that are closest. Flipping back and forth, that vertical axis of preference could be unfolded to return to the notion of the dimension that is drawn from west to east.

Unfolding models are classified into "External Unfolding Models" and "Internal Unfolding Models." In an external unfolding model, a perceptual MDS map is obtained from some proximities data, and then preference data are overlaid as ideal points. In an internal unfolding model, the marketer only has preference data and seeks to obtain both a perceptual mapping and the preference ideal points from the same data set. The external unfolding model is vastly more popular in the real world, it's what is described next, and its popularity is probably due to its statistical superiority—the internal unfolding models simply ask too much of one data set, and results and solutions tend to be unstable.

Thus, we proceed with an external unfolding model, fitting ideal points easily via regressions with just a few tweaks. Figure 6.31 shows the data set, with the standardized coordinates once more serving as predictors, along with the sum of their squared values. The dependent variable for each regression is one customer's ratings of the brands on a 7-point scale (where 1= "don't care for the brand" to 7= "one of my favorite brands." Customer 1 really likes the uncolas, and is not crazy about diet soft drinks. Customer 2 really likes the diet drinks and really none of the others. We run one regression per customer, obtain the regression weights, and use the regression weight for the new predictor (the sum of squares term) to adjust the others: new b_1 = old $b_1/-2b_3$, new b_2 = old $b_2/-2b_3$. New b_1 and new b_2 are the coordinates of the customer's ideal point.

	Standardized Coordinates Dimension			Customer Preferences Ratings (7 = "like very much")	
	1	2	SS*	C1	C2
Coke	0.641	-0.862	1.154	5	1
Pepsi	0.808	-0.637	1.059	5	2
Diet Coke	0.474	1.387	2.148	1	7
Diet Pepsi	0.641	1.162	1.761	2	7
7Up	-1.366	-0.412	2.036	7	2
Sprite	-1.198	-0.637	1.841	7	1

Figure 6.31
Preference Models: The Data Set

*SS = (Dim1^2)+(Dim2^2)

For customer 1, the b's are –2.50 (dim1), –0.47 (dim 2), and –3.46 for the sum of squares term, so the coordinates for the ideal point are: $new\ b1 = \frac{-2.50}{-2\times(-3.46)} = -0.36$, and $new\ b2 = \frac{-0.47}{-2\times(-3.46)} = -0.07$. For customer 2, the b's are –0.50 (dim1), 3.59 (dim 2), and –2.14 for the sum of squares term, so the coordinates for the ideal point are: $new\ b1 = \frac{-0.50}{-2\times(-2.14)} = -0.12$, and $new\ b2 = \frac{3.59}{-2\times(-2.14)} = 0.84$. (If the customer preference data had been ranks, where smaller numbers represented more liking, we'd reverse the signs on these coordinates to plot the ideal points. If we neglected to do so, we'd be plotting "anti-ideal" points—locations in the map that represented brands the customers liked the least.) The locations of the ideal points in Figure 6.32 are reasonable given the customers' data. Customer 1 had shown a clear preference for the uncolas, and Customer 2 showed a preference for diet drinks.

Once many ideal points are plotted, it is easy to see where there are segments of customers who might be good to target. The MDS map is complete—the perceptions form the basis of the map, and the ideal points indicate the preferences.

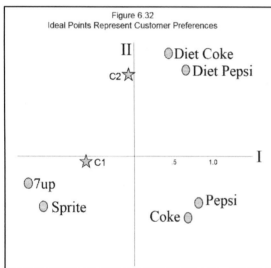

Figure 6.32
Ideal Points Represent Customer Preferences

Correspondence Analysis

These MDS models—classic metric, nonmetric, and individual differences scaling—and the supplemental external unfolding modeling of preferences represent easily 99% of the MDS work IRL. There are still more kinds of MDS models, and in particular, we close with a model that has become very popular for creating perceptual maps.

That model is called "correspondence analysis" (CA). CA produces vectors with coordinates to plot entities in space, wherein inter-point distances are interpretable, all much like MDS. One difference is that whereas MDS requires dissimilarities data as inputs, CA works on any non-negative valued matrix and matrices that are 2-mode, i.e., the row and column entities are different. For example, we might have a matrix with customers as rows and ratings on a 1 to 9 scale of products as columns. If we had such a matrix, we could use MDS, but we would first need to aggregate over the customers to create the derived dissimilarities "products by products" matrix. In CA, we'll plot the customer types and products in the same ("corresponding") space.

In particular, CA rose in popularity because we can use it to analyze frequency data in cross-tabs. Call "F" the frequency matrix (the cross-tab). We'll first take every element in the matrix, f_{ij}, and divide it by $1/\sqrt{f_{i+}}$ and $1/\sqrt{f_{+j}}$, the row and column sums of F (much like how we compute a correlation coefficient by dividing the cross-products terms by the relevant standard deviations).

Call that processed matrix H. We then factor H using a "singular value decomposition" (a procedure like the eigenvalue-eigenvector mechanism in factor analysis in Chapter 4): $H = P\Delta Q'$.[25] We will rescale the columns in P to obtain X, the coordinates to plot the row entities, and Q to obtain Y to plot the column entities (R is the set of row sums, C is the set of column margins, and I is the identity matrix): $X = R^{-.5}P(\Delta + I)^{.5}$ and $= C^{-.5}Q(\Delta + I)^{.5}$.

It is traditional in CA to use only 2-dimensions, and those coordinates are found in columns 2 and 3 of X and Y. The first column in either matrix contains intercept-like information that is ignored.

Time for an example! Figure 6.33 shows results from a study in which consumers were asked questions about their cars:

1. "Is the manufacturer (check one): _American, _European, _Japanese?"
2. "What is the make and model of your car?"
3. "Is your car primarily (check one): _the family car, _a fun, sporty car, _a car I take to work?"

The researchers took the information from question 2 and classified the car as large, medium, or small. Figure 6.33 shows the results in blocks of 3 columns—country of origin, car size, and car use.

Figure 6.33
Cars and Drivers

	American	European	Japanese	Large	Medium	Small	Family	Sporty	Work	Row sums:
Married	37	13	51	9	42	50	50	35	16	101
Married & kids	50	15	44	21	51	37	79	12	18	109
Single	32	15	62	11	40	58	35	57	17	109
Single & kids	6	1	8	1	8	6	10	2	3	15
Female	58	21	70	17	70	62	83	44	22	149
Male	67	23	95	25	71	89	91	62	32	185
Column sums:	125	44	165	42	141	151	174	106	54	334

The consumers were also asked questions about themselves, regarding marital status (married or single), whether or not they had children, and whether the respondent filling out the survey was male or female. Figure 6.33 shows family composition in the first 4 rows and gender in the last 2 rows.

We could use CA to look at any of the 6 sub-tables, but we will analyze them simultaneously (in a "multiple correspondence analysis"). The results are plotted in Figure 6.34. The car characteristics are depicted with a square symbol, and the consumer characteristics with a circle.

Figure 6.34
Correspondence Analysis of Cars and Drivers

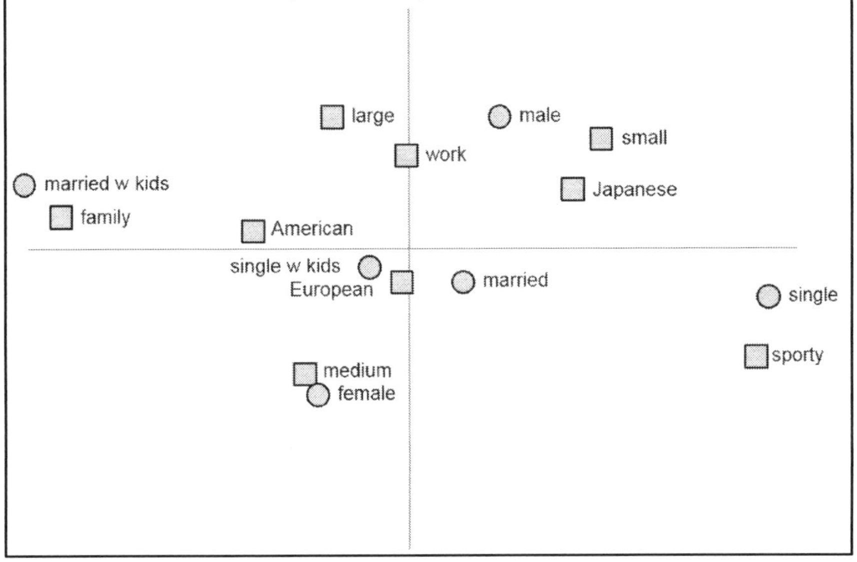

All inter-point differences are interpretable. Distances between points representing what had been the rows of the data matrix reflect the similarities between the household statuses. Distances between points that had been columns reflect the similarities between the cars and car attributes. Distances between points that represent mixed modalities, such as one point representing a row customer descriptor and one point representing a column car attribute, are interpreted as the extent to which a car attribute is one preferred by the customer.

[25] In fact, the vectors of P correspond to the eigenvectors of the symmetric matrix HH' (if H is consumers by brands, then HH' represents consumers by consumers; if H is brands by attributes, then HH' represents brands by brands), and those in Q are the eigenvectors of the symmetric matrix H'H (for an H that is consumers by brands, H'H represents brands by brands, and if H is brands by attributes, H'H represents attributes by attributes). The singular values in the diagonal matrix Δ are the square roots of the eigenvalues of HH' and H'H. Kewl, right?

For example, at the left, we see American cars bought for the family of two adults and kids. At the top right, we see men in small, Japanese cars that they drive to work. Men are also close to the attribute "large," which may be muscle cars or trucks (we'd need the raw data to know more). At the right, we see that singles drive sportier cars, and at the bottom of the plot, we see the women in cars that are not too big, not too small, from a European car maker.

Figure 6.35
Dominance Data in Sports: #Wins by Column Team over Row Team
1908 National League Baseball Season

	Boston Doves (Atlanta Braves)	Chicago Cubs	Cincinnati Reds	Brooklyn Superbas (now L.A. Dodgers)	Philadelphia Phillies	Pittsburg Pirates	St. Louis Cardinals	N.Y. Giants (now San Francisco Giants)
Boston Doves	-	16	14	10	12	15	8	16
Chicago Cubs	6	-	6	4	13	12	3	11
Cincinnati Reds	8	21	-	5	12	14	11	14
Brooklyn Superbas	12	18	16	-	17	13	9	16
Philadelphia Phillies	10	9	10	5	-	13	8	16
Pittsburg Pirates	7	10	8	9	9	-	2	11
St. Louis Cardinals	14	14	11	13	14	19	-	14
N.Y. Giants	6	11	8	6	6	11	8	-

MDS and CA both provide means of plotting brands and attributes and customer information. In MDS, we plotted the brands, and represented attributes as vectors and customers as ideal points. In CA, all entities—brands, attributes, customers, etc.—are represented in the same manner, as points in space. The simplicity of CA contributes to its popularity.

Summary

We close with a freebie. One of my esteemed readers suggested that I include more dominance data in this chapter (like the 3 Stooges data). Sports are a huge commercial enterprise, so let's consider a case of sports teams as brands. From the website baseball-almanac.com, I drew data from the last season of baseball that really mattered, 1908, the last year the Chicago Cubs won the World Series.[26]

Figure 6.35 contains the number of wins and losses in the National League from that 1908 season. There were several ties during the season that are not included in the table, but they are few (two between the Boston Doves and Cubs, and one for each of these pairings: Cubs and Phillies, Cubs and Giants, Reds and Giants, Pirates and Giants).

Analyzing those data just as we did the Stooges data, we obtain the scaling depicted in Figure 6.36. The scaling shows the teams with the most victories, and the inter-scale distances are interpretable as the extent to which one team dominates the others. The Cubs are at the top of the scale, but apparently the Pirates and Giants were valiant competitors as well, so any game among the three teams would be difficult to predict. The next teams are spaced out more, indicating clearer differences in abilities and track records.

Perceptual maps are useful to marketers, in thinking about positioning and in communicating new business opportunities. There are simple ways of creating perceptual maps by using means of survey ratings from customers, but a superior method of obtaining maps is to use MDS. There are different kinds of MDS models to choose from—classic metric, nonmetric, and individual differences models were described in this

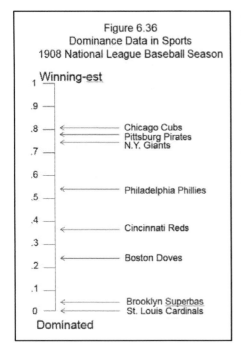

Figure 6.36
Dominance Data in Sports
1908 National League Baseball Season

Winning-est
1
.9
.8 — Chicago Cubs
     Pittsburg Pirates
.7   N.Y. Giants
.6
.5 — Philadelphia Phillies
.4 — Cincinnati Reds
.3
.2 — Boston Doves
.1
     Brooklyn Superbas
0   St. Louis Cardinals
Dominated

---

[26] The Cubs won the Series, beating the Detroit Tigers in 4 of 5 games. From baseball-almanac.com/ws/yr1908ws.shtml, words that bring tears to one's eyes: "The Cubs became the first team to record 3 consecutive World Series appearances and 2 consecutive World Series victories with both championship wins coming off the heels of a record 116 victory season of 1906. In 1908, Chicago's West Side franchise was more than just a winning baseball team, they had just become sports' first official 'dynasty.' From 1906 to 1908 the Chicago Cubs dominated baseball, winning 322 games vs. just 136 losses for a winning percentage of .703. That is the highest winning percentage any team has ever had over a 3 year span in baseball history." Sigh.

chapter. Attribute vectors help guide interpretation of the MDS solutions, and customer preferences can be overlaid as well, to see where pockets of segments exist, which help paint the picture of competition and market structure. Finally, correspondence analysis is a related technique, also providing perceptual maps on data that are frequencies, and two modalities such as brands and attributes or customers and brands.

Table 6.1: Helpful Tips for Multidimensional Scaling

MDS enables us to:
- ☐ Analyze perceptions of similarity / differences among p stimuli
- ☐ Understand resulting configuration and dimensions of perceptual space
- ☐ Infer from proximities data the dimensions relevant to respondents' comparisons
- ☐ Understand preferences among p stimuli, above and beyond perceptions

What decisions to make?
- ☐ Which p stimuli will form the set? Which to include, exclude, so p doesn't get too big and yet the map is interesting?
- ☐ Sample size: always an issue. MDS can be done on n = 1, but then we'd have problems with subsequent generalizations. Do we care about (wish to acknowledge explicitly in a model) individual differences? If so, use the INDSCAL model.
- ☐ Proximities data: how to collect the data, choosing from many judgment tasks, e.g., ranks (use a nonmetric model) or ratings (use a metric MDS).
- ☐ Number of dimensions: plot the Stress values or the variance accounted for, whichever the program produces.
- ☐ Interpretation: first, the configuration itself (clustering may be helpful); next, the dimensions and their labels, via regressions—vectors representing properties / attributes that we suspect might be the dimensions and on which we had respondents make ratings.
- ☐ Preferences for each stimulus (in addition to perceptions of stimuli)—ideal points, or vector preference model if more is better.
- ☐ You are now a bonafide MDS-er!

References

MDS texts:
- Kruskal, Joseph B. and Myron Wish (1978), *Multidimensional Scaling*, Beverly Hills: Sage. (Great primer.)
- Green, Paul E., Frank J. Carmone Jr., and Scott M. Smith (1989), *Multidimensional Scaling: Concepts and Applications*, Boston: Allyn & Bacon. (More info, well-written.)
- Davison, Mark L. (1983), *Multidimensional Scaling*, New York: Wiley. (Also well-written, lots of info on preference models.)
- Coxon, A.P.M. (1982), *The User's Guide to Multidimensional Scaling,* Exeter: Heinemann Educational Books.

Thumbnail sketch regarding software:
- SAS: first use proc distance to compute a distance matrix to model via mds (proc distance method=euclid out=outdist), then run proc mds on data=outdist, specify the number of dimensions, the level of measurement such as interval, and specify what to print such as pfinal, and what to plot) . For help: support.sas.com/documentation/
- SPSS: analyze, scale, mds, select vars, at lower right click on "model" and in that box keep default (ordinal) for nonmetrix MDS but change to "interval" for classic or metrix MDS, for "scaling model" leave Euclidean distances if you have 1 input matrix but change to "individual differences" if you're reading in more than 1 matrix, specify #dims. For help: search "IBM SPSS documentation," and open the "statistics base" manual.
- XLStat: first, create a proximities matrix: describing data, similarity/dissimilarity matrices, if your data are dissimilarities, click on dissimilarities so that bigger numbers mean more different, otherwise, you'll end with an mds plot where 2 points are close when they're different—weird), next run the mds: analyzing data, mds, highlight the whole proximities matrix (row and column labels also), might want to change the number of "dimensions" to something above 2. For help: www.xlstat.com, click on "support" and then "tutorials."

Chapter 7: New Products and Conjoint Analysis

Marketing Concept: New Product Design, Branding, and Pricing
Modeling Concept: Conjoint Analysis

Chapter Outline
1. Introduction
2. Why Conjoint
3. Designing a Conjoint Study
4. Conjoint Analyses

Introduction

Conjoint analyses are often used in the design of new products or product extensions. Most companies are capable of creating a number of different options, and conjoint gives guidance as to what features and attributes contribute to consumers' overall product preferences. Conjoint studies also help marketers with price-setting and brand-equity studies, because prices and brand names can easily be included among the set of attributes tested.

Conjoint studies are tremendously popular with marketers for several reasons. First, they simulate an element of the consumer decision-making process. Second, the data collection task is straightforward for the participants—they're asked to make judgments that are easy to do and that they make all the time. Third, once the marketer has the data, the analyses are easy to conduct. Conjoint is a powerful technique where you get a huge bang for just a little buck.

Why Conjoint?

Conjoint studies allow marketers to study how consumers make trade-offs. If we were designing a new car, we could interview or survey consumers and ask what they want. A driver might answer: a sports car with gorgeous lines that goes from 0 to 60 in 3 seconds, and also has good gas mileage and is priced under $20,000. Dream on. We could make a car with several of those features, but not all of them, or at least not profitably. In a conjoint, we'd present different kinds of car descriptions that span the attributes we're interested in testing, and we'll infer which attributes are truly the most important to the drivers.

If that sounds incredible, consider Figure 7.1. In this simple scenario, we're looking at energy drinks, and to keep things simple, we're only considering two features: brand and price. In a conjoint study, we'd put 4 pictures on a screen to show to a consumer: one picture is of Red Bull and there is a price tag indicating the 4-pack is $2.99. The other 3 pictures on the screen depict a 4-pack Red Bull with a price tag of $3.99, a store brand 4-pack for $2.99, and the store brand 4-pack for $3.99.

Next, we ask the study's participants to evaluate the 4 stimuli—how much they like each, how likely it is they'd buy each, etc. The evaluation is a global, overall judgment of each of the product profiles. All the consumers need to do is indicate which one they like most, next most, third most, and so forth, all the way to the one they like the least. The marketer isn't asking why the consumers like one thing over another, or for an explanation of how the consumers think they differ, but just an overall, gestalt judgment of the nature, "Do I like this one more than that one?" Consumers make this kind of judgment all the

Figure 7.1
A Simple Conjoint Study

	Red Bull	store brand		Red Bull	store brand
$2.99	1	3	$2.99	1	2
$3.99	2	4	$3.99	3	4

time, and so, in a conjoint study, they can do so easily and quickly.

In Figure 7.1, we have data from 2 consumers. The data are ranks, ranging from 1 (the most preferred combination) to 4 (the least preferred). The set of stimuli are designed to elicit trade-offs in the ranks or ratings data. You can begin to see the trade-offs even before we get into the official analyses. In Figure 7.1, both consumers tell us that their most preferred 4-pack energy drink is the Red Bull for $2.99. That's not surprising—most consumers prefer to pay less for most things they buy, and brands ought to dominate (otherwise, what are we marketers doing?). (Confirming this perspective, note that in contrast, the least preferred 4-pack for both consumers is the unbranded 4-pack priced at $3.99.)

Next, we ask what 4-packs the consumers want second most, and we see that at this point, the consumers' preferences diverge in very realistic directions, representing segments we see for most product categories. If for some reason the Red Bull at $2.99 were unavailable, the consumer on the left would pay $3.99 for the Red Bull brand. The consumer on the right forgoes the Red Bull brand to maintain the $2.99 price tag, even if it means chugging the store brand. With just 2 data points, we can classify the consumer on the left as someone who cares about brand equity or premium quality, and the consumer on the right as price-sensitive.

In studying trade-offs in consumer decision making, conjoint analyses help us discover which attributes are most valued, e.g., brand or price. The analyses also indicate which levels of those values are most desired, e.g., $2.99 to $3.99. These insights are hugely helpful to companies designing new products. Most companies are capable of producing many things, and using a conjoint, they can find out which design combinations are likely to pay off. These decisions can be made far in advance of beta development or product launches to market, thus offering guidance before much money is spent. Figure 7.2 contains a list of applications in which conjoint studies have helped companies streamline their new product development processes and decisions. The list goes on and on, because conjoint is so easy and helpful.

In addition to new product development, conjoint is also useful in branding and pricing studies, as the Red Bull example illustrated. Some brands are worth more than others, and conjoint can help us estimate that brand equity. Getting into the

---

Figure 7.2
Numerous Uses for Conjoint

Product Category	Attributes
Automobile tires	brand, tread life, price, design
Car	price, warranty, miles per gallon, seats 2, 4, or 6, country of manufacturer
Carpet cleaner	package design, brand, price, money-back guarantee or not
Credit cards	interest rate, annual fee, brand of issuer
Food processor	price, size of bowl, number of speed settings,
GPS device	location accuracy, display in color or monochrome, battery life, price
Hotels (external design)	size, pool type and location, landscaping, shape of building
Hotels (rooms)	entertainment access, room size, furniture in room, type of décor, bath size
Hotel service	price, quality, friendliness of staff, extent of customization of service
Mobiles	bundles of internet, voice and data, calls per month, monthly charge
Personal computers	brand, speed, software bundled, price, expansion slots
Roadway toll collection	number of dedicated lanes, price, how to apply, transferable
Salsa	brand, price, size of jar, color, spiciness
Soap	moisturize or deep-clean, formulated for man or woman, color, fragrance
Sports team logo	vividness of colors, clarity of team and city name, size of mascot

---

minds of consumers gives us a sense of their brand valuations; some customers hold steadfast to a brand, being price insensitive and forgoing all kinds of other attributes, whereas other customers flip readily because they don't value the brand as much as some other attributes.

Similarly, there are many ways to study price sensitivities and customers' willingness to pay. Once a product is in the marketplace, prices could be tweaked to watch customer reactions. For new products, of course, there would exist no sales data, and a tool like conjoint can provide analogous information. Conjoint analysis allows insights and good managerial decisions to be made, based on customer data, not just instinct, for new products, product modifications, line extensions, etc., far prior to expensive investment and potentially embarrassing launches.

Designing a Conjoint Study

There are two big decisions to make when designing a conjoint study—see the first two steps in Table 7.1. We must select the attributes we wish to study, and we must select the levels of those factors that we will test. For example, if price is going to be a factor, will we estimate only a simple "high" vs. "low" comparison? And what will those price points be, $2.99 and $3.99, or $2.99 and $3.49, etc.? If price is a particularly important attribute, perhaps the levels should be extended from 2 to 4 or more, such as $2.99, $3.49, $3.99, and $4.49, etc.

The challenge in designing a conjoint study does not lie in generating a list of factors. Typically, the first lists of "product features we should test" are quite extensive. Indeed, the challenge is usually to distinguish which factors should go into the study as critically important, and which attributes would simply be "nice to know" but are not as high a priority. If necessary, a quick, small sample pre-test could be run to elicit customers' thoughts on the relative importance of the factors, to help us prioritize and prune the list to no more than 4 or 5 of attributes that should be studied.

The concern is that if we include many factors, or many levels of each of those attributes, we'll end up creating a huge number of combinations, too many for a consumer to process sensibly. There are a few mechanical ways around this concern. For example, if we simply cannot cut a list of 8 factors down—they truly all seem important—then we might run one study in which we test factors 1–5, and in another study, factors 4, 5, and 6–8. We would combine the data to have customer judgment data on all 8 attributes. Note that in doing so, we assume that the samples are roughly the same (they might be, and the overlapping factors 4 and 5 can help with verification). In the end, though, we'd lose part of the very flavor that makes a conjoint a conjoint. We wouldn't have a study in which factors 1 and 7 appeared together, for instance, and thus the notion of trade-offs would be a bit diminished.

There are also ways to design a study in which all 8 factors might be used, but only a fraction of the combinations are tested. Keeping that number manageable enhances the likelihood that the consumer can complete the comparative task and report assessments that are still meaningful. The problem with this approach is that it doesn't allow us to estimate all the effects we'd want to examine (e.g., see more about "fractional factorial designs" in Chapter 8).

Once we know the conjoint study design—which attributes we're testing, and what levels of those attributes we're including—the next step is to create the combinations. The combinations can be actual products (e.g., different flavors of ice cream), but if creating mock prototypes is prohibitive (e.g., cars), the combinations can be presented as pictures and verbal descriptions. For example, to determine what features might make a new credit card appealing, a bank commissioned a conjoint test in which the customers compared different combinations depicted via bullet-point listings. The attributes were described in the cover letter soliciting the customer's participation, and then the credit cards were characterized as: "Card A, brand X, annual fee $20, …" vs. "Card B, brand Y, annual fee $20, …." The fact that we can count on the imaginations of customers is a real blessing, saving us tons of money in developing materials to test in consumer studies.

The question of the modality of the stimuli to be presented raises a couple of more issues. First, we've been talking about new products because they're easy to imagine, but the content of stimuli in conjoint studies can be just about anything (that's why we use the generic term, stimuli). In marketing, the conjoint could compare ad executions, or social media approaches, or package design, or salary structure for salespeople on commission, etc. In addition, it's important that to realize that some modality may yield useful information of some sort, but other modalities may be necessary for information of another sort. For example, in designing the optimal combination of attributes in a beverage start-up, interviews or surveys can assess customers' willingness to make trade-offs between antioxidants and price, but in-person testing will be required to facilitate taste-testing.

Next, we present the combinations to consumers. We can do this face to face, as in an old-fashioned interview, e.g., intercepting someone in a shopping mall, as they come out of a health club or popular restaurant, etc. Increasingly of course, we solicit a sample of people to participate via email and we include a link to our online study. Web sites are great in many ways, e.g., they allow for stimuli that are vivid (video, pictures) and informative (text), but they don't allow for product trial (e.g., "taste this"). C'est la vie; we can usually live with this limitation, and if we cannot, we run a study IRL.

We instruct the consumers to compare and judge the combinations they see. We can ask for any of a number of judgments. Usually we simply ask for their liking or preference, but we can have consumers make assessment along any criteria we wish, e.g., "Which of these ads make the car sound most eco-friendly?"

Figure 7.3 shows half of the combinations run in an ice cream study. A manufacturer was testing flavors and positioning elements to determine which new line they

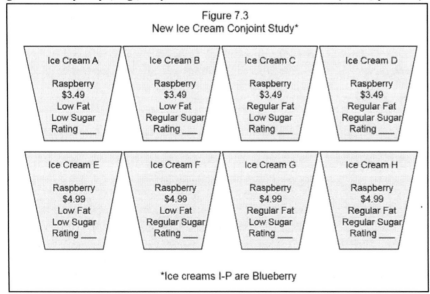

Figure 7.3
New Ice Cream Conjoint Study*

Ice Cream A	Ice Cream B	Ice Cream C	Ice Cream D
Raspberry $3.49 Low Fat Low Sugar Rating ___	Raspberry $3.49 Low Fat Regular Sugar Rating ___	Raspberry $3.49 Regular Fat Low Sugar Rating ___	Raspberry $3.49 Regular Fat Regular Sugar Rating ___

Ice Cream E	Ice Cream F	Ice Cream G	Ice Cream H
Raspberry $4.99 Low Fat Low Sugar Rating ___	Raspberry $4.99 Low Fat Regular Sugar Rating ___	Raspberry $4.99 Regular Fat Low Sugar Rating ___	Raspberry $4.99 Regular Fat Regular Sugar Rating ___

*Ice creams I-P are Blueberry

should roll out for the upcoming summer season. The ice creams were made so that consumers could taste them before commenting. During the first 2 weeks of July, local grocers' scanners were programmed to print an invitation for any consumer whose purchases included ice cream (along with the usual personalized coupons received upon payment) to attend an ice cream fare at a local hotel 5 days later.

The company produced beta versions of 16 ice creams. Half were raspberry (see Figure 7.3) and half were blueberry. The company also tested 2 price points ($3.49 vs. $4.99), and 2 health-related attributes (low fat vs. regular, and low sugar vs. regular). Thus this study considered 4 factors, each of which varied along only 2 levels, to keep things simple. It's a 2 (flavor) x (read "by") 2 (price) x 2 (fat) x 2 (sugar) experimental design. The 2 x 2 x 2 x 2 or 2^4 design results in 16 combinations. Each participant saw the descriptions on all 16 ice creams and tasted all of them.

The 16 ice cream descriptions form the left 5 columns of the data set in Figure 7.4. The ice creams, labeled A through P, are characterized by dummy variables as follows: for flavor, 1 = raspberry, 0 = blueberry; for price, 1= $3.49 and 0 = $4.99; low fat is 1 and regular (not low fat) is 0; low sugar is 1 and regular (not low sugar) is 0. The next column, labeled "rank," describes one person's likelihood of purchase. The judgments are ranks, meaning that 1 = "most preferred" through 16 = "least preferred." We're going to reverse the scale so that larger numbers imply greater preference; in Figure 7.4, the final column is "points = 17 – rank." Now we're ready to crunch.

Figure 7.4
Data for 1 Consumer

Ice Cream	Flavor	Price	Low Fat	Low Sugar	Rank	Points
A	1	1	1	1	2	15
B	1	1	1	0	4	13
C	1	1	0	1	6	11
D	1	1	0	0	8	9
E	1	0	1	1	9	8
F	1	0	1	0	13	4
G	1	0	0	1	11	6
H	1	0	0	0	16	1
I	0	1	1	1	1	16
J	0	1	1	0	3	14
K	0	1	0	1	5	12
L	0	1	0	0	7	10
M	0	0	1	1	10	7
N	0	0	1	0	14	3
O	0	0	0	1	12	5
P	0	0	0	0	15	2

Conjoint Analyses

There are different ways to analyze data that come from a conjoint study, but the most popular approach is to use a regression. Regressions are most frequently used in part because they're accessible (easy to run and explain), but in addition, the methodological literature continues to demonstrate that regression obtains conjoint results that are powerful and robust.

In the regression, the respondent's judgments (the variable called "points") serve as the dependent variable. The 4 design factors—flavor, price, low fat, and low sugar—are the predictors. We'll begin with the typical model, which estimates only the main effects of those 4 factors, without worrying about whether they interact in any manner (more about this matter shortly).

Running a regression on the data in Figure 7.4 yields a phenomenal $R^2 = 0.97$. More important for our needs are the regression weights, which help us determine the importance of the attributes in product design. The regression equation written in terms of the raw weights is:

predicted points = 1.625 – 0.25 flavor + 8.00 price + 3.00 low fat + 3.00 low sugar,

and in terms of the standardized beta weights it is:

predicted points = –0.027 flavor + 0.868 price + 0.325 low fat + 0.325 low sugar.

The flavor variable is not significantly different from zero, but the regression coefficients for price, low fat, and low sugar are all significant, $p < 0.0001$.

These results are interpretable, as in any regression, and offer clear direction for product launch. Ice cream flavor doesn't matter—as the predictor changes from 0 (blueberry) to 1 (raspberry), the effect on the dependent variable is negligible. In this particular application, it probably means that the customer likes both flavors, and either is acceptable. Once we obtain data from a large sample of customers, we might find segment differences in flavor preferences. Then our product launch decision is about whether we can support 2 flavors, but if not, we'd go with whichever segment appears to be the largest—those who prefer blueberry or raspberry.

The relative sizes of the regression coefficients tell us that price is the most important factor, with this customer preferring $3.49 to $4.99. That price differential is fairly large, so in subsequent studies we would likely zero in on more sensitive tests of price points between $3.49 and $4.99. The customer prefers low fat and low sugar, but cares more about price, and least about flavor.

Ta da! That's it—that's a conjoint. It's easy to see how the method's simplicity contributes to its popularity. There are several more issues worth discussing, including interactions, aggregation, and subsequent uses of the model.

Interactions

The conjoint model we just fit is known as a "main effects" model—it estimates the impact of each design feature on the consumer's preferences. The model is fine, and it represents 95% of the conjoints conducted in the real world. However, note that the model doesn't allow us to ask questions about how the factors might work in conjunction with each other. If we include interaction terms, we could study whether there were any combinations that were especially good or bad, to help us in the designing and planning.

Such a conjoint simply requires extending the regression to include interactions:[27]

predicted points = β_1 flavor + β_2 price + β_3 low fat + β_4 low sugar
$+ \beta_5$ flavor*price + β_6 flavor*low fat + β_7 flavor*low sugar
$+ \beta_8$ price*low fat + β_9 price*low sugar + β_{10} low fat*low sugar
$+ \beta_{11}$ flavor*price*low fat + β_{12} flavor*price*low sugar
$+ \beta_{13}$ flavor*low fat*low sugar + β_{14} price*low fat*low sugar
$+ \beta_{15}$ flavor*price*low fat*low sugar.

In this model, β_1 through β_4 estimate the effects of the 4 main effects, β_5 through β_{10} estimate the 6 two-way interactions, β_{11} through β_{14} estimate the 4 three-way interactions, and β_{15} represents the 4-way interaction.

Recall that we have 16 data points from the consumer (Figure 7.4). The full regression (above) requires 15 terms to be estimated. If we were to fit this model, we would have only a single degree of freedom remaining with which to estimate error variability. That model and estimation would be woefully underpowered, which means we couldn't be very confident about the results. Low power also means we'd probably find that none of the effects was significant.

A compromise is to fit a model in which we assume that the higher order interactions (3-way and 4-way) are negligible and not worth estimating. In addition, if, say, β_{15} were significant, many people would have difficulty comprehending what it means. Thus to proceed, we'd assume β_{11} through β_{15} are zero and therefore not include them in the model. Rather, we'd fit a regression with terms β_1 through β_{10} (the main effects and 2-way interactions). Doing so allows more stability and power, and yet we could still examine whether there are some interactions that suggest a particularly synergistic combination of features, or a combination we should avoid.

For example, if β_8, the coefficient for price*low-fat, were significant and positive, we'd know that getting a low price and low-fat offers a boost in consumer appeal, above and beyond just low price or just low-fat. Somehow, together they are a particularly winning combination.

In contrast, if β_{10}, the coefficient for low-fat*low-sugar, were significant and negative, we'd know that low fat and low sugar sounds like a tasteless, unappealing ice cream. If consumers reach for a treat like ice cream, they don't want it to taste like healthy granola. They want either the higher fat (creamier) to offset the low sugar, or regular sugar (sweeter) to offset the low fat.[28]

---

[27] A technical point: if you do plan to test for interactions, the dummy variables representing the design factors (e.g., flavor: raspberry or blueberry) should be coded –1 and 1 rather than 0 and 1. Either coding is fine if the model contains only main effects. But interactions are tested by creating product scores (e.g., multiplying the flavor dummy variable by the price (low or high) variable), and if they're coded 0/1, then the product term will have 3 sets of 0's, and 1's would only flag one cell (blueberry, high price). If the dummy variables are coded –1/1, then the product term will have 2 sets of 1's and 2 sets of –1's, which statistically will contrast the high-high and low-low cases (e.g., blueberry and high price, and raspberry and low price) against the high-low and low-high scenarios (e.g., raspberry and high price, and blueberry and low price). An interaction is properly defined as this second option.

[28] If you need help in interpreting an interaction between dummy variables in a regression, think like a correlation coefficient but for a 2x2 table, where each dummy variable is scored "low" vs. "high." A positive regression coefficient means that the higher scores are in the high-high and low-low cells (e.g., people like blueberry and high price, or raspberry and low price (you do have to look into the data further to figure out whether both are true or one is truer than the other)). A negative regression coefficient means the high scores are appearing in the high-low and low-high cells (e.g., people like the raspberry and high price or the blueberry and low price).

Aggregation

A second analytical issue to consider is how to examine conjoint results for more than one respondent. The data in Figure 7.4 represent the judgments of just 1 consumer. It's almost never the case that a marketer cares about 1 specific consumer, but rather a sample of consumers who represent vastly larger numbers of consumers in the marketplace.

Say we have a sample of 100 consumers. Now our spreadsheet would have 16 rows (like in Figure 7.4) replicated 100 times. There would be one block of 16 rows for each of the 100 consumers in our sample. The columns labeled ice cream, flavor, price, low fat, and low sugar would be identical from block to block. The only differences from block to block would be how the 100 consumers reacted to the 16 different ice creams; i.e., the rank and points columns would vary in each set of 16 rows.

If we combined the data before the regression, we would simply average over all the consumers' raw data. Thus, we'd take the average over all "ice cream A points" and then over all "ice cream B points," etc. At that point, we'd have a new data set, with just 16 rows, with the points variable in Figure 7.4 replaced by sample means. With this simplification down to 16 rows, we're back in business and can conduct a single regression on the mean perceptions.

Note of course that simplifications always come with a price. In this case, combining the data prior to running a single conjoint regression requires that we make the assumption that all our consumers are the same. They might be, but it is more likely that there are segments, so we might want to cluster the data first, and if we found, say, 3 segments, we would then compute 3 sets of means, and conduct 3 conjoint regressions, one per segment.

An alternative is to compute 100 regressions, one per consumer. When we obtain all the conjoint results, we'd have 100 sets of β's. At this point, we would build a data set with 100 rows, 1 per consumer, and the new columns would be the conjoint results, β_1 through β_4 (or β_{10}). Then we could see what other information that we have on the consumers might be correlated with these β's. For example, we might find that β_1 is correlated with income, and β_2 with age or gender. These β's could be clustered to look for segments, as well.

If the choice of aggregating before or after the conjoint were a no-brainer, we'd all just choose that superior option. It's a trade-off between the two (which is suitable, considering conjoints are all about studying trade-offs). If we take the first approach, and get the means on the raw data prior to running one conjoint regression, the approach has the benefit of being simple and the data have some statistical stability, being means. If we take the second approach, and run a regression on each consumer individually, combining the estimates after the conjoints carries the benefit of allowing for each consumer to have a voice. Both approaches have their advantages.

Après Conjoint

There are many analyses that complement a conjoint. First, people often raise the question, "Which of the attributes is the most important?" We can point to the factors that have significant β's with the largest absolute magnitude as obvious indicators. Concerns about interpreting coefficients in other regressions are somewhat ameliorated here because those concerns usually arise due to likely multicollinearity (correlations among the predictor variables). Here, the predictors are orthogonal (uncorrelated) by design—that is, every level (high or low, 0 or 1) of price was offered in combination with every level of all the other factors, in this factorial design. With independent predictors, we can more confidently interpret the magnitudes of the β's as reflecting their relative contributions and importance.

In addition, some conjoint analysts like to supplement that information with another assessment on which attributes are important. We begin by taking the mean rating of each level of each attribute. Ideally this is computed over the sample, but in Figure 7.4, we have only 1 respondent, so we'll pretend those data represent the sample of 100. Thus, for flavor, take all the ratings for raspberry (flavor = 1), i.e., 15, 13, …4, 6, 1, and get that mean. It's 8.375, and for blueberry (flavor = 0, the data 16, 14, …5, 2), the mean is 8.625. For price, the low price (1) mean is 12.50 (based on the data points 15, 13, 11, 9, 16, 14, 12, 10), and the high price (0) mean is 4.50. The low fat (1) mean is 10.0 and the regular fat (0) mean is 7.0. Finally (coincidentally), the low sugar (1) mean is 10.0 and the regular sugar (0) mean is 7.0.

Next, the ranges for each attribute are computed. For flavor, the range is small, 8.625 – 8.375 = 0.25. For price, it's 8, for low fat and low sugar, it's 3. The largest range is 8, so we would say price is the most important attribute.

Some modelers take it further. They'll add the ranges: 0.25 + 8 + 3 + 3 = 14.25, then compute the percentage of that total for each attribute range. Thus, the relative importance for flavor is 0.25 / 14.25 = 1.75%. For price, it's 56.14%, and for each of low fat and low sugar, it's 21.05%.

The second, larger follow-up to a conjoint is a simulation as to which product, arising from which combinations of the attributes, would be most desired and profitable to launch. Essentially, this is done by examining some transformation of the regression coefficients, such as the predicted values or even just the sum of the β's.

For example, fitting the main effects model to the data in Figure 7.4, recall that we obtained the following regression equation: predicted points = –0.027 flavor + 0.868 price + 0.325 low-fat + 0.325 low-sugar. We can plug in the values (0's or 1's) for each of the 16 ice cream profiles to obtain a sum indicative of relative preference. For ice cream A, we'd have –0.027 (1) + 0.868 (1) + 0.325 (1) + 0.325 (1) = 1.491. For ice cream B, we'd have –0.027 (1) + 0.868 (1) + 0.325 (1) + 0.325 (0) = 1.166, and so on. For the remaining ice creams, see Figure 7.5. Note that it's this kind of assessment that has led conjoint analysts to refer to regression weight as a "part-worth"—it's the part of the preference valuation contributed by the attribute associated with that particular regression coefficient.

Figure 7.5
Conjoint Predictions

model predicted points = -0.027 flavor + 0.868 price + 0.325 low_fat + 0.325 low_sugar

Ice Cream	Flavor ×(-0.027)	Price ×(0.868)	Low_Fat ×(0.325)	Low_Sugar ×(0.325)	predicted utility	e^U	estimated market share
A	1	1	1	1	1.491	4.44	11.7% (=4.44/37.93)
B	1	1	1	0	1.166	3.21	8.5
C	1	1	0	1	1.166	3.21	8.5
D	1	1	0	0	0.841	2.32	6.1
E	1	0	1	1	0.623	1.86	4.9
F	1	0	1	0	0.298	1.35	3.6
G	1	0	0	1	0.298	1.35	3.6
H	1	0	0	0	-0.027	0.97	2.6
I	0	1	1	1	1.518	4.56	12.0
J	0	1	1	0	1.193	3.30	8.7
K	0	1	0	1	1.193	3.30	8.7
L	0	1	0	0	0.868	2.38	6.3
M	0	0	1	1	0.650	1.92	5.1
N	0	0	1	0	0.325	1.38	3.6
O	0	0	0	1	0.325	1.38	3.6
P	0	0	0	0	0.000	1.00	2.6
sums:					11.93	37.93	

The largest predicted value is 1.518 for ice cream I (blueberry, low price, low fat, low sugar). On this index alone, we can defend launching this ice cream, with this particular combination of attributes. However, say we are unable to create a blueberry that doesn't result in a hideous purple mess. We can switch to raspberry, the next highest value (1.491) with little loss (indeed, insignificant loss, given that we know the flavor β is not significant). Alternatively, if we can pull off a good color for blueberry, but the recipes without sugar taste too tart, and we aren't happy with the low margins from the lower price, we'd obtain the value 0.325, the profile of ice cream N, and this value is quite a bit lower than the 1.518 starting point. How much lower depends on some assumptions.

We can study some scenarios, simulated by different assumptions in a sensitivity analysis. For example, say we know our unit costs are $2.50, we hope for 20% market share, and the ice cream market is 50mm buyers. We can multiply the predicted values by the margins ($4.99 or $3.49 minus $2.50), the market share, and the market size. Doing so offers a rough estimate of profits, from $37,125,900 for ice cream A, $29,033,400 for B, and so forth, to $0 for P, and worse, –$267,300 for H.

Instead of profitability, some marketers prefer to estimate market shares, using the predicted values as utilities in the standard formulation: $S_i = (e^{U_i})/(\sum e^{U_i})$. In Figure 7.5, the U_i's are in the column labeled, "predicted utility," so U_A is the desirability of ice cream A, and so forth. In the next column these utilities are in the exponential scale, and their sum is found at the bottom of the column. The S_i fraction is in the final column, yielding share estimates of: A = 11.7%, B = 8.5%, C = 8.5%, etc.

Summary

Conjoint analysis is a method by which a respondent makes an overall evaluation of a set of stimuli like brands, and from those choices, we derive information that tells us which of the features are most important to the respondent's judgments, and which levels of those attributes are most attractive. The data are broad evaluations, yet they allow for an understanding of micro level attributes and trade-offs.

The conjoint task forces the consumer to make trade-offs. The analysis quantifies the relative importance of attributes and determines the optimal levels of each attribute and the combination of attributes that should yield maximum appeal.

There is a small cottage industry of "conjoint experts." Probably many are perfectly fine. However, there's no apparent reason to pay for this service when it's so easy to run the study and its analyses.

There are other methods to use in conjoint studies—both in terms of data collection and in terms of data analyses. One technique that is particularly popular is called "choice-based conjoint" (CBC). In CBC, subsets of the combinations are presented, say 2 at a time, or a set of 4 or 5 at a time, and consumers are asked to choose the 1 out of the set. Another set is presented and another choice is made, for several iterations to make sure the consumers see the different attributes. The data are the counts of the number of times each attribute was in a selected stimulus, which may be analyzed using logit models given that the consumer's responses are discrete choices, with the product features as predictors, thereby yielding information about attractive product design.

Note that not all combinations are necessarily presented, and other than the "1 = yes" for the chosen brand in each set, other data points are rather ambiguous. For example, in a comparison of new product descriptions A, B, and C, if A is chosen, we don't know whether B would be preferred to C or the reverse. With that single choice of A, we also don't know quite what it is about A that made it attractive, until we begin to see over the next choice sets that the consumer repeatedly chooses the brands that are described with certain attributes in common.

CBC users defend it by saying it requires consumers to make judgments that are more like the ones they make IRL when purchasing—choices, rather than the ratings or rankings as emphasized in this chapter. There is also an interactive version, called "adaptive choice-based conjoint," in which consumers rate a few sets of a small number of stimuli, and depending on which attributes they seem to favor already, the algorithm pursues those attributes by presenting more of the product descriptions that contain those attributes, and fewer or none containing the less important or less desired attributes.

For both CBC and its adaptive version, recall that when we discussed the design of conjoint studies and the factors to include, we referred to another approach in which a fraction of the combinations are presented, and we qualified that technique as suboptimal because not all of the parameters of interest are uniquely estimable. Analyses are similarly constrained with these techniques, given that any combination that is not tested essentially yields missing data in the analyses. In contrast, the method we've focused on in this chapter is called "full profile conjoint" because the full set of all possible combinations are used as stimuli for the consumers to judge. In research comparing the classes of models, the results continue to demonstrate that simple is best—use all combinations in the full profile conjoint design, and a straightforward regression for the resulting data analyses. Thus, the best medicine is simply to make the tough choices about which features go onto a short list for inclusion in the conjoint study, and to run a full study with all possible combinations.

Table 7.1: Helpful Tips for Conjoint Analysis

Conjoint models help us learn:
- What tradeoffs do customers make among product attributes?
- Which features are the most important?
- What values of those features are optimal?

What decisions to make?
- Step 1: select which features or attributes will be included in the study.
- Step 2: determine what levels the attributes will take on as they vary. Be prudent in Steps 1 and 2, because together, the number of combinations that a consumer must consider increases quickly.
- Step 3: Create the stimuli.
  - Will they include all possible combinations ("full factorial" or "full profile") or a subset of them ("fractional factorial")?
  - Will the combinations of possible new products be presented as beta versions, or trial products (can we afford it?), artistic renderings, or verbal descriptions (most common)?
- Step 4: Gather data from N respondents.
- Step 5: In the conjoint analyses, shall we aggregate the data at once (i.e., take a mean over the N sets of ratings, and then run 1 conjoint), or shall we aggregate later (i.e., run N conjoints and take the means over the β's)? Latter is usually preferable, to allow initial variability in consumer tastes. We can then cluster the β's if desirable, and compute means within each segment.

Chapter 8: ROI, Experiments, and ANOVA

Marketing Concept: ROMI, Test Markets, Testing the Effectiveness
of Advertising, Promotions, Resource Allocation
Modeling Concept: Experiments, GLM (ANOVA, ANCOVA)

Chapter Outline
1. Introduction
2. Experiments
3. Brief Review of t-tests
4. Analysis of Variance
   a. One Factor
   b. Contrasts
   c. Verifying Market Segments
   d. Two or More Factors and Interactions
5. Analysis of Covariance
6. Experimental Design Issues
   a. Other Designs: Blocking, Fractional Factorials, and Friends
   b. Natural Observation
   c. Words o' Wisdom

Introduction

In this chapter, we tackle a tough question. Increasingly, marketers are being asked to be accountable—money is spent on some marketing action and the question is whether it yields a favorable result, one that is worth the expenditure. These ROI, or return on marketing investment (ROMI), questions may be posed about any action a company makes, including advertising, price changes, distribution actions, etc., as well as non-marketing actions, such as assessing the effectiveness of new management training programs, investments, installation of new software, machinery, etc.

It's fair that marketers be held accountable, as is true throughout the organization. However, it's important to recognize that much of a marketer's responsibility is difficult to measure and intended to have long-term consequences. Anyone can show a bump in sales if they drop a coupon, but a 3-year enhancement of brand attitudes is simply more difficult to demonstrate. Nevertheless, we can attempt to do so.

In this chapter, we'll look at experiments and the statistical model called analysis of variance (ANOVA). These techniques may be used to address more questions than just ROI, such as:

- considering the launch of brand extensions in test markets for a go/no-go determination or modification;
- planning resource allocation better, from an advertising budget spent across media, or in territory assignments of sales force personnel in different markets;
- assisting marketers in making decisions regarding the entire marketing mix, from product tweaking to price adjustments to discern the attractiveness of coupon offers to different segments.

Experiments

There are many kinds of marketing research techniques for gathering and analyzing data. They are generally classified into one of three categories. First, there are exploratory techniques, such as interviews and focus groups, which give the marketer an in-depth understanding of customers' thoughts and uses of a brand in the context of their lifestyles, motivations, and goals. Second, there are descriptive techniques, such as survey data or online purchase histories, which convey customers' attitudes and behaviors. Surveys don't capture depth like interviews, but their strength is in greater coverage of a random and representative sample of customers such that forecasting is possible. Third, there are causal techniques, such as lab experiments or test markets in the field, which are discussed in this chapter.

Causal methods enable marketers to establish cause-effect relationships between variables. Marketers believe that if they take some action on a marketing mix variable, they will see a favorable result in customers' attitudes or purchase behaviors. In essence, marketers believe in ROI—the question is how to obtain evidence that the marketing action was effective.

If we wish to establish that "X causes Y," philosophy of science says we should find three kinds of evidence. The first principle is "concomitant variation," meaning, if X causes Y, then X and Y should be correlated. (Recall from your basic stats class that the reverse is not true—if X and Y are correlated, X might cause Y, Y might cause X, or some other factor might cause both X and Y.)

The second principle is "sequential ordering." If X causes Y, we'd expect X to occur first, and Y would follow. This idea seems like a no-brainer, but it's more challenging to establish in the real world than you might think. For example, marketers want to claim that "increased advertising causes increased sales." However, in most companies, the advertising budget is usually determined to be a percentage of the previous year's sales. Setting the budget in this way makes it look like sales drive advertising spending, even though the assumption is that ad spending drives sales. It's a causal mess: sales in year 1 determine spending in year 2, which surely contributes to sales in year 2, but that makes it seem like sales in year 1 determine sales in year 2, or for that matter, that ad spending in year 1 determines ad spending in year 2. Argh.

The third principle is the "elimination of other possible explanations," that is, if one may posit that X, Q, or Z may cause Y, it would be desirable to show that Q and Z do not, thereby leaving the X→Y relationship as most plausible. For example, if marketers want to say that a recent increase in their brand's sales is due to recent promotional efforts, they need to eliminate extraneous sources of variability. An example of an extraneous factor is seasonality, which would be problematic if the timing of the study were to occur at the point during the year when sales would have picked up naturally.

There aren't a lot of guarantees in life, but we can come closest to supporting a causal statement if we conduct an experiment. We can create two advertising campaigns, launch one in several (randomly selected) markets and the other in other markets (also randomly selected), and watch subsequent sales. We will obtain a fairly clean answer to the question "Does ad 1 perform better than ad 2?" by having manipulated one variable (advertising) and studied its impact on another (sales).

In addition to advertising and sales, pricing decisions befuddle many managers, and experiments offer a great solution. If we wish to answer the question, "Will a price cut lead to a significant sales increase?" we would exert control over the price points, and we would study the effect on sales or some other measure (e.g., customer satisfaction).

The simplest experimental design has two cells (or two "conditions"). We could take one action in one condition and do nothing out of the ordinary different in the other condition. Alternatively, we could do something new in both conditions. For example, medical experiments compare the effectiveness of a new drug against either no drug (or a placebo), or the best drug currently prescribed, or two new treatments might be compared to see which should be developed further.

The two-condition experiment in marketing is analogous. We can compare sales "at our current price" vs. sales stimulated with a "$1 coupon," or we could compare sales bumps with a "$1 coupon" vs. those with a "$1.50 coupon."

An experiment proceeds as follows. The units of observation (usually people, but they could be business customers) are randomly sampled so that the results will have external validity. External validity is an important quality of experiments that allows us to generalize our findings to the broader target population, not just to the sample of people on whom we have data. Thus, we cannot sample only our friends or people at the nearby coffee shop, for example.

We then randomly assign the sample of customers to one of the two conditions. We can flip a coin (or use the function in Excel, randbetween(1,2)); and if the coin comes up heads (or Excel says 1), the customer is assigned to condition 1, and if it's tails (or Excel says 2), the customer is assigned to cell 2. Random assignment is important so that the results will have internal validity. Internal validity is the other important quality of experiments that allows us to attribute the results to our intervention, not to some other confounding factor. Thus, we cannot put all the customers we recruit on Monday into one condition, and those from Friday into another. The marketing conditions would have been confounded with the day of the week, so results of the study would be ambiguous.

The thing we manipulate (e.g., factors such as a coupon for $1 or $1.50, a package design for a perfume that is "modern" or "floral," an ad with a "celebrity" or a "regular person," etc.) is an independent variable, or the explanatory factor, or predictor. The result we measure (e.g., sales, enhanced brand attitude or memory, generating more word-of-mouth in a social network, etc.) is called the dependent variable, or criterion measure, or response function.

If we have designed a proper study, i.e., with random sampling and random assignment, and if the dependent variable differs across the two conditions, then we can be reasonably confident that it was caused by the independent variable we manipulated. The resulting causal evidence would be indisputable ROI.

Yet complexities arise because it can be difficult to achieve both internal and external validity in the same study. To enhance internal validity, we'd ideally be in a lab or office or online, with a great deal of scientific control exerted over the participants' environment. But people who participate in such studies know that what they're doing is a little peculiar, thus rendering some doubt about generalizability.

Conversely, to enhance external validity, ideally we'd run a large-scale field study, and in several randomly selected markets, we'd manipulate something such as price or advertising, and call these "test markets." In other markets, we wouldn't interfere, and just allow business to continue as usual—these would serve as "control markets." After some period of time, we'd compare sales from the test markets to sales from the control markets. Unfortunately, the real world is messy, with many factors varying along with our manipulations, including local customer tastes or competitor actions. As a result, we cannot be as insistent that sales differences were caused by our intervention alone.

There is no perfect solution to this inherent trade-off. Most social scientists would encourage both types of studies. Many marketing research firms run simulated test markets on virtual reality shopping monitors, for example. Others conduct tests within a single market to at least minimize problems of local tastes, for example.

We do the best we can, but you can begin to appreciate that while ROI is a simple concept, it can be somewhat challenging to measure. Still, we try. To demonstrate how to compare something like sales in a set of test markets to sales in control markets, or for ROI, to compare sales prior to and after some marketing intervention, we'll need some statistics, so now the fun begins (mwa ha ha).

Brief Review of t-tests

A 1-sample t-test is conducted as follows. We select a random sample of size n from our target population, collect data on them, compute the sample mean, and use it to test our hypothesis about the population mean.

Specifically, say variable X represents customers' attitude toward a brand on a 1 to 7 scale, where 7 = "like very much." We'll put X in as a column in a spreadsheet. Our data set will have other variables in other columns, e.g., Y, Z, Q, etc., but for now, we're focusing on the variable X.

For a sample of size n, the customers' data points running down the X column are labeled: $x_1, x_2, ..., x_n$. We'll compute a mean, in the usual way: $(x_1 + x_2 + \cdots + x_n)/n$. That sample mean is denoted $\bar{x}$. It is an estimate of the population mean, μ. The estimate $\bar{x}$ is sometimes also referred to as $\hat{\mu}$.

If all we wanted was a description, we'd be done. But usually underlying this process is a guess as to what μ might be. That is, implicitly or explicitly, we're working with a simple model: $x_i = \mu + \epsilon_i$. We believe each person's data point is a function of the population mean as well as some error for each person ϵ_i. The population mean μ is fixed and we're trying to estimate it. The errors ϵ_i are random, and they make the data points x_i random.

If we had only a single guess to represent the brand attitude of the whole sample (and thereby the population), we'd guess $\bar{x}$ as the estimate of μ. There are individual differences, or heterogeneity in attitudes, thus, this guess will be off for many of our respondents. Some customers will have a more positive attitude, and others will have a more negative attitude.

If we make some assumptions, such as that all the n data points are independent (e.g., no customer copied the survey answers of another), and the population distribution is a normal bell curve,[29] then we can test the null hypothesis, $H_0: \mu = c$ (where c is some constant value, e.g., perhaps the attitude measured last quarter, prior to our releasing a new ad campaign). The alternative hypothesis is that H_0 does not hold, or, $H_a: \mu \neq c$ (because we'll want to know if we're off in either direction, we'll always use a non-directional alternative hypothesis, or a 2-tailed test).

To test H_0, we'll compute the sample variance, $s_x^2 = (1/(n-1))\sum_{i=1}^{n}(x_i - \bar{x})^2$, the standard error, $s.e. = s_{\bar{x}} = (1/\sqrt{n})s_x$, and then the t-statistic, or the z-statistic if $n \geq 30$ (which is usually the case in marketing research studies), $t \text{ or } z = (\bar{x} - c)/s_{\bar{x}}$. If $z \geq 1.96$ or ≤ -1.96, we conclude with 95% confidence that our guess stated in H_0 was wrong. If the null hypothesis were true, we wouldn't expect to see such a large z-value very often (we'd obtain a z as extreme as the one we obtained only 5% or less of the time). Given that we did obtain a big z-value, it is more likely that the null hypothesis probably does not hold.

That refresher should have cleared the ol' neural cobwebs. Before proceeding to 2-sample t-tests, we pause to "behold the power of n!" Let's take the equation for z and rewrite it from $z = (\bar{x} - c)/s_{\bar{x}}$ to spell out the standard error, $z = (\bar{x} - c)/(s_x/\sqrt{n})$ and finally to bring the square root of n from the denominator of the denominator up to the numerator, $z = (\sqrt{n}(\bar{x} - c))/s_x$. This reformulation shows us that for any given mean $\bar{x}$ and standard deviation s_x, we enhance the likelihood of our detecting a significant result (i.e., increase the power of the test) by obtaining a larger sample, n. So some day when you're CEO and your research department wants to spend money getting data, don't scrimp and ask for a smaller sample size. You'll be hurting yourself. There are tests for statistical power (i.e., to answer the question, "How big should

---

[29] This model is monstrously robust, so we'll be okay even if we don't have a perfect normal distribution. Our observed sample distribution shape could be a little rougher, bumpier, a tad less symmetric, or a smidge skewier (lop-sided).

my sample be?"), but two rules of thumb are these: 1) at least 30 consumers per cell or per condition to enhance the statistical properties, and 2) at least 100 consumers per cell or per condition to enhance the believability of the results.

Next, let's consider a 2-sample t-test. We select two random samples, of sizes n_1 and n_2. They may both be from the same target population, if we're planning on conducting an experiment on them, or they could be from different populations, if we're planning to test whether the groups (e.g., men and women, brand users and non-users) are the same or different. We collect data on both groups, and we'll note with the first subscript whether they're in group 1 or 2: $x_{11}, x_{12}, \ldots, x_{1n1}$ and $x_{21}, x_{22}, \ldots, x_{2n2}$. We estimate the population means μ_1 and μ_2 using the sample means, $\bar{x}_1$ and $\bar{x}_2$, just as before.

We posit the null hypothesis, $H_0: \mu_1 = \mu_2$ (the groups are roughly the same) and the alternative, $H_a: \mu_1 \neq \mu_2$. To test H_0, we'll compute the "sum of squares" for each sample. Sum of squares, or SS, actually stands for the sum of squared deviations of each sample data point around its mean. It is simply: $SS = \sum_{i=1}^{n}(x_i - \bar{x})^2$. Note the SS is the numerator in computing the variance (equation above). The denominator, $n - 1$, is referred to as the degrees of freedom, or df. We assume homogeneity of variance; that is, $s_{x1}^2 = s_{x2}^2$; customers' attitudes will vary in group 1, and they'll vary to about the same extent in group 2. We care more about whether the means in the groups are the same or different. With that assumption, we pool the SS to get a good estimate of that homogeneous variance, $s_p^2 = \frac{SS_1 + SS_2}{df_1 + df_2} = \frac{\sum_{i=1}^{n1}(x_{1i} - \bar{x}_1)^2 + \sum_{i=1}^{n2}(x_{2i} - \bar{x}_2)^2}{(n_1 - 1) + (n_2 - 1)}$, and use s_p^2 to get a better estimate of the standard error, $s.e. = s_{\bar{x}1 - \bar{x}2} = \sqrt{s_p^2 \left(\frac{1}{n_1} + \frac{1}{n_2}\right)}$. We create a 2-sample t-test, $= \frac{(\bar{x}_1 - \bar{x}_2) - (\mu_1 - \mu_2)}{s_{\bar{x}1 - \bar{x}2}}$, and compare our calculated t to the t-tables with $(n_1 - 1) + (n_2 - 1) = df_1 + df_2 = n_1 + n_2 - 2$ df. If our t exceeds the critical value, we're confident that μ_1 and μ_2 are probably not equal.[30]

At this point, we know how to operate with 1 or 2 groups. But what if we wanted to compare 3 groups? We might compare groups 1 and 2, then 2 and 3, and 1 and 3, using three 2-sample t-tests. However, that approach is statistically suboptimal: first, the tests aren't independent because we're using the data more than once. Second, the tests aren't as powerful as they might be because we're not using all the data simultaneously. If there were 100 customers in each of the 3 samples, each t-test would be based on 200 data points. We'll turn to a technique that uses all 300 data points, from all 3 groups combined, so the sample size is effectively bigger, and the test more sensitive. This technique is called analysis of variance (ANOVA), and it's a natural extension of t-tests to 3 or more groups. (The statistic we'll compute for ANOVA is called F on $df_{numerator}$ and df_{error}. When there are only 2 groups, so $df_{numerator} = 1$, it is equivalent to a t^2 on df_{error}.)

Analysis of Variance (ANOVA)

Let's say we run an online experiment. We get a marketing research firm to help us recruit a random and representative sample. The customers solicited for the sample go online, and land on a home page that was randomly assigned to them—featuring a product description with a low, medium, or high price point, and we record their interest on a 0 to 100 point scale: "How likely is it you would buy this product?"

We could also test differences on naturally occurring groups, rather than experimentally imposed groups. For example, we might wish to compare customers who have self-identified as loyal to brands A, B, or C, with customers who vary in groups based on age, income, frequency of purchasing, word-of-mouth activity, whatever. ANOVA is just a statistical method so we can use it to make these comparisons as well, but ANOVA's greatest strength occurs when used in conjunction with experiments. The difference between the experimental scenario and the self-selection scenario is that only in the first can we draw causal conclusions. In the second, if we see differences between the brands, we may wish to say it's the brands that generate the differences, but there might be something about the customers themselves that propels them to the different brands, which then perpetuate the different brand data. Whether the interpretation can claim causality or just the existence of group differences, let's look at how it's done.

One Factor

A "one-factor analysis of variance" is the term used for an ANOVA when we're comparing the means from some number of groups that vary along one factor. Figure 8.1 illustrates an example in which we've shown 3 groups of customers different price points. Price is the one factor—the groups are different in this one way. The low price yielded the highest mean on the 0 to 20 point scale of "How likely is it you would buy this?" As we might anticipate, as the price increased, fewer customers were interested, resulting in lower scores on a purchase intentions or willingness to pay (WTP) scale.

---

[30] For critical values of t, see appendices in most statistics texts. Alternatively, enter t.dist.2t(t,df) in Excel to obtain the p-value—the probability that we'd get a t as big as the one we got, or bigger, if the H_0 were true. We'll reject H_0 if p < .05.

Note that each price point mean, $\bar{x}$, is associated with a distribution, because customers vary in their opinions about the attractiveness of the purchase, even when everyone in the same group is exposed to the same price point. We randomly assigned each participant in the study to one condition—low, medium, or high price—so a priori we expect that these customers were approximately the same kinds of people, at least prior to our exposing them to the different price information. As a result, we can conclude that the differences on WTP for the 3 groups are attributable to the prices and nothing else. In addition, we acknowledge that there will be individual differences, or heterogeneity among customers in their reactions to their group's price point. We assume this variability is approximately the same from condition to condition. This assumption is known as "homogeneity of variance," which allows us to aggregate (or "pool") the data, as we did in the 2-sample t-test.

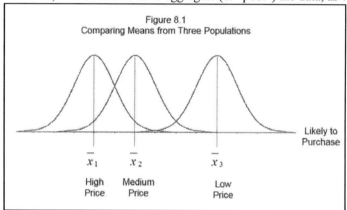

Figure 8.1
Comparing Means from Three Populations

We use ANOVA to look at mean differences, but it gets its name, analysis of variance, from the fact that we compare how much the means for the groups differ to how much people differ within each group. You might recall that in regression, we can partition variability in the dependent variable into that which is explained by the predictor variables and that which is unexplained, random error. Analogously, for ANOVA, we say that the total sum of squares is comprised of variability between the group means as well as variability within each group: $SS_{total} = SS_{between\ groups} + SS_{within\ groups}$.

Obviously, we'll have a computer crunch these pieces, but seeing the equations helps you learn. The number of groups ranges from 1 to "a" (e.g., a = 3 price points) and the number of participants in the study in group 1, 2, etc., is "n," such that the overall sample size is N = a × n. (We could let the sample sizes differ in each group, but we're keeping $n_1 = n_2 = n_3 = n$ for simplicity.) The total SS is calculated by comparing every person's data point, x_{ij}, regardless of which group they're in, to the overall, grand mean, $\bar{x}..$ as in: $SS_{total} = \sum_{i=1}^{a} \sum_{j=1}^{n} (x_{ij} - \bar{x}..)^2$. The variability from group to group is what really interests us because it reflects whether the different prices result in different WTP scores. Thus, we compare the $\bar{x}_i$'s to the grand mean $\bar{x}..$ as in: $SS_{between\ groups} = \sum_{i=1}^{a} \sum_{j=1}^{n} (\bar{x}_i - \bar{x}..)^2$. The last piece is the variability within a group, assessed by comparing each person in group "i" to the mean for that group: $SS_{within\ groups} = \sum_{i=1}^{a} \sum_{j=1}^{n} (x_{ij} - \bar{x}_i)^2$.

That was a little crunchy, so let's look at an example. Say we have 4 customers reacting to each of the 3 price points (for 12 customers total, a ridiculously small sample). The first group saw the high price and they gave ratings on a "likely to purchase" scale of: 4, 5, 6, 5. Group 2 saw the medium price and their data were: 5, 6, 6, 7. Group 3 saw the low price and their scores were higher: 9, 10, 11, 10.

As Figure 8.1 suggests, the means of the 3 groups look different: $\bar{x}_1 = 5$, $\bar{x}_2 = 6$, and $\bar{x}_3 = 10$. The overall mean in the sample is $\bar{x}.. = 7$. The calculations for SS_{total}, $SS_{between}$, and SS_{within} are in Figure 8.2 (makes ya glad for computers). Note that, as promised, $SS_{total} = SS_{between} + SS_{within}$, 62 = 56 + 6.

Next, as we've seen in the equation for a simple variance, $\sigma^2 = \frac{\sum_{i=1}^{n}(x_i - \bar{x})^2}{n-1}$, the numerator is an SS and the denominator is a df. Here too, we adjust the SS by their df. The results are called "mean squares" (MS) in

Figure 8.2
Calculating SS_{total}, $SS_{between}$, and $SS_{w/in}$

SS_{total} = $(4-7)^2 + (5-7)^2 + (6-7)^2 + (5-7)^2$
$+ (5-7)^2 + (6-7)^2 + (6-7)^2 + (7-7)^2$
$+ (9-7)^2 + (10-7)^2 + (11-7)^2 + (10-7)^2$
= 62.00

SS_{betw} = $(5-7)^2 + (5-7)^2 + (5-7)^2 + (5-7)^2$
$+ (6-7)^2 + (6-7)^2 + (6-7)^2 + (6-7)^2$
$+ (10-7)^2 + (10-7)^2 + (10-7)^2 + (10-7)^2$
= 56.00

$SS_{w/in}$ = $(4-5)^2 + (5-5)^2 + (6-5)^2 + (5-5)^2$
$+ (5-6)^2 + (6-6)^2 + (6-6)^2 + (7-6)^2$
$+ (9-10)^2 + (10-10)^2 + (11-10)^2 + (10-10)^2$
= 6.00.

ANOVA. Specifically, $MS_{between} = \dfrac{SS_{between}}{(a-1)}$, and $MS_{within} = \dfrac{SS_{within}}{(a(n-1))}$. For these data, $df_{between} = (3-1) = 2$, $df_{within} = 3(4-1) = 9$, so $MS_{between} = 28.000$, $MS_{within} = 0.667$.

We then compare those variance estimates in a ratio called an F-test: $= MS_{between}/MS_{w/in}$ and the F has $(a-1)$ and $(a(n-1))$ degrees of freedom.[31] (I saw a joke online: "There's a fine line between numerator and denominator!") For our data, F = 41.98, on 2 and 9 df. For $\alpha = .05$, the critical value F = 4.26, and Excel returns p = 0.0000273 (far less than 0.05). The p-value tells us to reject the null hypothesis.

Note that in ANOVA with 3 groups, $H_0: \mu_1 = \mu_2 = \mu_3$. The alternative "Ha: at least one μ is different" is not very specific. It could be that all 3 means are different, or it could be that just 1 mean is different but the other 2 are the same. The precise nature of the group differences can be isolated using a follow-up analysis called a "contrast," as we'll do shortly.

If we consider that the ANOVA model is as follows,[32]

$$x_{ij} = \mu + \alpha_i + \varepsilon_{ij}$$

where $\alpha_i = \bar{x}_i - \bar{x}_{..}$, the effect of being in group i (the group i mean compared to the overall, grand mean), we may also write the null hypothesis that we're testing as: $H_0: \alpha_1 = \alpha_2 = \alpha_3 = 0$. Whether we state H_0 in terms of μ's or α's, the point is, if we cannot reject it, the groups have means that are statistically the same, that is, equally allowing for sampling variability. If we reject the null, then not all the means are the same; at least one is different.

It is customary to put all of this information into a summary ANOVA table, like Figure 8.3. Computer outputs provide the analysis in this format as well. The rows are labeled as variance between or within groups. The sums of squares are the values in the SS column (per their respective equations and the values that we computed "by hand" in Figure 8.2). The characteristic of ANOVA that it is a decomposition of sources of variability can be seen by the fact that the $SS_{betw} + SS_{w/in} = SS_{total}$.

Figure 8.3
Summary ANOVA Table

source (of variation)	SS	df	MS	F
between	56	2	28.000	41.98 on 2,9 df
within	6	9	.667	
total (corrected for the grand mean)	62	11		
	These will sum.	These will sum.	MS = SS/df	F = Ms_{effect} / MS_{error}

That summation property holds for the degrees of freedom as well—there were 12 data points, and the SS_{total} term uses 1 df to estimate the grand mean, so $df_{total} = 12 - 1 = 11$. There are 3 groups, hence 3 group means, but once we know the grand mean, they are constrained, so $df_{betw} = a - 1 = 3 - 1 = 2$ df. Within a group, there are n observations, and they too are constrained by our knowing (having estimated) the group mean. Thus, within a group, there are $n - 1$ df, and there are "a" groups. So, $df_{w/in}$ (or df_{error}) = $a(n-1) = 3(4-1) = 9$.

Next in the table come the mean square values; $MS_{effect} = SS_{effect} / df_{effect}$, whether the effect is "between" or "within." The F statistic is usually $MS_{betw}/MS_{w/in}$ (but more complicated designs might vary this form slightly).

All of this is still just for one factor. We'll proceed to 2 and more factors shortly. But we take a moment to understand contrasts, and to look at an important use of 1-way ANOVA in marketing.

Contrasts

In a 2-sample t-test, if we reject the $H_o: \mu_1 = \mu_2$, the interpretation is unambiguous. If $\bar{x}_1 > \bar{x}_2$, then we say $\bar{x}_1$ is significantly greater than $\bar{x}_2$ (or vice versa if $\bar{x}_2 > \bar{x}_1$). In ANOVA, we have 3 or more groups, so when we reject the $H_o: \mu_1 = \mu_2 = \mu_3 = \mu_4 = \mu_5$, say, we know that at least one of those μ's is different from the others. Perhaps 2 are different. Perhaps they're all different. To find out more detail about the nature of the group differences, we run contrasts.

---

[31] Critical values of F are tabled in the appendices of most statistics texts. Alternatively, enter f.dist.rt(F,df1,df2) in Excel to obtain the p-value, and reject H_0 if p < .05.

[32] The group effect α_i has nothing to do with the 95% confidence level and the Type I error rate α. The latter never has a subscript, if that helps.

Suppose we ran a promo in 3 stores in each of 5 test market cities: Los Angeles, Las Vegas, New York, Boston, and Atlanta. We gathered sales data and average over the 3 stores to obtain the 5 means: $\bar{x}_{LA}$, $\bar{x}_{Vegas}$, $\bar{x}_{NY}$, $\bar{x}_{Boston}$, and $\bar{x}_{Atlanta}$. We run an ANOVA and obtain a significant F-test for the main effect of city, so we reject the omnibus null hypothesis: $H_o: \mu_{LA} = \mu_{Vegas} = \mu_{NY} = \mu_{Boston} = \mu_{Atlanta}$. At this point, we probably want to know more—which means aren't the same? We can create a statistical test that contrasts 1 (or several) of these 5 cities against another 1 (or another subset) of these 5 cities. For example, we might wonder whether there is an East Coast– West Coast difference. To answer that question, we would posit: $H_o: (\mu_{LA} + \mu_{Vegas})/2 = (\mu_{NY} + \mu_{Boston} + \mu_{Atlanta})/3$. Someone might suggest that the 2 northeastern cities are probably different from Atlanta, so we could run yet another comparison, contrasting those sets: $H_o: (\mu_{NY} + \mu_{Boston})/2 = \mu_{Atlanta}$. Note that in the second contrast, the data from the markets in L.A. and Vegas don't even enter into the analysis. We might break that second contrast down even further and test whether $H_o: \mu_{NY} = \mu_{Boston}$.

The ANOVA model (or computer algorithm) estimates and tests these contrasts as follows. We attach contrast coefficients to the 5 means to represent the comparisons we wish to make: $c1\ \bar{x}_{LA} + c2\ \bar{x}_{Vegas} + c3\ \bar{x}_{NY} + c4\ \bar{x}_{Boston} + c5\ \bar{x}_{Atlanta}$. The only constraint is that they must sum to 0: $c1 + c2 + c3 + c4 + c5 = 0$. The contrasts above are defined as:

contrast#1 = $.5\ \bar{x}_{LA} + .5\ \bar{x}_{Vegas} - .33\ \bar{x}_{NY} - .33\ \bar{x}_{Boston} - .33\ \bar{x}_{Atlanta}$,
contrast#2 = $.0\ \bar{x}_{LA} + .0\ \bar{x}_{Vegas} + .5\ \bar{x}_{NY} + .5\ \bar{x}_{Boston} - 1\ \bar{x}_{Atlanta}$,
contrast#3 = $.0\ \bar{x}_{LA} + .0\ \bar{x}_{Vegas} + 1\ \bar{x}_{NY} - 1\ \bar{x}_{Boston} + .0\ \bar{x}_{Atlanta}$.

Next, we estimate how much variability in the data may be explained by a contrast. Recall that the variability is captured in the sums of squares (SS) terms. So we compute: $SS_{contrast} = (n \times contrast^2)/(\sum c_i^2)$. The value n is the number of observations in each cell (3 stores for us). The term in the denominator is simply $c1^2 + c2^2 + c3^2 + c4^2 + c5^2$.

Each contrast uses a single degree of freedom, so the $MS_{contrast} = SS_{contrast}/1$. We then form the F-test as: $MS_{contrast}/MS_{error}$, where the MS_{error} term is that in the ANOVA table that had served as the denominator for the test of this very main effect.

Say the mean sales figures had been: $\bar{x}_{LA} = 40$, $\bar{x}_{Vegas} = 35$, $\bar{x}_{NY} = 60$, $\bar{x}_{Boston} = 50$, and $\bar{x}_{Atlanta} = 40$. Then contrast#1 = $.5(40) + .5(35) - .33(60) - .33(50) - .33(40) = -12.45$. $\sum c_i^2 = .5^2 + .5^2 + (-.33)^2 + (-.33)^2 + (-.33)^2 = 0.83$. SScontrast#1 = $(3)(-12.45)^2/0.83 = 558.46 = $ MScontrast#1. The MS_{error} in the big overall ANOVA had been 59.0, so the F = 558.46/59 = 9.47 on 1 and 95 df. The p-value is .003.

Next we compute contrast#2 = $.0(40) + .0(35) + .5(60) + .5(50) - 1(40) = 15$. $\sum c_i^2 = .5^2 + .5^2 + 1^2 = 1.5$. SScontrast#2 = $(3)(15)^2/1.5 = 450 = $ MScontrast#2, for F = 450/59 = 7.63 on 1 and 95 df, for a p-value of .007.

The third is contrast#3 = $.0(40) + .0(35) + 1(60) - 1(50) + .0(40) = 10$. $\sum c_i^2 = 1^2 + (-1)^2 = 2$. SScontrast#3 = $(3)(10)^2/2 = 150 = $ MScontrast#3, F = 150/59 = 2.54 on 1 and 95 df, for a p-value of .114.

The first contrast is significant—there is something different between the coasts. The second contrast is also significant, indicating that the Atlanta sales are different from those in New York and Boston, and the third contrast is not quite significant, indicating Boston's sales and New York's sales are statistically equal.

The reason that contrasts are useful is that they take the comparison of 3 or more means down to tests that each have only 1 degree of freedom. In the 2-sample t-test, we said that we'd only need to look at the means—if one is lower than the other, then we'd know it's significantly lower. In ANOVA, a factor that defines 3 groups has 2 df, 4 groups have 3 df, etc. Our example had 5 cities, or 5 groups, and therefore we had 4 df. Each contrast, however, defined subsets of the 5, such as 1 city vs. another, or 2 cities vs. the other 3, etc., and in this simplification, when a contrast pops as significant, its interpretation is now similarly unambiguous.

Verifying Market Segments

In a segmentation study, we cluster customers based on the similarities of their data. We then try to understand differences between the groups by staring at the various profiles of those means in tables and plots. However, it is essential to test whether the apparent group differences are truly statistically significant differences.

Thus, for marketers, one hugely useful application of 1-way ANOVA is to validate a segmentation scheme arising from a cluster analysis. To do so, we run a 1-way ANOVA, where the segments define the different groups in the ANOVA, and each variable on which we suspect the segments to be different serves as the dependent variable in an ANOVA. Prior to the ANOVA, we know we have groups 1, 2, and 3, and we might suspect that the groups are "heavy or frequent," "medium," and "light" purchasers, but the F-test in ANOVA will tell whether that descriptor truly helps distinguish the groups.

Consider these recent studies:

- Customers who buy frozen yogurt were significantly more likely to be singles living alone than people living in households of 5 or more people. Frozen yogurt was also purchased significantly less by African-American and Asian-Americans, and Hispanic-Americans preferred sherbets.

- Marketers often test whether apparent profile differences are significant for segments of heavy (frequent) users vs. light users. They have found the following significant differences: 1) heavy purchasers of ketchup and candies almost certainly have kids; 2) heavy users of orange juice, cake mixes, and toothpaste represent higher incomes; 3) frequent purchases of beer tend to have less education and watch more TV daily.
- Segments of customers who purchase various financial investments differ significantly on income, education, and risk tolerance, and differ significantly in their desire to invest in companies that offer advisors.

Two or More Factors and Interactions

We've seen that ANOVA is a logical extension of t-tests to 3 or more groups. It is also an extension to the analysis of two or more factors. A factor is what is manipulated (or measured) to form the groups in our experiment. Figure 8.1 had depicted a scenario in which we varied one factor, price. Typically we will manipulate more than one factor at a time (for efficiency's sake and because we're rarely interested in how one factor works in isolation). We'll begin the usual way, via randomly sampling participants (customers, stores, test markets, etc.) and then we will randomly assign each to one condition. The conditions now are defined by a combination of two or more experimental factors, such as price and advertising, or price and advertising and packaging, etc. We then obtain measures on dependent variables of interest.

There are two reasons to run studies in which we combine multiple factors. The first is the economics of the sample size. If we ran a study on pricing, with 30 customers in each of 3 cells, and another study on advertising, with 30 customers in each of 3 cells, we'd need 180 customers total. If instead, we ran a 3x3 factorial with 10 customers in each of the 9 cells (each price level with each ad), we'd only need 90 customers total. The statistical power for testing effects of pricing (ads) would be the same as the larger first study because, as you'll see shortly, we temporarily aggregate over ads (pricing).

The cooler reason to manipulate several factors in a single study is that in addition to answering questions about one factor at a time ("main effects"), we'll be able to examine interactions. An interaction is the joint impact of 2 or more factors on the dependent measure. Thus, in a two-factor design in which we manipulate both price and advertising, we can pose three questions: 1) Is one ad more effective than another? 2) Is one pricing level more effective than the others? 3) Do the ads and price interact—is there any particular combination of the ads and prices that is especially effective, or detrimental?

The underlying model in 2-factor factorial (all combinations) ANOVA for any customer's data point reflects all these pieces:
$$x_{ijk} = \mu + \alpha_i + \beta_j + (\alpha\beta)_{ij} + \varepsilon_{ijk},$$
where α_i is the effect of the ads i (i = 1, 2, ... a), β_j is the effect of price j (j = 1, 2, ... b), and the $(\alpha\beta)_{ij}$ term is the combined effect of ads and price in cell i,j, and ε_{ijk} is the variability of each participant, k = 1, 2, ..., n from the mean in their i,j cell. The variability is parsed accordingly:
$$SS_{total} = SS_{Ads} + SS_{Price} + SS_{AdsxPrice} + SS_{error},$$
calculated as follows: $SS_{total} = \sum_{i=1}^{a} \sum_{j=1}^{b} \sum_{k=1}^{n} (x_{ijk} - \bar{x}...)^2$, $SS_{ads} = \sum_i^a \sum_j^b \sum_k^n (\bar{x}_i - \bar{x}...)^2$, $SS_{price} = \sum_i^a \sum_j^b \sum_k^n (\bar{x}_j - \bar{x}...)^2$, $SS_{ads \times price} = \sum_i^a \sum_j^b \sum_k^n (\bar{x}_{ij} - \bar{x}_i - \bar{x}_j + \bar{x}...)^2$, $SS_{w/in} = \sum_i^a \sum_j^b \sum_k^n (x_{ijk} - \bar{x}_{ij})^2$.

Figure 8.4 shows the results for a 2x3 study that was run in which we manipulated advertising in addition to our low, medium, and high price point factor. Two ads were tested. One ad reflected the current positioning of the brand, and the other ad tried to portray a more upscale, luxurious position. Consumers' purchase intentions were measured as the pre-market test-dependent variable (in-market tests would yield sales for the dependent variable). The ANOVA table indicates that varying the type of ad didn't matter by itself (the p-value for the main effect was > .05). Price was significant, as was the interaction. So how do we know which ad and price affected consumers most positively?

The means are presented in a table (Figure 8.5) and plots (Figure 8.6). Both formats are popular in analytic reports and consulting white papers. The ad means were fairly close to each other (as the insignificant F-test for ad indicated). The price means look different—at least the low price

Figure 8.4
ANOVA Table for 2x3 Factorial: Purchase Intentions (or Sales)

Source	SS	df	MS	F-test	p-value
A (Ad)	5.30	1	5.30	0.75	0.3951
B (Price)	74.46	2	37.23	5.27	0.0127*
A x B (Ad x Price)	52.60	2	26.30	3.72	0.0392*
Error (5 test markets in each cell)	169.60	24	7.07		
Total	775.36	29			*p<.05

df_{Ad} = #ad-1
df_{Price} = #price-1
df_{AxB} = $(df_A)(df_B)$
df_{error} = (#ad)(#price)(n-1)

These will sum. These will sum. MS = SS/df   F = Ms_{effect} / MS_{error}

mean looks higher than the other two. The interaction shows how consumers' reactions were contingent upon a combination of these two factors.

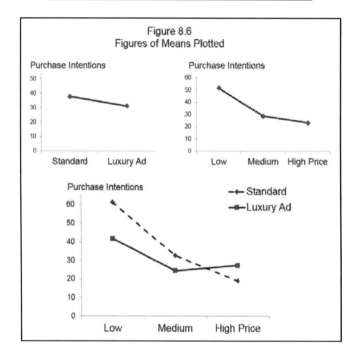

Figure 8.5
Table of Means: Purchase Intentions (or Sales)

Ad:	Price: Low	Medium	High	
Standard	61.4	32.7	19.1	37.7
Luxury	41.8	24.5	27.3	31.2
	51.6	28.6	23.2	

Figure 8.6
Figures of Means Plotted

The interaction tells us that the lack of effect for the ad (per the insignificant main effect) is a little deceptive. We can't actually say that the ads were the same or that one never fared better than another. In fact, the standard ad did better when it was paired with low and medium price points. And the luxury ad did better when it was coupled with the higher price. Together the interaction results show statistically what we expect as marketers—consumers are sensitive to consistent cues between the marketing mix variables.

The analyses are complete. They're intended to inform the managerial decisions that must be made, and so, which ad and price should we choose to take to market? The insignificant main effect for an ad implies that the ad choice doesn't matter, in isolation. Looking at the means, it's true that 37.7 is greater than 31.2, but the ANOVA tells us that it is not significantly greater—the difference is attributable to error.

The means for the price factor (which are significant, and therefore the choice does matter) suggest demand will be greatest for the low price point and least for the high price point. If we prefer a position with a low price, we can see that we'll yield the most volume. We can of course forgo volume if we wish to have a premium price point and image, and if our margins are better as a result. The price means also tell us that it would be silly to select the medium price point. It's true that raising price from medium to high drops purchase intentions (or subsequent sales), but that drop doesn't appear to be dramatic. (We could test whether or not the drop is significant by comparing the medium to high means via a contrast. If indeed it is not, we might as well price higher.)

The interaction indicates that we should present either the standard ad with the low price or the luxury ad with the high price. The choice between the two involves managerial aspiration regarding desired positioning, as well as examination of volume vs. marginal trade-offs.

In general, beyond our pricing and advertising study, Figure 8.7 shows sample patterns of what results might look like if the main effects for factors A and B are significant or not, with the interaction being significant or not. The lack of an interaction is well known to produce approximately parallel lines—implying that the effect of factor A or B is not contingent upon levels of the other factor.

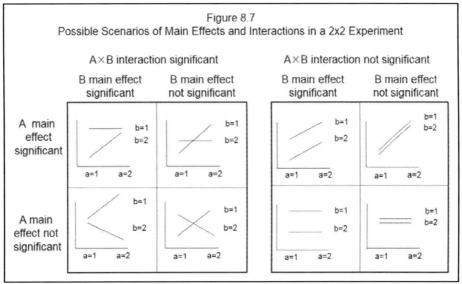

Figure 8.7
Possible Scenarios of Main Effects and Interactions in a 2x2 Experiment

Experiments and ANOVA generalize nicely to 3 or more factors. We might run a test in which we varied price and ad and package design, for example. If we were to do so, we would estimate three main effects (the impact of each factor on its own), three 2-way interactions (price and ad, price and packaging, and ad and packaging), as well as a new higher-order effect, the 3-way interaction between all the factors. If the 3-way interaction is significant, it would signal that the combined effects of price and ad on purchase intentions (or sales) would vary depending on the different kinds of packaging. Adding terms, the model extends to:

$$x_{ijk\ell} = \mu + \alpha_i + \beta_j + \gamma_k + \alpha\beta_{ij} + \alpha\gamma_{ik} + \beta\gamma_{jk} + \alpha\beta\gamma_{ijk} + \varepsilon_{ijk\ell},$$

where γ represents the new third factor, $k = 1, 2, \ldots c$ levels of package designs.

For example, in a recent, real-world example, an online music provider experimented with its marketing mix to draw more sales. The company varied 3 factors: factor A was the type of referral program offered to the customer. It included: 1) a control group for which the message said (as their website and emails always said), "Tell your friends about us!," 2) a second option that offered 50% off the price of a download if they would recommend the service to three friends, and 3) an option for a free download if they recommended the service to one friend. As you might expect, the free download telling just one friend was the most attractive (best payoff and least effort). The ANOVA results also showed that the second option yielded no more sales than the control group.

The second factor, B, was a price promotion, offering 1, 2, or 5 downloads for $0.99. The results yielded a significant main effect for this factor also, with the 5 downloads being the most attractive. The opportunity to download 2 songs was no more attractive than 1, statistically speaking.

The third factor, C, was whether the customer was contacted via an online social network or a purchased list of emails from a marketing research vendor. The network contact was preferred. This effect was significant but not as strong as the main effects for factors A and B.

At this point, you might be thinking that the company should go with the promotional campaign of: A = free download with referring a friend, B = 5 downloads for $0.99, and C = contact via networks. However, think again, because these main effect results were modified by an interaction between A and C. The results indicated that the choice of A = 50% off for referring 3 friends did fairly well if the customer had been contacted via a social network rather than email; after all, on the network, it would be easy to forward the promo. The company was happy to implement the choice that the results highlighted, because it believed that networks were the way of the future.

Analysis of Covariance (ANCOVA)

When we test an effect in ANOVA such as the main effect of factor A (on its own) or the A×B interaction (jointly), etc., the F-tests are essentially of the form, $F = (MS_{effect})/(MS_{error})$. The F will be large and significant if the effect is large, e.g., if ad 1 is really different from ad 2. The F will also be large if the error term is small. We can't control the extent of individual differences in customers' perceptions, but we can try to statistically control for extraneous sources of variability.

For example, say we wish to launch a new salsa nationwide, and we've been testing several concoctions, combining different colors, vegetables, and so forth. At the moment, our focus is on spiciness, and we're testing 4 levels of heat. We can't randomly assign a person to being one who prefers mild or spicy flavors, so after the taste test part of the study, we collect additional information on the respondents, including an index of how frequently they eat spicy cuisine.

That additional measure is called a covariate. It is likely to affect the dependent variable, but it's not something we're interested in—it's a nuisance variable. We'll acknowledge it and statistically control for it, to try to see whether, above and beyond a person's basic taste predilection, there are differences among the 4 test salsas. We control for covariates in the analysis of covariance.

In ANOVA, we model the test on the spiciness factor as: $x_{ij} = \mu + \alpha_i + \varepsilon_{ij}$. The α_i indicates the effect of the manipulated factor—the spiciness of the salsa we're testing. In ANCOVA, the model includes a term for the covariate (labeled "c" for simplicity): $x_{ij} = \mu + \alpha_i + \beta(c_{ij} - \bar{c}) + \varepsilon_{ij}$. The α represents the spiciness factor still, and the β conveys the effect of the covariate (mean-centered).

One way to understand the ANCOVA model is to think of it as a mix of ANOVA and regression. Imagine the following. Say we're interested in the dependent variable measuring WTP or sales or a scale of "how good does this taste." We could run a regression predicting this dependent variable as a function of how frequently the customer ate spicy foods. That regression would look like: $x_{ij} = \beta(c_{ij} - \bar{c}) + \varepsilon_{ij}$, or $x_{ij} = \hat{x}_{ij} + \varepsilon_{ij}$ where $\hat{x}_{ij} = \beta(c_{ij} - \bar{c})$.

Turn these inside out and the residuals would be: $r_{ij} = x_{ij} - \hat{x}_{ij} = \varepsilon_{ij}$. Instead of calling $x_{ij} - \hat{x}_{ij}$ a residual, let's call it an adjustment to the dependent variable, $x_{ij(adjusted)}$.

Then we bring in the experimental factor to see if it has an impact on this adjusted score. That is, very roughly speaking, we can think of ANCOVA as being an ANOVA applied to the dependent measure that has been adjusted by the covariate: $x_{ij(adj)} = x_{ij} - \beta(c_{ij} - \bar{c}) = \mu + \alpha_i + \varepsilon_{ij}$. Naturally the values for α_i and ε_{ij} and such will not be the same in the ANCOVA as they would have been in the ANOVA without the adjustment for the covariate. In particular, we hope that many of the ε_{ij}'s are much smaller.

ANCOVA is an extension of ANOVA that offers a great deal of flexibility. It helps us remove extraneous variation from the error term on the dependent variable, which helps to increase the precision of the analysis.[33]

Experimental Design Issues

When people hear the word "experiment," they often conjure up a vision of test tubes and beakers and labs. The experiments described in this chapter should dispel that simple notion. In this section, we'll see still more kinds of studies and ways of measuring impact.

Other Designs: Blocking, Fractional Factorials, and Friends

First, there are many kinds of experimental designs. The experiments we've been using are full factorials—every level of one factor is run in conjunction with every level of the other factors. Factorials are extremely important and they comprise easily 95% of experiments that are run. Let's briefly look at a couple of others to give you a sense of what's out there.

We'll begin with a simple "randomized block design." Every day, brand managers of the zillion consumer packaged goods in major grocery chains wonder about their marketing mix. Say one wishes to assess the relative effectiveness of 3 promotions: a $0.25 coupon, a $0.50 coupon, and a $1 mail-in rebate. A sample of stores is selected randomly, and those stores are randomly assigned to one of these 3 conditions. The offers are made available to consumers in the store, right under the shelf-facing of the product. We could run this study, collect sales data, and get some insights about price sensitivity, the attractiveness of the offers, and together, a sense of their effects on contribution margins and ultimately ROI.

---

[33] One final helpful tip: when you fit ANOVAs and ANCOVAs in SAS, SPSS, or whatever your favorite statistical computing package is, make sure you select the option to compute the "Type III SS." Those SS handle unbalanced data better; it's important to keep your cell sample sizes (n's) as equal as possible—otherwise, power is diminished, which means you're less likely to detect effects.

If we did so, it is possible, not likely but possible, that the random sample of stores would end up drawing all very small traffic stores. If that were to happen, the test results would be oddly biased, likely underestimating the impacts of the promotions.

To make sure that problem doesn't arise, we'll use a randomized block design. We take the sample of stores, and rank them by their annual sales. Our experimental factor has 3 levels (3 kinds of promotions), so we'll divide the list of stores into 3 blocks—those with the highest sales, lowest sales, and the rest in between. We then randomly assign each of the large stores into 1 of the 3 promotions conditions. Then we take the middle block of stores, and randomly assign them to 1 of the 3 conditions, and we do the same for the last block of smaller stores, we perform the blocking prior to the random assignment of the experimental condition to roughly match the stores by sales volume across the 3 conditions.

The blocking factor takes into account that yes, more sales result from bigger stores, but that finding isn't particularly shocking, nor is it relevant to our questions about the promotions. A blocking factor is essentially a nuisance factor—it controls for something we know is likely to be important but is not of central interest in the study.

The rest of the experiment proceeds as normal—we'd issue the promotions and wait to gather the sales data. We'd test these data in an ANOVA model with this form: $x_{ijk} = \mu + \alpha_i + \beta_j + \varepsilon_{ijk}$. The data point x_{ijk} stands for sales in experimental promotion condition i, block j, for store k. The grand mean is μ as always. The α_i's reflect the effects of the experimental factor—the promotions. The β_j's reflect the blocking factor. The last term is the usual error term, recognizing that the store (k) sales will vary, even with an experimental condition (i) and block (j). We fully expect the main effect for the blocking factor to be significant (in fact, if it's not, we went through the trouble of blocking for no good reason). We also assume that there is no interaction between the blocking factor and the experimental factor—indeed there is not even an interaction term in the model. That's because we designed this study so there couldn't be—there will be big stores that get the $0.25, $0.50, and $1 promos, and small stores that get all 3, so sales shouldn't vary contingently over those 2 factors. Our interest in this blocking design is solely on the experimental promotional factor. We included a block factor to simply control for store size.[34]

Another class of designs that marketers should know about are "fractional factorials." We have been working with full factorials, meaning, if we have 2 factors with 2 and 3 levels respectively, then our design is a 2×3 factorial, in which we will run all 6 conditions, and we will obtain data from all 6 of those cells. Six conditions seems manageable, but imagine if we were interested in studying more factors, say 5—even with just 2 levels of each factor, we'd have $2 \times 2 \times 2 \times 2 \times 2 = 32$ conditions. That's a lot. If the experiment we're conducting is a test market, we'd need at least 32 markets. If the experiment we're conducting is a conjoint study, we'd be showing 32 combinations to some poor, beleaguered consumers.

One option is to run a subset of conditions. Say we have just 3 factors, A, B, and C (each with 2 levels) to keep things simple. A full factorial would be a $2 \times 2 \times 2$, or 2^3 design. Instead of running all 8 conditions, we might run 4, which is a fraction—half—of the full factorial, usually written 2^{3-1}. The question is how to choose which 4 of the 8 conditions to run so as to maintain coverage over all three factors, A, B, and C.

Figure 8.8 shows a table with 8 cells, based on the $2 \times 2 \times 2$ ($A \times B \times C$) structure. The checks in 4 of the cells indicate that these are the conditions proposed to be run; i.e., not all 8. Say we do so, and obtain 4 means. You can see from the columns that 2 of the means will capture the effect of c1 and 2 of the means will capture the effect of c2. That comparison is the main effect for factor C. But also note the following. If we ignore factor C for a moment, then we have a mean in the a_1b_1, a_1b_2,

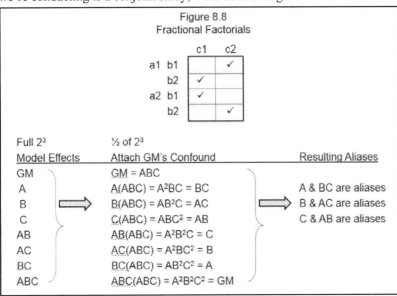

Figure 8.8
Fractional Factorials

	c1	c2
a1 b1		✓
b2	✓	
a2 b1	✓	
b2		✓

Full 2^3 Model Effects	½ of 2^3 Attach GM's Confound	Resulting Aliases
GM	GM = ABC	
A	A(ABC) = A²BC = BC	A & BC are aliases
B	B(ABC) = AB²C = AC	B & AC are aliases
C	C(ABC) = ABC² = AB	C & AB are aliases
AB	AB(ABC) = A²B²C = C	
AC	AC(ABC) = A²BC² = B	
BC	BC(ABC) = AB²C² = A	
ABC	ABC(ABC) = A²B²C² = GM	

effect for factor C. But also note the following. If we ignore factor C for a moment, then we have a mean in the a_1b_1, a_1b_2,

---

[34] Blocking designs serve a purpose similar to that described previously for ANCOVA. The blocking is a control that is done mechanically at the start of the study. ANCOVA is a control that is done statistically after the data are collected, and can be used if blocking is difficult to do, or we didn't think of controlling for certain variability until the study was already run.

a_2b_1, and a_2b_2 cells, and what are these but the structure of the AB interaction. That is, the main effect of C is confounded with the AB interaction. In the terminology of fractional factorial designs, C and AB are aliases.

Furthermore, the effects of C and AB aren't the only ones confounded. The way to determine the alias patterns is found beneath the 2^3 table. All of the effects that are in a full 3-factor model comprise the first column, from the grand mean to the main effects, to the 2-way and 3-way interactions. In the next column, we make the often chosen assumption that the grand mean (something we don't care much about) is confounded with the highest way interaction, in this case a 3-way (something others don't tend to understand). We then take the symbols for the 3-way, ABC, and attach it to every effect, e.g., A becomes A(ABC), etc. Where there are 2 of some factor listed, erase them, and what remains is the effect that is confounded with the original effect in that row. Thus, in that row for A, we have A(ABC), and once we delete the A's, we are left with BC. Hence, the main effect for factor A and the BC interaction are aliases.

If we don't like these results, for example if we want to estimate both A and BC, then we can start over and confound the grand mean with a different term, until we get an aliasing pattern that suits us. Next, once we know what will be aliased, we still need to understand which conditions to run. IRL, there are research consultants who would charge an arm and a leg for this, so now you will have this tool for free. Figure 8.9 contains the table of effects for all the components of the 3-factor model. The grand mean is a function of all 8 cells; the main effect of factor A contrasts the first 4 cells listed (all with a1) against the last 4 cells (all with a2); etc. The main effects are easy enough to determine. The trick to the interactions is that the pattern of 1's and -1's is just the product of their factors; e.g., the first interaction is AB, and its pattern of 1's and –1's is obtained by simply multiplying the 1's and –1's in the A and B columns.

| | | | | | Figure 8.9 | | | |
| | | | | | Fractional Factorial Designs | | | |
Condition	GM	A	B	C	AB	AC	BC	ABC
$a_1b_1c_1$	1	-1	-1	-1	1	1	1	-1
$a_1b_1c_2$	1	-1	-1	1	1	-1	-1	1
$a_1b_2c_1$	1	-1	1	-1	-1	1	-1	1
$a_1b_2c_2$	1	-1	1	1	-1	-1	1	-1
$a_2b_1c_1$	1	1	-1	-1	-1	-1	1	1
$a_2b_1c_2$	1	1	-1	1	-1	1	-1	-1
$a_2b_2c_1$	1	1	1	-1	1	-1	-1	-1
$a_2b_2c_2$	1	1	1	1	1	1	1	1
Condition	GM	A	B	C	AB	AC	BC	ABC
$a_1b_1c_2$	1	-1	-1	1	1	-1	-1	1
$a_1b_2c_1$	1	-1	1	-1	-1	1	-1	1
$a_2b_1c_1$	1	1	-1	-1	-1	-1	1	1
$a_2b_2c_2$	1	1	1	1	1	1	1	1

Next, the point of the fractional factorial is to run 4 of the conditions that label the rows, not all 8, so which 4 do we run? In this example, we started with the observation that the main effect of C is confounded with (i.e., the same as) the interaction of AB. So, in the table at the bottom, we have lifted and kept the subset of rows in which the signs in the C column match the signs in the AB column. Once we see the signs matching, all we have to do is read off the conditions that label the rows. Specifically, we'll run the following conditions: $a_1b_1c_2$, $a_1b_2c_1$, $a_2b_1c_1$, and $a_2b_2c_2$.

It's a little tricky to even write the model we're testing, for example, this version would be legitimate: $x_{ijkl} = \mu + \alpha_i + \beta_j + \gamma_k + \varepsilon_{ijkl}$ as would this: $x_{ijkl} = \mu + \beta\gamma_{jk} + \beta_j + \gamma_k + \varepsilon_{ijkl}$. In any event, the ANOVA table will have fewer rows, that is, fewer sources of variability, than the usual 2^3 would produce, and we'd have to make assumptions to interpret the F's accordingly.

Now that we know how to do fractional factorials, it's worth closing them out on a sobering note. When we characterize effects like C and AB as aliased, it means that the design is so restricted that we don't have enough df to estimate both C and AB, so their results collapse into each other. If the effect is significant, we don't know if it's attributable to C or AB. That confounding is a huge problem. Some analysts feel comfortable simply assuming that C (or AB) is nonexistent, and hence the effect must be due to AB (or C). These fractional factorials are used a lot in conjoint studies, and notice the implication—if the effect is significant, does it mean that C is important to the product design, or that AB is? Can you confidently assume it's one or the other?

There are many more types of experimental designs, e.g., nested designs (in which one factor is manipulated within the hierarchical context of another), between-subjects design vs. within-subjects design (whether the consumers are exposed to more than one experimental condition, and how that affects the analysis), differences between fixed and random experimental factors (determined by how the levels of the factors are sampled, and which determine the generalizability of the study's findings), and more. Different designs offer flexibility in running studies, but it's important to know that many of them modify the form of the F-statistics that must be used to test the significance of the effects.

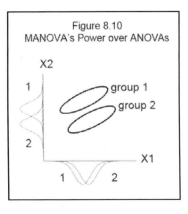

Figure 8.10
MANOVA's Power over ANOVAs

Analyses are also altered if we wish to model more than one dependent variable simultaneously, such as sales and customer reviews. With multiple dependent variables, we'd run a "multivariate ANOVA," or MANOVA, replacing one mean per group with a vector of p means per group. MANOVA sets up test statistics that are matrix analogs to F's, based on sums of squares of effects on each variable as well as their cross-products.

MANOVA can be handy because there can be true statistical power in the added information contained in multiple variables. For example, in Figure 8.10, we see the scatterplots of data on two dependent variables, x_1 and x_2, for each of 2 experimental groups, group 1 and group 2. If we ran a univariate ANOVA on either x_1 or x_2, we may or may not see significant groups differences, as indicated by a good amount of overlap in their marginal distributions. However, in the 2-d plot, we can see that using the information on both variables simultaneously distinguishes the groups perfectly—we would certainly find a significant difference between the groups if we ran a MANOVA on those data.

Natural Observation

Sometimes we want to test whether groups of data are significantly different, but the study doesn't lend itself to a design in which we exert control over all the variables. For example, sometimes all we have are longitudinal data, like in Figure 8.11, and the question is how to characterize what's happened.

Diagrams like these are frequently seen when we try to assess the effectiveness of health care or social marketing interventions, monitor blogs prior to elections, or listen to customer tweets about our brand. If we have bots scanning the web for increased volume of chatter or artificial intelligence coding text analyses for the valence of discussions, we don't have an experiment and we have no control over how the data unfold. Typically, we'll compare the mean levels of sales (or

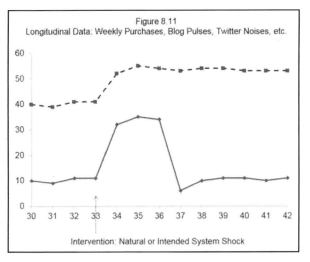

Figure 8.11
Longitudinal Data: Weekly Purchases, Blog Pulses, Twitter Noises, etc.

Intervention: Natural or Intended System Shock

attitudes or whatever) prior to, during, and after the intervention. The intervention might be something we created, such as a new ad or product launch, or it might be something that happened outside of our control, e.g., a competitor action, a meltdown of our celebrity spokesperson, or a global event of some sort, etc.

The solid line in Figure 8.11 is a typical result of introducing coupons or price-based promotions—when the promotion is launched, sales show an uptick, and when the promo is over, sales return to the previous base rates (or even show a slight decline at first, reflecting the fact that consumers have purchased to the point of creating an inventory). The dashed line is the result we hope for, which is a more permanent increase.

Recall that we had characterized highly controlled ("lab") experiments as being strong in terms of internal validity and field experiments (like test markets) as being strong on external validity. That means that in terms of our certainty regarding causal statements, we're in the best position off with controlled experiments. Next would be so-called field experiments in which, say, we randomly assign stores to promotional conditions, but there are known extraneous factors (such as competitive action) that we cannot control. A little less internally valid still would be the so-called quasi-experiment, which is characterized primarily by the fact that we hadn't randomly assigned conditions. For example, if we have stores all over the U.S., and one state begins to impose an added tax, we can try to analyze the effects, pre- and post-imposition, by comparing that state to others, but it's a weird event, outside of our control. There's a "treatment condition" (the one state) and a "control condition" (the other states), which we could compare in ANOVA, or via dummy variables in a regression. But there was no random sampling or random assignment. So it might look like an experiment and it might smell like an experiment, but it's not an experiment. Without random sampling and random assignment, we'd called it a quasi-experiment. Finally, the position imbuing the least confidence in causal statements would be when we've had zero control over anything and all we are doing is watching and measuring. In these situations, we can think in terms of time series, look for trends, and measure the movements of the naturalistic observations.

Words o' Wisdom

Finally, let's consider two unrelated notes about using experiments in the real world. First, it's long been considered that the function tying advertising exposure to consumer behavior is probably not a simple linear one. Imagine a plot in which the horizontal axis measures ad exposures from zero to 10 (or however many ads have been purchased in the last quarter or year, etc.). The vertical axis captures how much the customer knows about the product, or likes the ad, or thinks they'd buy the product. The function is usually posited to be a curve that first increases, then peaks, and then begins to decline. The idea is that when consumers know little about the new flavor of 7Up (say), then each time they see the ad, they learn a little bit more and if they are at all inclined to the soft drink and uncola category, their expected liking increases as well. But you know yourself, you get to a point…(just like hearing a formerly favorite song on the radio for the zillionth time), when consumers know pretty much all there is to learn from the ad, their interest declines, and indeed, soon the ad becomes irritating (and by association, the brand attitudes are thought to get tainted a bit as well). This description of one particular function—the form of the relationship between ad exposure and ad or brand liking—is just to remind us to consider the functional forms in our data, no matter what we're studying. Prior to any serious crunching, it's never a bad idea to generate a lot of scatterplots. If we saw curvilinear relationships, we can insert terms to try to capture such forms, e.g., just as in regression, where we can insert X and X^2, or X and $X \times Y$, for example.

The second concern is far more pervasive and disappointing. Companies don't seem to mind spending gobs of money on fun stuff like design or advertising or hey, corporate compensation, but they seem to choke when research and experimentation are proposed. It's true that conducting a study may seem daunting, but the alternative is to go ahead, and rely on the senior managers' supposedly insightful "guts," launch the new product (or whatever) and watch it fail at the rate of 70% or more, as per averages. The cost (in money and time) of the experiment will seem like beans in comparison after the fact. Even that bastion of managerial dominion, *Harvard Business Review,* has gotten into the spirit (j/k)—an article by Almquist and Wyner argues for the use of experiments to measure ROI and understand factors that affect it, and an article by Anderson and Simester reminds people interested in analytics to keep it simple so that the results can be useful and actionable.

Summary

An analysis of variance (ANOVA) is like an extension of a t-test, applicable to two or three or more groups. In addition, those groups may be defined by one or two or more experimental design factors. ANOVA is particularly useful in conjunction with an experiment, whether the experiment is conducted through online surveys or in test markets throughout the world. The combination of an experiment and ANOVA enables drawing conclusions about causal relationships between manipulated factors, like a marketing mix variable, and subsequent measured responses, like attitudes or sales. A one-way ANOVA is also very useful in validating the interpretation of a segmentation study—the input clusters define the ANOVA groups, and the groups may be tested as to whether what looks like segment differences truly are significant, or for that matter, what looks like segment similarities might actually be statistically different.

References

Intro texts and readings:
- Iacobucci, Dawn (1994). "Analysis of Experimental Data," in Richard Bagozzi (ed.), *Principles of Marketing Research*, Cambridge, MA: Blackwell, 224-278.
- Iversen, Gudmund R. and Helmut Norpoth (1987), *Analysis of Variance*, Sage. (Great, succinct intro.)
- Keppel, Geoffrey and Thomas D. Wickens (2004), *Design and Analysis: A Researcher's Handbook* (4th ed.), Englewood Cliffs, NY: Prentice Hall. (Great intro, especially for non-quant people; i.e., lots of good verbal explanations.)
- Snedecor, George W. and William G. Cochran (1980), *Statistical Methods*, (7th ed.), Ames, IA: Iowa State University Press.
- Wildt, A. R., and Ahtola, O. (1978), *Analysis of Covariance*, Beverly Hills, CA: Sage
- Snedecor, George W. and William G. Cochran (1980) *Statistical Methods* 7th ed., Ames, IA: The Iowa State University Press.

Experimental design:

- Berger, Paul D. and Robert W. Maurer (2002), *Experimental Design: With Applications in Management, Engineering, and the Sciences*, Belmont, CA: Wadsworth.
- Box, George E. P., J. Stuart Hunter, and William G. Hunter (2005), *Statistics for Experimenters: Design, Innovation, and Discovery* 2nd ed., New York: Wiley.
- Kirk, Roger E. (1982), *Experimental Design: Procedures for the Behavioral Sciences* (2nd ed.), Belmont, CA: Brooks/Cole.
- Winer, B. J., Donald R. Brown, Kenneth M. Michels (1991), *Statistical Principles in Experimental Design* 3rd ed., NY: McGraw-Hill.

Dealing with missing data:

- Little, Roderick J. A. and Donald B. Rubin (1987), *Statistical Analysis with Missing Data*, NY: Wiley.
- Searle, S. R. (1987), *Linear Models for Unbalanced Data,* New York: Wiley.

Thumbnail sketch regarding software:
- SAS: use proc glm, list the factors (class a b;), then a model statement (model y=a b a*b /ss3;), that last term to get the Type III sums of squares (helps if your data aren't perfectly balances, e.g., if there are missing data), and a means statement (means a b a*b;). For help: support.sas.com/documentation/
- SPSS: go to analyze, choose general linear model, univariate, select your predictor and dependent variable, don't forget to click on all the interactions if you have more than one predictor factor. For help: search "IBM SPSS documentation," and open the "statistics base" manual.
- XLStat: modeling data, anova, highlight the dep var Y, then the qualitative predictor factors X, on the options tab click on all the interactions you want, on the outputs tab click on "Type III SS." For help: www.xlstat.com, click on "support" and then "tutorials."

Chapter 9: Diffusion and Forecasting

Marketing Concept: Product Sales into the Marketplace
Modeling Concept: Diffusion Models, Market Sizing, Test Market Forecasting

Chapter Outline
1. Introduction
2. Marketing Diffusion Model
3. Market Sizing
4. Test Market Models

Introduction

It's exciting to launch a new product into the marketplace and watch sales grow. New products are risky, given their high failure rate, but they're the lifeblood of most companies' growth portfolio. They can complement a company's current offerings, or they can encourage current customers to purchase more frequently.

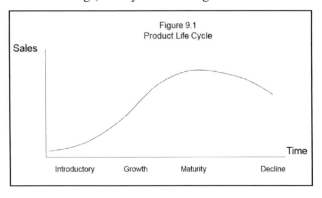

Most marketers hold to the concept of a product life cycle, as depicted in Figure 9.1. A new product is introduced to customers, and with time, sales grow, reach a point at which they seem to maintain, and eventually begin to decline. If decline they do, then replace them we must (so might say Yoda).

Discussions about strategic purposes of new products, or reasons for their failing and methods to avoid it, or marketing actions to take during the different stages of the product life cycle, etc., are not the topics of this chapter—for more, see *MM* or *Marketing Management* by moi. The models in this chapter were developed for application to watching early sales for a new product.

Marketing Diffusion Model

Figure 9.2 shows a normal curve that serves as the foundation of diffusion models. The idea is that for any new product or service or idea, there is an initial small part of the marketplace that finds the new item faster than everyone else. We all know friends who are techno-geeks, and they like to read pcworld.com and cnet.com to see what new gizmos

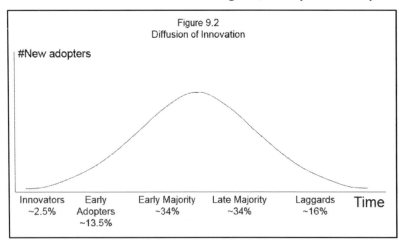

will be available soon. Next thing you know, they have the latest whiz-bang e-toy and they're telling all their friends about it. (The people who are innovators in one product category (e.g., hi-tech) aren't necessarily or even likely innovators for other product categories, e.g., movies, fashion, etc.)

Not quite as zealous as the innovators but still more progressive than most of the market are the customers called "early adopters." Any lag in adoptions, e.g., from the innovators to the early adopters, or from the early adopters to the groups yet to be described, can be attributed to a number of factors, probably several of which will be relevant for any product launch. For example, some product categories launch new products

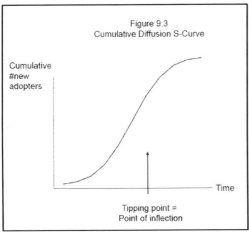

Figure 9.3
Cumulative Diffusion S-Curve

using skimming (high) prices, and customers who are high-involvement (care a lot about) a particular product category will happily pay the higher prices, whereas other customers might wait for the prices to come down a bit. It's also the case that new products might not be as easily accessible or as widely distributed as they will be later, so while the innovators might make the extra effort to find the new gadget, later adopters might wait until it's easier to find.

The next customers to adopt are creatively labeled the "early" and "late" majority. These customers are obviously not as innovative as the first two groups—they might be risk-averse, waiting for the earlier adopters to find the bugs, the company to fix them and launch 2.0, etc. The last group, the so-called laggards, might not ever adopt the new product because it's just not that important to them. If they do adopt, they'll be the last in the market to do so, very likely doing so as the innovators are trying out 3.0, and so on. The numbers under the labels in Figure 9.2 are the rough proportions of customers assumed to fall under each category for any product. We don't take these numbers hyper-seriously, but the idea is that they basically follow the shape of a normal curve; the early and late majority comprising 2/3rd's of the market, etc.

Figure 9.3 looks different in form, but it is simply the numbers of new customer adoptions from Figure 9.2 cumulated and plotted. Normal curves plotted cumulatively take on this distinctive s-shape. The point in time when adoptions pick up speed and seem to spread into the marketplace like wildfire (or go viral online) is the point of inflection (in calculus) or the tipping point (colloquially).

An interesting comparison across new product launches is to see how quickly one new product rather than

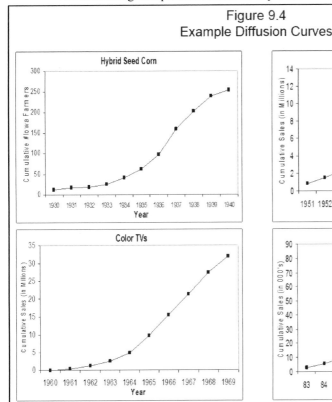

Figure 9.4
Example Diffusion Curves

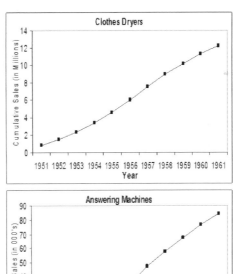

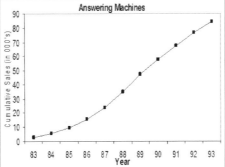

another finds the tipping point (going from left to right on the horizontal axis) as well as how rapidly the adoptions shoot up (i.e., how fast the rate of the curves increase—whether the middle of the s-shape is nearly vertical as in fast growth or nearly flat as in slow growth). Figure 9.4 plots examples from 4 publicly available data sets illustrating adoption by farmers of a particular (biogenetically enhanced) corn seed in the 1930s, dryers in the 1950s, color TVs in the 1960s, and answering machines in the late 1980s. Hybrid corn is slow to take off (think of the economics of the time), as were color TVs (they were expensive initially). The s-shape for clothes dryers is rather flat (the free alternative of a clothesline was already in use) as is that for answering machines. Marketing models want to quantify these statements about initial adoption and later growth being fast or slow.

One of the older models in marketing is called the diffusion model, and its job is to capture these growth tracks. The diffusion model that marketers use looks like this:[35]

$$n_t = \left[p + q\left(\frac{N_{t-1}}{M} \right) \right]\left(M - N_{t-1} \right).$$

Here's what the terms mean: n_t is the number of new adopters or sales in units that occur at time t. Time points might be annual, quarterly, weekly or hourly, etc. Sales (in units volume) doesn't have to actually be sales—it could represent something like the number of new subscribers to Netflix or the number of new subscribers to our modest little blog RSS feed. In social marketing efforts, adoption could represent action (e.g., signing up young adults to vote), or awareness (e.g., spreading information that condoms prevent all kinds of things), etc. What is important is that the numbers represent new adopters. The model doesn't handle repeat purchases (we'll deal with that in other models). The model also doesn't handle sales or profits measured in dollars (so if you wish to apply the diffusion model to sales data that are captured in currency, you have to first assume an average price, and divide back out to get sales data in units or volume).

Next in the model are two parameters that we'll be estimating—p, which is the "coefficient of innovation," and q, the "coefficient of imitation." If p is high, it means that there were strong early sales. If p is low, it means it took longer for the sales to take off. By comparison, q reflects the strength and speed of continued sales. A high q means the product is getting into the rest of the marketplace very quickly, even to customers beyond the innovators. A low q means the product is diffusing relatively slowly throughout the rest of the market (i.e., among the regular folk, the non-innovators). Just to help you calibrate what's high vs. low for p and q—a large-scale meta-study obtained an average p = .04 and an average q = .30, and like these averages, the p:q ratio is frequently on an approximate 1:10 scale.

Figure 9.5 shows 4 scenarios—all possible combinations of low and high p and q. Recall that low p means early adoptions will be slow, and this characteristic is true for the two plots to the left. In contrast, high p means the adoptions are rapid in the beginning, as is seen in the two plots to the right. The two plots on top reflect low q—slow growth among the majority of adopters (after the early buzz dies down). The bottom two plots reflect high q's, which indicate strong, steady, continued growth among the majority in the marketplace.

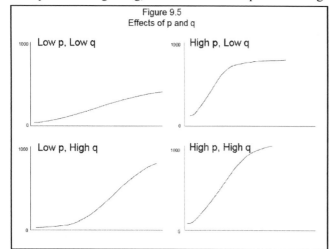

Figure 9.5
Effects of p and q

Marketers who want to make a big, showy flash entry into the marketplace with lots of early sales need to appeal to the innovators—go for high p. Marketers who want to increase the overall size of the pie and have many eventual buyers need to appeal to the imitators (there's more of them then there are innovators)—they should go for high q. Innovators are said to be affected by external influences, meaning, for example, marketing efforts such as advertising. In contrast, imitators are said to be affected by internal influences, primarily the word-of-mouth and reactions of customers who have already tried the new product.

Next, the term N_{t-1} is the number of customers who have already adopted the innovation so far by time t-1. The term M is the best guess at the potential size of the market; the maximum possible, the total number of customers in the target segment, all of whom are expected to eventually adopt the innovation. Thus, comparing these terms in the ratio, $(N_{t-1})/M$ is the proportion of the total market potential who have already adopted, and the difference term, $M-N_{t-1}$, is the number of potential customers out there who haven't yet adopted but whom we expect to see do so with time.

Our sales data cover n_t and N_{t-1} and we'll use the model to estimate p and q. We can use the model to predict M, but it is often better to obtain an independent estimate of M (using market sizing methods we'll discuss later in the chapter), and certainly it would be a good idea to compare estimates of p and q for two different estimates of M, to verify that they converge to reasonably similar values. Also note that while M is important in that it affects the height of the curve or the overall level of sales, it does not affect the shape of the curve, such as when sales begin to grow.

[35] Bass, Frank (1969), "A New Product Growth Model for Consumer Durables," *Management Science*, 15 (5), 215–227.

So how do we use the magical diffusion model? To solve for the estimates we want, the model parameters p and q, we begin with the model:

$$n_t = \left[p + q\left(\tfrac{N_{t-1}}{M}\right)\right](M - N_{t-1}),$$

multiply all the terms out:

$$n_t = pM - pN_{t-1} + qM\left(\tfrac{N_{t-1}}{M}\right) - qN_{t-1}\left(\tfrac{N_{t-1}}{M}\right).$$

In the third term (above) there are M's that cancel, and in the last term, we have a squared N term:

$$n_t = pM - pN_{t-1} + qN_{t-1} - q\left(\tfrac{N_{t-1}^2}{M}\right).$$

Next, let's combine the terms attached to the N_{t-1} pieces:

$$n_t = pM + (q - p)N_{t-1} - \left(\tfrac{q}{M}\right)N_{t-1}^2.$$

At this point, the rearranged diffusion model looks like a regression (if you use your imagination): call "pM" the intercept, and "(q – p)" a regression coefficient for N_{t-1}, and "–(q/M)" a regression coefficient for N_{t-1}^2, then we'd have:

$$n_t = c + bN_{t-1} + aN_{t-1}^2.$$

We have initial sales data for n_t and we can lag and cumulate them to form N_{t-1}, and square them to obtain N_{t-1}^2. If we use N_{t-1} and N_{t-1}^2 as predictors and n_t as the dependent variable, then the regression will estimate the three coefficients we need. (Note that it's not terribly important whether b and a are significant—indeed they're often not—if the number of data points being modeled is small.) As stated above but repeating it to be clear, the terms are defined as:

$$a = -\left(\tfrac{q}{M}\right), \qquad b = (q - p), \qquad c = pM.$$

That's nice, but we don't really want a, b, and c; we want p, q, and M. No problemo. Solving for the model parameters, we use the c = pM relationship to solve for p:

$$p = {^c}/_M$$

and plug that p into the equation for b, b = q – p, to obtain q:

$$q = b + p = b + {^c}/_M$$

where both of these are predicated on having a value for M. For the moment, let's pretend the size of the potential market is 20,000 units.

Figure 9.6
The Good Ol' Zenith HDTV Example

Year	units sold (000s)
1	14
2	121
3	648
4	1460
5	2536
6	4102
7	5705

Figure 9.7
Working Up the HDTVs

Year	n_t units	N_{t-1} cumulative	N_{t-1}^2 cumulative squared
1	14	0	0
2	121	14	196
3	648	135	18,225
4	1460	783	613,089
5	2536	2243	5,031,049
6	4102	4779	22,838,841
7	5705	8881	78,872,161
	total:	14,586	

After all that abstraction, let's see those equations in action. Figure 9.6 shows a now classic data set—the sales in 1000s of units of Zenith HDTVs. Figure 9.7 shows the pre-processing necessary before running the regression. The first sales figures will serve as n_t. To the right, we lag and cumulate those sales and that column will serve as N_{t-1} (so, in this column, 14 is offset as the sales that preceded the 121, and the 135 is the sum of 14 and 121, etc.).

We pop the three variables into the regression:

$$n_t = c + bN_{t-1} + aN_{t-1}^2 + \varepsilon$$

and we obtain these results (with a spiffy $R^2 = 0.989$):

$$n_t = 298.31895 + 1.09468\,N_{t-1} - .00005524\,N_{t-1}^2 + \varepsilon.$$

With these results, we solve for p = (298.31895/20,000) = 0.0149, and q = (1.09468 + 0.0149) = 1.1096. We have seen the rough averages for p = .04 and q = .30, so is our p very small and q very large? Yes and no. It is important to keep in mind that the stated averages for p's and q's are first aggregates over many different kinds of product categories, and hence may not be terribly relevant. In addition, they've been estimated on curves shaped like those in Figures 9.3–9.5, in which sales have peaked and the marketplace is largely saturated, at least among the potential of the first targeted segment of customers. In the HDTV data, even 7 years into the launch, the product was still relatively young (and expensive), and growth was still climbing. Nevertheless, it is true that we can characterize the p as small (slow early adoption) and for the moment, q is large (faster later sales).

We saw a guesstimate of M = 20,000. Estimates of potential market size can come from several places: first, we can derive an estimate for M from this regression; second, we could use the largest cumulative value (i.e., 14,586 in Figure 9.7) as a lower-bound; third, and best (but requiring more work) is the option to obtain an independent estimate (described later in this chapter). To use the regression, we can solve for M in the following manner:

$$M = -\frac{q}{a} = -\frac{\left(b+\frac{c}{M}\right)}{a},$$

multiplying both sides of the equation by "a":

$$Ma = -\left(b + \frac{c}{M}\right) = -b - \frac{c}{M}.$$

Now multiply both sides by M:

$$M^2 a = -Mb - c,$$

and collecting the terms to one side:

$$M^2 a + Mb + c = 0,$$

which we can solve using ye ol' quadratic formula. Shake off your middle school cobwebs:

$$M = \frac{-b \pm \sqrt{b^2 - 4ac}}{2a},$$

in this case,

$$M = \frac{-1.09468 - \sqrt{1.09468^2 - 4(-.00005524)(298.31895)}}{2(-.00005524)} = \frac{-1.09468 - \sqrt{1.1983 + .0659}}{-.00011}$$

$$= \frac{-1.09468 - 1.12438}{-.00011} = \frac{-2.2191}{-.00011} = 20,173.32$$

or rounding up to 20,174 (since these are indivisible units).

Using this newly derived M, alternative estimates for p and q are: p = (298.31895/20,174) = .015, q = (1.09468 + p) = 1.109. Just for comparison, using the value 14,586 (Figure 9.7) as a very rough lower-bound, we'd obtain p = (298.31895/14,586) = .0204 and q = (1.09468 + p) = 1.1151. It would be helpful to be confident in a value for M, to plan for budgetary reasons and such, but the good news from a modeling perspective is that even with 3 different guesstimates for M, the estimates for p and q didn't vary hugely. We'll see more on M shortly.

Some diffusion modelers stop here, but why, when there are more intriguing questions to answer? New questions arise, such as approximately when we might see the peak of the distribution in Figure 9.2, and what will the sales be at that point in time? Such estimates can help us in planning when to build additional plants, hire additional staff, etc. The time at which we'll see peak sales is t_P, and the sales level that we'll see at that peak are s_P. They're both easy formulations using p, q, and M:
$$t_P = \left(\frac{1}{p+q}\right) \ell n \left(\frac{q}{p}\right) \quad \text{and} \quad s_P = \frac{m(p+q)^2}{4q}.$$
The term "peak" implies that the number of new adopters begins to fall afterward, but remember that we're still in the majority portion of the curve. That is, there are still many new customer adoptions ahead, so it's not a time to withdraw marketing support. Furthermore, recall that this model doesn't consider repeat purchases, nor of course does it consider the real world marketing concern of the sales of this TV priming the market for the launch of the subsequent TV model, so we need to keep the marketing dollars flowing.

Before we close on diffusion and turn to the question of market sizing, there are 5 more issues to discuss. First, one concern with this model is that while not many data points are required to begin estimating and forecasting future scenarios, indeed there must be at least a few! Of course we cannot have sales data points without sales, and sales presume the new product has been launched. Thus, the model has been criticized as being limited in its utility as applied to make decisions about launching new products. The criticism is fair, and it motivates other models that we'll see shortly. However, defenders of this model say we can argue from analogy—there are collections of p's and q's online that we might borrow; e.g., in launching DVRs, we might borrow from lessons learned and p's and q's obtained when launching Plasma TVs, VCRs, etc.

Second, the model provides solid estimates when the sales curve has reached the tipping point (just past the midpoint of the early/later majority adopters or beyond). However, if sales haven't yet started to slow, the growth of the sales curve will look more linear. The regression will give a large estimate for b, the coefficient associated with the linear term N_{t-1}, and a miniscule estimate for a, the coefficient associated with N^2_{t-1}, because the sales curve hasn't shown any downturn yet that could be captured by that quadratic term. The main problem with that estimate being small is that it appears in the denominator of the equation for M, and hence that estimate is likely to be hugely inflated. It's helpful to keep in mind that the regression coefficients "b" and "c" should be positive, and "a" negative, because the model parameters should all be positive (i.e., p is a proportion of innovators, q is a proportion of imitators, M is a market size), and recall the relationships between the regression coefficients and the model parameters: $c = pM$, $b = (q - p)$, and $a = -\left(\frac{q}{M}\right)$. If "a," the coefficient for the squared term comes in so small as to not be significant or even slightly positive, take a look at a plot of the data, perhaps there has not yet been a downturn or previous peak in sales. If not, this model won't be as useful as for data that have already shown a peak in new adopters.

Third, some plots of sales show an increase and then a flattening or even decline before a final return to a strong upturn. The pauses in the growth pattern are referred to as saddles, and they're usually attributed to there being two (or more) segments underlying the purchase patterns—that there seems to be a bit of a lag between the first customers (innovators and early adopters) and the later customers (early or later majority). In the popular business press, this delay has been referred to as a chasm. It's important to simply recognize that such a thing may exist. If the data look as described, it can be sensible to fit two diffusion curves rather than one. Marketers might try to close the gap (if so desired) with trial discounts, etc.

Fourth, the diffusion model is impressive in its applicability, and it is intuitively appealing to capture the natural impetus of customers trying new products, through the phenomena of being innovative and word-of-mouth affecting imitators. Yet notice that marketing efforts aren't even present in the model. To address this concern, a more general model has been developed that can incorporate terms representing, say, price at time t, or advertising dollars spent at time t–1 and so on. While that particular model is fit through some complications, ordinary regressions approximate those results fairly well. If we add terms to our regression, say $n_t = c + b\,N_{t-1} + a\,N_{t-1}^2 + w_1\,Price_t + w_2\,Ad_{t-1}$, we'd still have estimates of a, b, and c, to use in calculating p, q, and M, and in addition, we'd have estimates for the effects of price and advertising. Furthermore, all these effects are estimated simultaneously, so that each coefficient is the result of having partialled out, or statistically controlled for, the other effects. An alternative, again keeping the modeling simple, would be to fit the original diffusion model, obtain a, b, and c to derive p and q, and then take the residuals from that model and model them as a function of the pricing and advertising variables. However, marketplace actions are fraught with chicken-and-egg problems—did advertising increase sales, or were sales inching up on their own, and with the sales successes, more marketing resources were allocated, and the like. Those kinds of associations make it smarter to estimate all of these effects at once, rather than parsing the model, obtaining the original p and q, then adding back in advertising terms, and pretending the effects work independently. In addition, this approach using residuals tends to result in parameters estimates that are not as close to the ones obtained by fitting all the terms at once (whose parameters were close to those of the complicated model).

In his book, *Diffusions of Innovations*, Everett Rogers offers several factors that predictably influence the speed of diffusion. For example, diffusion of a new product is likely to be more rapid if a) it has a clear relative advantage to other products already in the marketplace; b) it is compatible with the customers' lifestyle and, e.g., current equipment; c) it is something where trial is easy and inexpensive; and d) it's something that customers can observe an innovator using, hence facilitating their imagining the product's utility for themselves. Diffusion is slower when: a) the new product is complicated and its benefits are unclear, and b) there is risk, as in high prices or untested features, etc. To date, these factors have been treated from a qualitative perspective, but each could be quantified and used to generalize the model further.

Market Sizing

One of the first questions that arises as managers begin to ponder new product development is whether there is a market for the new product. More precisely, the question is whether the market is large enough or price-insensitive enough that the new product is likely to be profitable. The best technique for estimating the size of a market is relatively simple, and it can be refined to the extent necessary (e.g., ballpark estimates vs. numbers to insert in spreadsheets for budgets). This technique is also the one we've intimated as a means of obtaining a good estimate of M, independent of the diffusion model in which it's used.

Markets are sized by beginning with a number attached to the maximum size of the relevant population as a universe, and then focusing in on increasingly relevant groups to obtain an estimate of the number of possible target customers. If you like Venn diagrams, think of a large bubble representing the entire population, and a series of smaller, concentric bubbles inside representing our efforts to focus in on the target population as cleanly as possible. For example, the entire population might be "all consumers in Indonesia." If that's the case, go online and find out Indonesia's population. If we need to target adults as the purchaser, then we need to know the age distribution as well. If the product is targeted to children and they are effective at "pull" (influencing their parents), then we might need to capture numbers on children instead.

No diffusion, no [illegible] of test

The logic is obviously easy. The skill is determining the factors that are relevant to reduce the population numbers to a base of relevant target customers. At the most abstract level, we can summarize this approach with the following rough model:

$ Sales Potential = Market Potential (units) $\times$ Probability of Purchase $\times$ Price.

Marketers have control over prices that are set, and of course we must keep in mind that a price point helps determine the attractiveness of a product to a customer, hence affecting the probability that they purchase. Our effect on market potential and probability of purchase is more complicated and less direct than simply quoting a price, but we can make our products as fabulous as possible.

The sales potential model shows the simple form of the market sizing technique—it's a series of figures that are chained together (indeed, these models are sometimes referred to as chain models). The chain is often comprised of a series of proportions and probabilities (ignoring price for the moment). For example, imagine that you're sitting through one of those obnoxious "consulting" interviews, and the interviewer asks you a question out of the blue, about a product line you're not working on and know nothing about, such as, "If I made artistic lenses for men's reading glasses, how big is the U.S. market?" Take a deep breath and think it through. String together the following:

market size = U.S. population (~310,000,000) $\times$ 0.47 (a little less than half are male)

$\times$ 4/8 (reading glasses are mostly for men in their 40s, 50s, 60s, and 70s)

$\times$ 2 (each owns at least 2 pairs of reading glasses) = 145,700,000 so far.

Just roughing out an estimate, such as that above, we can take it forward and use it, or we can obtain better estimates of the pieces, consider the insertion of additional factors, or both. In taking the estimate forward, it is a good idea to run a sensitivity analysis. In this scenario, here's how it would work. Set up a spreadsheet with headers: U.S. population, proportion male, reading glasses ownership, etc. The last column would be "model predicted result," from whatever model we're using to get this estimate, such as the diffusion model.

Then, change the estimate of any piece (e.g., obtain a more precise estimate of the population or the number of readers anyone owns, etc.), insert it into a new line in the spreadsheet and into the model, see what the model yields with the new input, and insert the new model result in the proper location in the spreadsheet. If the change on the input resulted in minimal change in the output, that means that the model is pretty robust (or insensitive) and that the precision of that particular input isn't terribly important. When model outputs vary more as a function of different estimates for some model component, then we know that that variable is particularly important (it impacts the model a lot), so we need to be sure that the number for that model input is as precise as possible. Again, the logic isn't complicated and estimates of pieces are often online. We just need to be smart about what elements go into the model.

Test Market Models

Part of the fun of models is that there is often more than one way to do something. In this section, we'll look at two commercial forecasting models that offer an alternative way of looking at new adoptions. Both proceed to capture repeat purchasing as well.

Assessor

The first is a classic marketing model called "Assessor."[36] This model is intended to get a read on likely market receptivity before launching a new product. It was created in part to address the concern that real world test markets are sometimes impractical. They can be very expensive, they require up and running plants for manufacturing or personnel to be hired and trained for customer services, competitors can see what you're developing and have often played leap-frog, bringing to market a version of what you're testing, etc. So, pre-test market models, or simulated test models, have become popular when you are trying to identify products that could be successful, or to find what needs to be tweaked (including price or the proposed ad campaign) before launch.

Assessor comprises an 8-step procedure: 1) screen and recruit customers, 2) survey them for current brand attitudes and preferences, 3) show them an ad for the current brands and for the new brand, 4) survey them regarding the ad materials, 5) simulate a shopping trip, e.g., show a virtual reality shelf-facing of the new brand in among the current brands, 6) record which brand they choose, 7) send them home to use the brand with their family, and 8) follow up with a survey about how they liked the brand.

---

[36] Silk, Alvin J., and Glen L. Urban (1978), "Pre-Test-Market Evaluation of New Packaged Goods: A Model and Measurement Methodology," *Journal of Marketing Research*, 15 (May), 171–191, now offered at MarcResearch.com.

The model begins simply enough, stating that the new brand will achieve market share M as a function of trial T and share of repeat S: $M = T \times S$. There is then a model for T and another for S. Trial is thought to be a function of several factors. First, there is a probability that the product will be purchased for the first time, F, assuming there is complete awareness and availability. F is often estimated by the proportion of the new brand choice in step 6 above. K represents the extent of knowledge or awareness in the market; that is, while F assumes that K is at 100%, the K factor is in the model to adjust the model to the true level of awareness. Managers can enhance K by spending a lot on advertising. Similarly, D represents distribution or the extent to which the product will be available anywhere. Managers can control D or at least input a good quantification of it, as the proportion of retail outlets in which the new brand will appear, and that number can be further weighted by the sales volumes per stores. C represents the proportion of consumers who will receive a sample of the new brand, and U is the proportion of those who will use it. Together, then, a trial is modeled as FKD + CU and we subtract off their product to erase the joint double-counting (FKD)(CU): $T = FKD + CU - (FKD)(CU)$.

Next, managers formulate an estimation of the share of repeat purchases, S, as a function of a transition matrix, like we did in Chapter 3 to study brand loyalty and brand switching. For now, it's easy enough to track that $= \frac{R(k,m)}{1+R(k,m)-R(m,m)}$. R(k,m) is the probability that a customer who bought any of the existing brands, k, during their last shopping trip will purchase the new brand, m, this time. R(m,m) are the customers who are already loyal to the new brand—they bought brand m last time and this term reflects the probability that they'll buy brand m this time also. Initial estimates of the numbers of switchers and loyals come from the data obtained in step 8 in the Assessor procedure.

Finally, there is another part of the Assessor model to capture preferences. The structure of this part of the model is like comparative utilities (again, discussed in Chapter 3 regarding logits). Basically, consumers are predicted to prefer a brand if their utility for that brand is greater than their utility for the other brands. The terms utility and preference are used essentially interchangeably. These preference estimates can also be useful in estimating the F term in the T model. This model has been widely used in the CPG arena to help many marketing managers make relatively accurate forecasts of customers adopting and repurchasing their brands.

Bases

The second model is also a classic marketing model, called Bases (now a part of Nielsen). Bases begins like the Assessor model, saying that a new product will achieve market share M as a function of trial T and repeat R: $M = T \times R$. Sometimes that equation is further tweaked by adding a term to represent how much additional volume might be expected at any given point in time due to promotional sales.

Next, the trial term T is modeled as a function of several terms. First, P represents cumulative penetration thus far. It's like N_{t-1} in the diffusion model. In the Bases formulation, P is a function of two factors we've seen before, in the Assessor model, K, the knowledge (or awareness) factor, and D, the distribution factor. In addition, Bases brings in an estimate for customer purchase intentions (I) for the new product. Furthermore, those purchase intentions are scaled, usually downward, calibrated (C) by managerial judgment based on in-house data and experiences of the extent to which that intention score is likely overestimated. Thus far, we have: $P = C \times I \times K \times D$. The next terms in the T model include: U, the average number of units bought; Si, a seasonality index; TM, the size of the target market (like M in the diffusion model); and CDI, a term called category development index, essentially a wiggle room factor to reflect the strength of the product category in the target market. Together, the trial forecast is:

$$T = P\,U\left(\tfrac{1}{Si}\right)(TM)\left(\tfrac{1}{CDI}\right) = \left(\frac{PU(TM)}{(Si)(CDI)}\right).$$

The Bases model for share of repeat builds on the logic of Assessor:

$$R_t = \sum_{i=1}^{\infty} N_{i-1,t} Y_{it} U_i,$$

where R_t is the repeat volume estimate for week t, $N_{i-1,t}$ is the cumulative number of customers who repeat purchased at least i-1 times by week t (so, e.g., $N_{0,t}$ is the volume of initial trials). Y_{it} is a conditional term—given that $i - 1$ repeat purchases were made up to week t, how many will repeat on the ith purchase. Last is that U term again, the average number of units purchased. (Note that the summation goes to infinity—those Bases people are funny little optimists, aren't they.)

Permeating the Assessor and Bases models is a fundamental belief in the underlying concepts about marketing and consumer behavior, that a customer must be aware of a brand or product before they will seek it out, it must be available for purchase, and then purchase and perhaps repeat can follow: awareness → availability → trial → repeat. If we believe that marketing actions can affect these elements, then there need to be factors in the models that reflect those relationships. For example, greater advertising spending can help both with brand awareness to enhance initial purchase as well as to shorten the purchase cycle to enhance the repeat rate. In addition, at least among consumer packaged goods, it's known that customers falling off and turning to competitors' brands is not a good thing—if we can get repeat even just once to obtain a second purchase, we're likely to see repeat again and again (second purchases are highly correlated with the third, and fourth, etc.), so we must be confident in our products, our value proposition, or we must issue valuable coupons, or try some other tack.

Few firms will try to create such testing environments on their own—they're more inclined to hire a marketing research agency to do so. This chapter has illustrated the models so the manager can make thoughtful requests of the researchers and understand the content and processes of the methodology.

Summary

It's amazing how frequently in business a forecast of future sales is desired. There are many modeling approaches to try to predict likely future scenarios. The diffusion model, and the Assessor and Bases models, are three examples of forecasting models—they are structured by logic, they require certain measures and assumptions, and they result in projections about sales.

Forecasting simply means prediction, just like in standard regression models. It's never a bad idea to begin with a regression—it's a model that is well understood (by you, the model builder) and others (to whom you'll be communicating results), and it's a robust and powerful statistical methodology. In addition, as simple as regression is as a model, we can finesse a number of things and make the model far more sophisticated. For example, while correlations and regressions assume linear relationships, we can build in nonlinearities by squaring a predictor. We can include dummy variables to represent predictable factors (such as holiday season sales) or intervention factors (such as sales promos). We can increase the stability of our model against random perturbations by leveraging past knowledge and data, computing something smoother like a moving average ("tomorrow's weather will look much like today's"; "the next brand of toothpaste that you buy will probably be the same as your last").

Most forecasting models are rather straightforward applications of regressions and chaining models. In the real world, managers are convinced about the results of one model over another mostly by demonstrations of the models' relative accuracies. One R^2 that exceeds another by what seems like a small amount can translate into the making or savings of millions of dollars. And ultimately, what contributes to a greater R^2, and what makes one model superior to and more useful than another, is the intelligence behind the design and the model elements.

References

For a catalog of average (historical) p's and q's for numerous product categories for analogical reasoning or comparison:
* Bayus, Barry L. (1992), "Have Diffusion Rates Been Accelerating Over Time?," *Marketing Letters*, 3 (3), 215-226.
* Sultan, Fareena, John U. Farley, and Donald R. Lehmann (1990), "A Meta-Analysis of Applications of Diffusion Models," *Journal of Marketing Research*, 27 (1), 70-77.

Additional diffusion materials:
* Rogers, Everett (2003), *Diffusion of Innovations*, 5th ed., New York: Free Press.
* Danaher, Peter J., Bruce G. S. Hardie, and William P. Putsis, Jr. (2001), "Marketing-Mix Variables and the Diffusion of Successive Generations of a Technological Innovation" *Journal of Marketing Research*, 38 (Nov.), 501-514.

Diffusion models do not need special software; just use the regression procedure in your favorite statistical computing package.

Chapter 10: Word-of-Mouth and Social Networks and Network Analyses

Marketing Concept: Social Networks
Modeling Concept: Network Analyses

Chapter Outline
1. Introduction
2. Social Networks Methods
   a. Micro-Analysis: Actor Indices
   b. Meso-Analysis: Subgroups within the Network
   c. Macro-Analysis: Studies of the Network as a Whole
   d. Statistical Network Models
3. Word-of-Mouth Principles

Introduction

Social networks seem to be everywhere these days. It's hard to remember life before Facebook. Brand characters like BK's Burger King, Tony the Tiger, the Maytag repairman, and Betty Crocker have their own pages. Companies are using this medium for traditional marketing activities—posting ads, information, coupons, and such, as well as experimenting with new means of engaging customers—hosting customer discussions, asking brand fans to "friend them," etc. Brand communities and customer clubs like Swatch.com, Harley's hog.com, or Volkswagen's vw-club.de are supported, often with no apparent or immediate commercial gain, as if seeking popularity as an end in itself.

Of course, social networks have always existed, as friends, tribes, nations, members of clubs who come together for mutual interests, etc. In marketing, one of the ways that networks were thought about long before they could be tracked is in their role supporting word-of-mouth communication used to diffuse information about new products. Even Red Bull, when it was small and entrepreneurial (i.e., with a shoestring budget) launched via seeding samples in trendy clubs and bars to generate buzz (about the drink's buzz).

For most marketers, social networks end there. But savvier marketers can take advantage of the fact that networks generate data. The great news is that network models are big bang for the buck—they're relatively easy to use and yet very illuminating.

Social Network Methods

All kinds of sociometric studies have been conducted—tracking patterns of friendship among children and respect among monks, emotional support for the chronically ill, emails flowing among co-workers, etc. All kinds of methods have been used to collect the network data, including self-report interviews and surveys (e.g., name your three best friends), observation (e.g., time spent together), and of course increasingly, electronic history traces. And all kinds of questions have been asked and answered, for example:

- dating sites tend to show homophily, or similarity and attraction (i.e., "birds of a feather flock together" is in effect far more frequently than "opposites attract"),
- industry regulators worry about a lack of objectivity of corporate boards because directorships often show a lot of overlap in the executives serving on each others' boards, naturally raising concerns about mutual gains ("you scratch my back and I'll scratch yours"),
- counter-terrorism teams use networks to smoke out criminals because bad guys frequently rat on each other ("no honor among thieves"),
- it has been shown consistently that friendships develop in predictable patterns, namely, social connections are highly correlated with physical proximity (we're lazy and don't venture far from our own offices).

Studies on networks that are not social have also been popular. Much of epidemiology is the study of who passes cooties to whom. In transportation, experts try to design efficient routes from point to point such as those exemplified by an airline's hub-and-spoke system or a city's metro. In communications, networks use satellites as hubs and try to offer sufficient bandwidth so as to support customer demand for voice and data. In web analytics, we study frequencies of activated paths to identify strong sources and attractive site destinations, information that marketers can use to set online advertising pricing.

At first glance, these network examples are so diverse that it would seem they have nothing in common. Yet they all share the basic elements of networks—each has a set of "actors" or "nodes" that are connected via "relational ties" or "links." In this chapter, we'll keep things simple by consistently choosing to refer to actors and ties. Network methods are used to analyze the structure of interconnections and identify patterns of interest.

In marketing networks, the actors are frequently customers, as in studies of family purchase decision making or buyers and sellers dynamically negotiating an exchange. Actors might be employees whose communication ties in small, new firms show more widespread flow than those who work in hierarchical, bureaucratic companies. Actors might also be firms, as when marketers study power conflicts among distribution channel members, or cooperative alliances in global joint ventures.

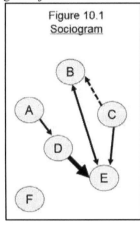

Figure 10.1
Sociogram

Figure 10.1 shows a network drawn as a graph, known in network studies as a sociogram. This sociogram shows 6 actors who are connected by ties that vary in strength and directionality. Some network analysts prefer to work only with binary information—a pair of actors is connected or not—whereas other networkers like to retain the information contained in the tie strengths. In addition, the figure also depicts some ties as mutual and others as asymmetric. These qualities may be inherent to the information sought (e.g., if B is a classmate of E, then E is a classmate of B) or they may arise as a function of how the relational tie data are gathered (e.g., A goes to D for advice, but D does not reciprocate, instead D seeks help from E).

Diagrams of network connections illustrate many structural properties, such as the popularity of E, the isolation of F, the group of mutually connected actors B, C, and E (called "cliques" in network studies), and so forth. As networks get larger, it's more illuminating to analyze the network systematically by transforming the graph into matrix form, in network studies, called a "sociomatrix." Figure 10.2 shows the matrix form of the relationships in Figure 10.1. In the matrix, the actors comprise the rows and the columns, and the element in the ith row and j^{th} column describes the relationship between actors i and j. For example, there is no tie from B to C and a weak one from C to B, so the B,C data point is 0 and the C,B data point is a 1 (stronger ties in Figure 10.1 are represented with larger values in Figure 10.2). Let's see how the matrix form enables analyses.

Imagine the matrix in Figure 10.2 with even more actors, so that there would be far more rows and columns. Now the matrix starts to resemble a spreadsheet, and we can run through a variety of statistical models that we might apply to these data. Most statistical models are focused on understanding the associations among the columns, which usually represent variables measured on the row entities, which are usually customers. Furthermore, many statistical models (such as regression) assume that the observations in the rows are independent. In networks, the rows are absolutely not independent—the whole point of networks is that some actors (rows, columns) are tied. Analysts who don't know about networks would view the violation of the independence assumption as a problem to work around, but network modelers don't see the interdependencies among the observations as a mere statistical nuisance—instead, the interdependencies are the very thing of interest.

There are many kinds of network models, measures, indices, etc., and it helps to simplify things by recognizing that most of them fall into one of three classes. There are network methods for analyzing the patterns at the micro level of the actors, the meso level of the subgroups within the larger network, or at the macro level of the whole network itself. Figure 10.3 illustrates these levels, and we proceed to consider examples of each.

Figure 10.2
Sociomatrix

	A	B	C	D	E	F
A	-	0	0	2	0	0
B	0	-	0	0	2	0
C	0	1	-	0	2	0
D	0	0	0	-	4	0
E	0	2	0	0	-	0
F	0	0	0	0	0	-

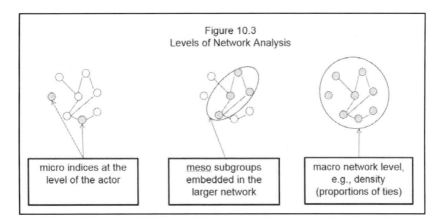

Figure 10.3
Levels of Network Analysis

| micro indices at the level of the actor | meso subgroups embedded in the larger network | macro network level, e.g., density (proportions of ties) |

Micro: Actors

The most frequent question posed about the actors in a network is about their centrality. An actor's centrality is an index that reflects the extent to which the actor is in the thick of things and therefore, the extent to which the actor is important relative to others.

The simplest index is called "degree centrality," C_D, and it captures the number of connections each actor has. Figure 10.4 shows a sociomatrix for g actors and depicts a row sum and a column sum. Given that the sociomatrix elements i,j reflect relational ties extending from i toward j, the row sums capture the level of activity or number of ties extended from actor i. This sum, within a row (for actor i) over columns (partners j) is referred to as i's out-degree: $C_{D-out}(i) = \sum_{j \neq i}^{g} x_{ij}$. This outgoing index is sometimes called expansiveness, and could reflect extraversion, for example. If the social network ties reflected "person who tweets to lots of people," then the out-degree would reflect something like chattiness.

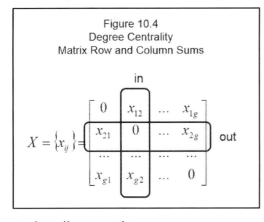

Figure 10.4
Degree Centrality
Matrix Row and Column Sums

$$X = \{x_{ij}\} = \begin{bmatrix} 0 & x_{12} & \cdots & x_{1g} \\ x_{21} & 0 & \cdots & x_{2g} \\ \cdots & \cdots & \cdots & \cdots \\ x_{g1} & x_{g2} & \cdots & 0 \end{bmatrix}$$

in

out

Conversely, the column sums capture incoming activity from others toward actor i, so these sums are called in-degrees. The in-degree for actor i is obtained by summing the matrix elements within the ith column for actor i over all rows: $C_{D-in}(i) = \sum_{i \neq j}^{g} x_{ij}$. The in-degree is often referred to as reflecting the popularity of the actor, because it is higher when many other actors seek this actor out, perhaps to friend them on Facebook. When few or no actors seek this actor out, the actor's in-degree is smaller, and the actor is said to be less popular.

If network ties are all symmetric (e.g., "actors i and j are co-workers"), then the row sums will equal the column sums. If inter-actor ties are measured with strengths, the in- and out-degrees reflect the weighted ties. Degree centrality is by far the most commonly used actor index in network studies for two reasons: first, it is easy to understand conceptually and second, it is trivially easy to compute, even for large-scale, online networks.

There are other kinds of centrality indices that capture other network structural qualities. For example, "closeness centrality" expresses which actors seem to be relatively interconnected with many others in the network compared with the actors who are more distant with ties to others that are fewer in number or weaker in strength. The index C_C is computed for each of the g actors by first finding the shortest distance between each pair of actors, i and j (that shortest distance is called the geodesic), d_{ij}. Closeness is defined by taking the reciprocal of the average geodesics connected to actor i: $C_C(i) = 1/\sum_{j=1, i \neq j}^{g} d_{ij}$. Figure 10.5 shows a comparison of two network structures. Both networks have the same number of actors, and both have the same number of ties. The difference is that the star actor is relatively closer to the others in the left network than in the right network.

Another actor criterion is called "betweenness centrality." It captures the number of times an actor is found on the shortest tie (geodesic) between any pair of actors: $C_B(i) = \sum_{j<k}^{g} (g_{jk}(i)/g_{jk})$. Figure 10.6 illustrates two networks, where the star actor has a higher betweenness centrality score on the left than on the right. In the network to the left, the star actor serves as a bridge between the others. In a company, this actor might be the sole person who can speak

"marketing" and "engineering," for example. Both groups depend upon this bridge person. Thus, even though this star actor has only 2 ties (i.e., the degree centrality isn't huge), the actor is very important to the flow of information throughout the network. In the network at the right, there are additional ties connecting the subgroups. Even if they are weak ties (per the dashes), they serve as connectors, thus reducing the importance of the star actor as a go-between or gatekeeper.

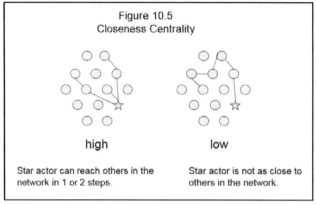

Figure 10.5
Closeness Centrality

high

low

Star actor can reach others in the network in 1 or 2 steps.

Star actor is not as close to others in the network.

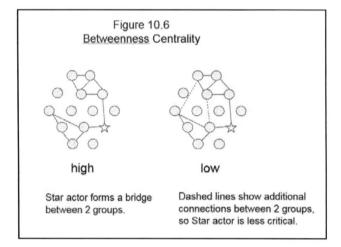

Figure 10.6
Betweenness Centrality

high

low

Star actor forms a bridge between 2 groups.

Dashed lines show additional connections between 2 groups, so Star actor is less critical.

Meso: Subgroups

A middle ground between micro and macro is the meso study of networks. In network models, this class of inquiry concerns identifying subgroups that are embedded in the larger network. There are many ways to define and analyze such groups, but two distinctions are important and popular: cliques and structural equivalence. Cliques look for sets of actors who are tightly interconnected. Structural equivalence identifies actors who are similar vis-à-vis their connections with others.

Cliques are defined as a subset of 3 or more actors, all of whom are connected pairwise (a dyad—2 connected actors—doesn't count as a clique). Figure 10.7 shows a network on the left with two cliques, and a network on the right with the same number of actors and ties but no cliques. Whether the actors are consumers or companies, the tight grouping depicted in Figure 10.7 at the left shows how cliques are indicative of cohesiveness.

Cliques can be beneficial, as when the ties represent communication and sharing information. Cliques in other applications can be more troublesome, for example, as in coalition formation and negotiation disputes. Whether a quality of a network (centrality, cliques, etc.) is good or bad depends on the setting and the content of the relational tie data measured and represented in the network.

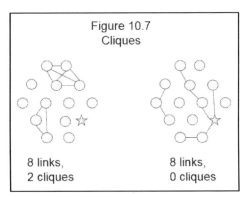

Figure 10.7
Cliques

8 links,
2 cliques

8 links,
0 cliques

Strictly speaking, a clique is defined as a "maximal complete sub-graph," meaning that it's the largest number of actors who are completely connected to each other. So, for example, Figure 10.7 shows a clique of size 3 and another of size 4. In the network to the right, there is a set of 3 actors that has 2 of the actors tied, but the third dyad is not, so the 3 actors do not form a clique, whereas the triangle of 3 fully connected actors in the left network is a clique. You might imagine too that as the potential clique size grows, the likelihood that all actors are interconnected lessens. For example, a clique of 5 actors would require all 10 pairs of ties to exist, and if even 1 did not, the connections would not comprise a clique.

Many networkers think this definition is a little restrictive, so there are other definitions of clique-related characteristics that capture whether a group of actors are highly interconnected, even if it's not the case that they're all connected pairwise. One such more relaxed definition of a clique uses the criterion of "k-core." A network has a k-core clique if each actor in the clique is connected to at least k others in that group. Thus, say for k = 3, a clique of 10 might exist, as long as each of the 10 is connected to at least 3 of the others in the set of 10. Another more relaxed definition of cliques is called an n-clique, and it works by identifying groups in which all of the pairs of actors are connected, but perhaps not directly. A network has an n-clique if each actor in the clique is connected to all the others, either directly or indirectly through a series of ties of length n. For example, for 10 actors and n = 2, the idea is that actor i is connected to all the other 9 actors either directly (e.g., i and j are friends) or through one other person (i is a friend of a friend, represented by i→k→j).

The first definition of cliques, as maximal complete sub-graphs, may be pure, and it helps envision the ideal form sought by a technique identifying subgroups within the larger network, but it should be clear that either the k-core or n-cliques criteria would be more realistic and more likely to be useful in the analysis of real world network data. The k-core cliques relax the clique restriction on actors, and n-cliques relax the clique restriction on direct ties. In modeling, it is a good idea to begin with the pure definition to find the number of most compact, complete cliques, the number of which would presumably be a lower-bound when relaxing the assumptions and applying the k-core or n-cliques methods.

The other major meso-technique in network analysis is finding sets of actors who are structurally equivalent. In structural equivalence, it doesn't matter whether the actors in the group are themselves interconnected. Rather, two or more actors are identified as structurally equivalent if they are similar vis-à-vis their ties to others, specifically, if they have the same patterns of connections to others in the network. For example, Figure 10.8 shows two starred actors, both of whom are connected to exactly the same set of 3 others. Here too, we begin with the strict definition, but other versions of the techniques are more relaxed; they're probabilistic in the sense that if one of the ties for one of the stars were missing, but the others were identical to the other star, the two starred actors would be defined as stochastically (statistically) equivalent.

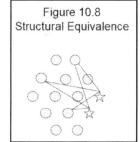

Figure 10.8
Structural Equivalence

Sets of structurally equivalent actors are found using cluster-like techniques. A popular method is called "con-cor," which stands for converging correlations. The technique begins with the raw sociomatrix, X, and if the ties are symmetric, it computes the correlation matrix for all the columns in the sociomatrix. The columns of that correlation matrix are computed for their inter-correlations, the correlations among the next set of correlations are computed, etc., repeatedly until the correlations themselves all converge to ±1. The rows and columns of the matrix are then permuted into blocks of 1's indicating a mass of ties that the actors share in common, making them roughly equivalent. (For sociomatrices that are not symmetric, the technique begins by first stacking X on top of its transpose, X' in which all the rows of X become the columns of X' and all the columns of X become the rows of X'. Including X and X' is important so that the information about incoming ties in X is complemented with the outgoing ties in X'.)

There are other techniques for finding structurally equivalent actors. A technique related to factor analysis (Chapter 4) is the extraction of the eigenvectors of X and X' or the row and column vectors from a correspondence analysis on X and X' (recall the method from Chapter 6).

Before leaving the topic of structural equivalence, it is worth noting a popular contemporary use. Recall in the presentation of cluster analytical techniques of Chapter 2 that recommendation agents are effectively seeking patterns of similarity. At Facebook and LinkedIn, the recommendation engine looks for people, say persons A and B, whose sets of established connections look similar, to recommend friends of A as potential friends to B (and vice versa). At Amazon, the recommendation agent looks for customers whose purchases are similar to make recommendation about SKUs: items that A has bought that B might find interesting (and vice versa).

In networks like Facebook and LinkedIn, the sociomatrices comprise the actors as both the rows and columns, representing one modality—the actors in the network. In networks like Amazon, the data matrix is called two-mode—customers comprise the rows and SKUs for purchase (or cultural events attended, etc.) form the columns. For Facebook, recommendations are made based on culling the data to look for rows (or columns, or both) that show similar patterns. For Amazon, recommendations are based on looking for rows (customers) that resemble each other with respect to the columns.

In an altogether geekier application, structural equivalence is also used to assist analyses of the network sort and others on monster-sized data sets. The technique is used to first simplify the set of actors from some number like one million (customers) down to say a dozen (segments), wherein each of the actors within a group are so similar and structurally equivalent that they can be treated as a unit in other analyses.

Finally, real world uses of social networks can easily blend the notion of cliques, in which friends form a group, and structural equivalence, in which similar customers form a group. Companies like Groupon, issuing coupons to groups, count on the groups being populated in large part by people making their friends aware of offers while simultaneously being formed by people with similar preferences and purchase proclivities.

Macro: Networks

There are a few measures that can be used to characterize a network as a whole. One is to compute its density, which is the proportion of ties that exist compared to the number of pairs of actors in the network that could be connected. A proportional measure of density isn't that informative on its own, but it can be very helpful when comparing structures of two or more networks. For example, we might expect the communications among employees to yield a denser network for an entrepreneurial comprising R&D and engineers in biotech than, say, a more competitive or hierarchical and bureaucratic firm.

Other techniques allow networkers to use one sociomatrix to predict another, as when examining sequential network structures, for example in longitudinal studies to learn whether the network structure in an organization's early days looks like or helps to predict how the firm develops subsequently, or whether a network structure looks the same before and after some perturbation such as a change in industry regulations or economic conditions. This technique has also been used to compare cross-cultural networks, such as by looking at network properties at companies with greater or lesser marketing orientations, or whether local offices of multinational firms have similar structures in different countries.

Statistical Networks Models

Many network techniques share the property that they are descriptive in nature. There is no question that those descriptions can be rich and compelling—the graphs alone make many people's eyes pop. Beyond being descriptive, there are a few classes of network models that are inferential. They posit probabilistic models that may be used to formulate and test hypotheses about actors and their patterns of interrelationships in networks.[37]

For example, when we look at data, we might identify a person who seems to have more friends on Facebook than others, or a person who exerts seemingly more tweets than the average person, or a CEO who seems to sit on more boards than most CEOs, or a company that might be involved in more alliances than others in its industry, etc. Statistical models can tell us whether those patterns are statistically significant, or just large but within the bounds of statistical sampling and typical results.

To test such propositions, we'll call an actor i who relates to partner j with tie strength k (x_{ij} in a sociomatrix like Figure 10.2), and a partner j who relates to i at level m (x_{ji} in a sociomatrix), for actors i = 1, 2, ..., g, and partners j = 1, 2, ..., g, and tie strengths k, m = 1, 2, ..., C. Then define a large indicator matrix of order $g^2 \times C^2$: $Y_{ijkm} = 1$ if $x_{ij} =$ k and $x_{ji} = m$, and = 0 otherwise. We can model the probability that the (i,j) dyad takes on the relational values (x_{ij}, x_{ji}) = (k,m), denoted π_{ijkm} as follows:

$$\ell n\, \pi_{ijkm} = \lambda_{ij} + \theta_k + \theta_m + \alpha_{i(k)} + \alpha_{j(m)} + \beta_{j(k)} + \beta_{i(m)} + \rho_{km}.$$

The λ's assure that the probabilities sum to 1.0 for each dyad, and the θ's are like grand mean effects for the level of the relational ties (e.g., is the overall outgoing tie of strength 0.5 or 1,250?). Then the model gets interesting. The α

[37] Iacobucci and Hopkins, "Modeling Dyadic Interactions and Networks in Marketing," *Journal of Marketing Research*, vol.29, 5-17; Iacobucci, "Modeling Multivariate Sequential Dyadic Interactions," *Social Networks*, vol.11, 315-362.

parameters will reflect the combination of the expansiveness of the actors and the strengths or volumes of their outgoing ties, and conversely, the β's will capture the incoming effects. The α's and β's are analogous to out-degrees and in-degrees, but they're more versatile than simple counts, and recall this is a probabilistic model, so we can test hypotheses about whether there are any significant differences among the actors in their outgoing or incoming tie patterns. The final parameter, ρ, reflects the extent to which ties in the networks are reciprocated and mutual, vs. asymmetric.

The network model is easily fit, and the parameter hypotheses tested, using a straightforward set of logit models (just as in Chapter 3). It is also a model that is easily extended, in ways that the descriptive techniques cannot. For example, if we measured a network at multiple points in time, we would extend the definition of Y to $Y_{ij,k1,m1,k2,m2,...,kt,mt}$ and fit a model that would include α's say at the multiple points in time, $\alpha_1, \alpha_2, ..., \alpha_t$, as well as new parameters that would reflect auto-correlative relationships, $\tau_{k1,k2}$, or dominance patterns in one actor's behaviors influencing partners more than the reverse, say ω_{k1m2} vs. ω_{m1k2}. More generally, multivariate ties may be fit, e.g., if a company was measured for its social ties vs. its reporting lines, etc., we could see whether the α's or β's varied as a function of the kind of relational tie, and whether they were themselves correlated or distinct.

Finally, unlike most network methods, these models allow us to incorporate attributes of the actors into the model. If we're not really interested in actors i and j, but really more interested in segments "old" and "young," then we would code all actors into one of these sets, and model the sets. For example, we might guess that at work, younger people are more likely to go to the more experienced older people for advice and help on work projects. Then we would test whether younger people are more expansive than older people, and older people more popular than younger people. We'd posit: H_0: $\alpha_{oldk} = \alpha_{youngk}$ and H_0: $\beta_{oldm} = \beta_{youngm}$, test them, and see. Way awesome.

Another issue that this modeling approach highlights is that IRL, social networks can be huge. Unlike the sociomatrix in Figure 10.2, it would be inefficient to store very large networks as sociomatrices. Imagine all 905 million members of Facebook as the rows and columns of a network spreadsheet. It would be huge. Furthermore, that format of storage would also be inefficient because most of the matrices' cell entries are zeros—most people on Facebook know fewer than .000001% of all the others on Facebook.

Thus, instead of storing network data as a full and sparse matrix, they are more often stored as a data set listing the ties in the network. For example, in Figures 101 and 10.2, the network has 6 ties. The data set would be stored with variables: "actor i," "partner j," and "tie from i→j," specifically: (1,4,2), (2,5,2), (3,2,1), (3,5,2), (4,5,4), (5,2,2).

Word-of-Mouth Principles

Whether online or IRL, marketers have always been interested in at least one form of network—word-of-mouth. When a friend tells another about some new product or offers a recommendation for a good hair stylist or dentist, the recipient trusts this information. People can be skeptical of advertisements, because the purpose of ads is to be persuasive. In contrast, a friend typically doesn't have any commercial interest in offering the advice. Thus word-of-mouth is a powerful force.

Figure 10.9
Word of Mouth Networks

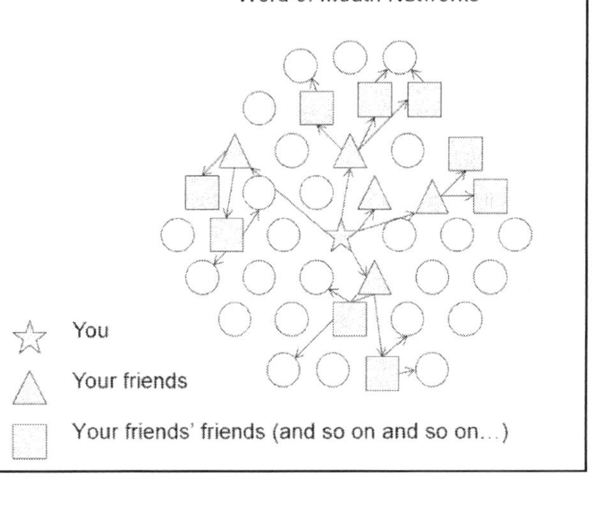

☆ You

△ Your friends

☐ Your friends' friends (and so on and so on...)

In word-of-mouth networks, communications flow between customers diffusing knowledge of new products throughout the marketplace. Figure 10.9 depicts a word-of-mouth network that radiates from the center, a starred actor who discovers a new techie gadget that is so cool, the actor wants to tell others about it. The starred actor tells friends (the triangles), who in turn share the information with their friends (the squares). In just a few steps, and sometimes fairly quickly, quite a number of customers have learned about the new product from the information that radiated out of a single source. Indeed, a frequently asked question is how to post something online and "make it go viral," meaning, generate fast-moving and far-spreading word-of-mouth or email diffusion, etc.

Marketers may not have much control over whom customers inform, but there are predictable effects depending on the customers' choices, as illustrated in Figure

10.10.[38] For example, it's natural that customers may wish to inform their friends about the new product, figuring their friends might want one themselves. Furthermore, people spend more time interacting with close friends (again, whether in person or online), so there would be more opportunity and more conversations in which the topic of a new product could arise, relative to the smaller number of conversations with mere acquaintances. Yet ironically, customers telling their friends about new products won't spur diffusion and word-of-mouth that much. The phenomenon at play is variously called "homophily" or "similarity and attraction." The concept is basically that people are more likely to be friends with (attracted to) people who are similar to themselves (similarity more in attitudes, but also often in demographics). Thus, a customer who reads cnet.com and learns about the new product and buys it probably has friends who do the same, so when the customer tells the others, they already have knowledge of the new product.

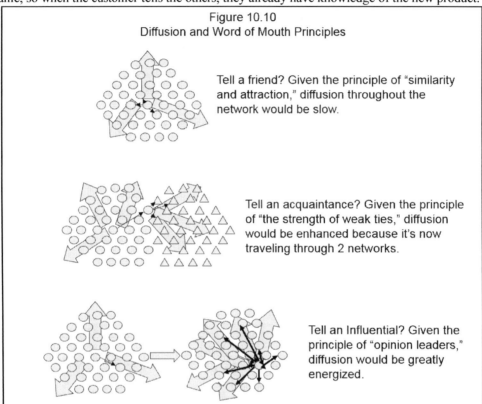

Figure 10.10
Diffusion and Word of Mouth Principles

Tell a friend? Given the principle of "similarity and attraction," diffusion throughout the network would be slow.

Tell an acquaintance? Given the principle of "the strength of weak ties," diffusion would be enhanced because it's now traveling through 2 networks.

Tell an Influential? Given the principle of "opinion leaders," diffusion would be greatly energized.

By comparison, marketers might wish customers would inform people like co-workers or people at their coffee shops, or other people the customers don't know as well. If the customer is informing people who are not close friends, it may well be the case that the recipients of the information are not very similar to the source customer. The source customer and a co-worker might not interact all that frequently, but they may in fact have complementary and overlapping subsets of knowledge. Diffusion would be enhanced because the news is now traveling through both networks. If the knowledge sets are slightly different, then when the customer mentions the new product to a co-worker, it may indeed be informative. The underlying phenomenon at work is called "the strength of weak ties." The friendship tie between the customer and the co-worker isn't very strong (it's weak), yet it's very useful in the spread of new information (thus it has its strengths).

What marketers drool over is the possibility of finding a customer who will be a brand advocate or zealot, energetically informing others about their new product (cf., Zuberance.com). In network studies, these actors are referred to variously as "influentials," "opinion leaders," "market mavens," etc. These are key network players. They have expertise in some domain and keep up-to-date on developments in that world. As a result, these opinion leaders are seen as authorities and are often highly influential. They're likely to tell more people, and whoever received this person's advice would take it as trustworthy and would more likely act upon the recommendation.

---

[38] Marketers can certainly offer incentives to their customers to share their good news, though of course, those very incentives weaken the credibility of the persuaders in the eyes of those receiving the recommendations.

It should be rather obvious that if a marketer has access to a network, finding these important players is trivial—they are the actors with high centrality. While opinion leaders are easy to find in networks, it is noteworthy that there already exist scales that measure opinion leadership (e.g., on 7-point scales from strongly disagree to strongly agree), using items such as "I like introducing brands and products to my friends," "I like helping people by providing them with information about many kinds of products," and "People ask me for information about products, places to shop, or sales."[39] If network data are available, centrality indices are ideal, but if they are not, these scales provide at least some alternative.

Summary

In a myriad of settings, people and firms are interconnected, and information about how they are connected is not redundant with information about who they are, thus network models are complementary to traditional data sources such as surveys or secondary data. Network analytics is a body of techniques that facilitates the description of structures of relationships. We saw micro-level analyses (degree centrality, closeness and betweenness centrality), meso-level analyses (finding cliques and groups of structurally equivalent actors), and macro-level analyses (such as calculating the density of a network). Inferential models were also introduced, to facilitate testing on model parameters, such as α, β, and ρ. There are still more kinds of networks, including brand association cognitive networks, in which the actors are concepts, say brands and brand attributes, and relational ties connect brands with attributes that are most characteristic, from the point of view of the customers.

References

Texts:
- Knoke, David and Song Yang (2008), *Social Network Analysis* 2nd ed., Thousand Oaks, CA: Sage (Great intro.)
- Scott, John (1991), *Social Network Analysis: A Handbook*, London: Sage. (Also great intro.)

Articles on network models:
- Iacobucci, Dawn, and Nigel Hopkins (1992), "Modeling Dyadic Interactions and Networks in Marketing," *Journal of Marketing Research*, 29, 5-17.
- Iacobucci, Dawn, and Stanley Wasserman (1988), "A General Framework for the Statistical Analysis of Sequential Dyadic Interaction Data," *Psychological Bulletin*, 103, 379-390.
- Wasserman, Stanley, and Dawn Iacobucci (1991), "Statistical Modelling of One-Mode and Two-Mode Networks: Simultaneous Analysis of Graphs and Bipartite Graphs," *British Journal of Mathematical and Statistical Psychology*, 44, 13-43.
- Wasserman, Stanley, and Dawn Iacobucci (1988), "Sequential Social Network Data," *Psychometrika*, 53, 261-282.

Applications:
- Romàn, Sergio and Dawn Iacobucci (2010), "Antecedents and Consequences of Adaptive Selling Confidence and Behavior: A Dyadic Analysis of Salespeople and Their Customers," *Journal of the Academy of Marketing Science*, 38, 363-382.
- Üstüner, Tuba and Dawn Iacobucci (2011), "Does Intra-Organizational Network-Embeddedness Improve Salespeople's Effectiveness? A Task Contingency Perspective," to appear in the *Journal of Personal Selling & Sale Management*, 31 (4) or 32 (1).

For a nice network analysis package, go to www.analytictech.com, and at the left, click on UCINET,

---

[39] See Feick and Price, "The Market Maven" *Journal of Marketing*, vol.51, 83-97.

Chapter 11: Marketing Models
Classic Models, Big Data, to ∞ and Beyond

Introduction

In this final chapter, we take a step back, as well as a leap forward. We step back to look at several classic marketing models. These models helped established the analytical side of marketing and any good marketing modeler would know them. We then leap forward and consider something modelers are already encountering and will only certainly grow in future analyses, and that is "big data." Finally, we leave modeling by broadening the discussion to understand optimal model choices for different kinds of data, and offering suggestions of solid, high quality data sources.

Classic Marketing Models

When quants in marketing hear the term "marketing models," it can mean one of two things. One class of models includes the many multivariate statistical methods that we've seen, like factor analysis, MDS, clustering, etc. These are models that we've called marketing models because we've been using them to answer marketing questions. Yet marketers share these models with the rest of the world, e.g., biologists use cluster analysis and psychologists use factor analysis.

Another class of "marketing models" includes models that were developed wholly to address a specific marketing issue. We've seen three of these models in Chapter 9—the diffusion model, the Assessor model, and the Bases model. Someone outside of marketing could pick up the Bases model, say, and generalize it to be applicable to their world. However, it would take some doing, because the kinds of questions it was designed to answer, the kinds of variables used as inputs, and the kinds of predictions produced as outputs, are all very marketing-like in content.

These marketing-dedicated models deserve a bit more mention. They've achieved their status because they were so effective in addressing the questions they were built to answer. These are important models, for their historical and current popularity and impact in academia and industry. Thus, in the sections that follow, we briefly describe several more marketing models: Hotelling's Law, the Defender model, Scan*Pro, Adbudg, CallPlan, and Syntex. We then close with discussions about decisions that need to be made in modeling and structural modeling in general.

Hotelling's Law

You've heard the mantra, "location, location, location" for real estate, restaurants, retail outlets, shopping centers, etc. "Geo-balance models" help with site selection, and they grew out of a simple model called Hotelling's law.[40]

Here's the heart of the problem. Imagine a small town with a single central road that runs east and west called Main Street. A baker wants to set up shop. If the baker is the only baker in town, the shop can be set up anywhere along Main Street. But say that while the baker is at City Hall filling out the paperwork to register the business, the clerk mentions that another bakery is also preparing to open soon. Now, where should Bakery A and Bakery B set up shop?

The model is crafted along a line (the east-west orientation). The length of that line is ℓ, the model analog to the size of the market, say $\ell = 35$ pies that could be sold on any given day (from both bakeries combined). The bakeries

---

[40] Hotelling 1929; also see Hess and Samuels 1971.

are denoted A and B, and the traveling distances from the end points of Main Street to the nearest bakeries are denoted a and b. The terms x and y are the distances from the bakeries A and B to the middle of town. Main Street looks like this:

$$0 \text{——}^{a}\text{—— A ——}^{x}\text{——midpoint ——}^{y}\text{—— B ——}^{b}\text{—— 35.}$$

Together, the distances $a + x + y + b$ sum to $\ell = 35$. The quantity of pies that bakery A will sell, according to the model, is $q_1 = (a + x)$. These are the customers living to the west (and northwest and southwest). The model says it would be silly for those customers to go to bakery B. Similarly, the quantity of pies that bakery B will sell is $q_2 = (b + y)$. Its customers live to the east (and northeast and southeast) of the midpoint of Main Street. The two shares, q_1 and q_2, must sum to ℓ; that is, $(q_1 + q_2) = (a + x) + (b + y) = 35$.

Hotelling's law says the optimal solution is for both bakeries to set up shop right next to each other and right in the middle of Main Street. Then, store A draws half of the town's customers—all those who live to the west side of the two bakeries, and store B draws the half of the town who live to the east. You might think, why do the bakeries have to be side-by-side? If one bakery was planned for the left side of Main Street and the other for the right end of Main Street, apparently these "optimizing economists" (or "selfish bakers") would seek to modify their location plans to build closer to the center of Main Street to scoop up more of the other shop's business. (Good grief.) Let's see how and why.

The model speaks to pricing for the bakeries: bakery B might want to price p_B higher than bakery A's p_A, but p_B can't exceed p_A by more than it costs a customer to travel from shop A to shop B. We'll call the cost of customer travel c for each of the 35 units along Main Street. The point of indifference is $p_A + cx = p_B + cy$. Use that equation with the constraint that $a + x + b + y = \ell$ (recall above) to solve for x and y. Crunch crunch crunch. Hotelling's law says the profits for the two bakeries are: $\pi_A = (c/2)[\ell + ((a - b)/3)]^2$ and $\pi_B = (c/2)[\ell - ((a - b)/3)]^2$.

So let's return to give advice to the baker filling out forms at City Hall. Take either bakery, say bakery B. The profit equation indicates that bakery B can make the most if "b" is as large as possible (in the π_B equation, there is a term $-(-b)$). So bakery B wants to move away from ℓ , heading west as far as possible. Meanwhile, bakery A wants to move away from 0, heading east as far as possible. The two bakeries will meet at the midpoint, and can coexist there. Weee.

Obviously the law only works with piles of simplifying assumptions. For example, the bakeries have to offer comparable pies, service, etc. That is, one bakery cannot be inherently more attractive than another. Marketers don't tend to believe their brands are commodities, so this assumption seems limiting. Analogously, the model assumes the customer bases are interchangeable. Yet most cities have more and less desirable places to live, e.g., if the east part of town is wealthier, we'd set up shop closer to them.

Yet even for the model's weirdnesses, anecdotal evidence suggests it sort of works. For example, historically, shopping malls began to be developed in part because stores had been clustering already (à la Hotelling's prediction), or think of gas stations on on the corners of the same intersection. Furthermore, on a more macro scale, we know there are industry clusters—locations that a priori may have no particular advantage over another, but as they become populated with some critical mass of similar companies, the area becomes magnetic to other competitors.

The geodistance models are often applied to business problems such as these with literal physical location and distance issues, but as with MDS, we can apply the model more broadly to consider perceptual distances. To see how, note that the model is also called "the principle of minimum differentiation." The bakeries are not only in approximately the same location, but as mentioned per the assumptions, they sell the same stuff at the same prices. Indeed, isn't it the case that we more often see copycats in the marketplace rather than true originals? If BMW creates an SUV, so does Mercedes, whereas instead, Mercedes could have begun developing a sports car that also flies (or whatever). If United Airlines begins offering seats with more leg room, American could take its proverbial bakery in a different direction and specialize in something else, but instead, they're likely to meet the UA leg room feature. The notion of Main Street running east and west also brings the analogy to the political system. Where a conservative candidate would please the conservatives more, and a liberal candidate would please the liberals more, in the end, both candidates are usually very moderate, which is to say they've located their political platforms pretty near the center so as to be as "close" to all voters as possible, and the candidates become nearly interchangeable in their claims about their positions.

Defender

Let's now turn to a model that was developed to address questions of marketing strategy. Here's the scenario: a competitor launches a new product. How should we respond? Should we change our price, spend more on advertising, or improve our own product to try to regain ground that we fear will be lost to the new competitive entry? The creators of the "Defender" model[41] painted a Hotelling-like picture to answer these questions.

Imagine a perceptual map of dishwashing detergents. The soaps differ along two dimensions: efficacy and mildness. If we're in Hotelling's town, then the east-west corridor (formerly called Main Street) will represent efficacy, and now there is also a street running north-south, and it will represent mildness. Thus, the Defender model extends Hotelling's distances into two dimensions.

Among the current brands of dishwashing detergent, Ajax stakes out efficacy, so it has coordinates like (9,1). Ivory stakes a claim on mildness, and it is located at (1,9). There is a third brand, Joy, with coordinates (5,5) that claims to be both (but note that on either single dimension it is dominated by Ajax or Ivory).[42]

The model first posits the probability that a consumer will prefer and buy brand j of all brands if the utility for j exceeds the utility for the other brands (recall the logic presented in Chapter 3 for logit models and brand choice). Aggregating the consumers' utilities yields estimates of brand shares. The utilities are defined as weighted sums of the scores of the brands on the attributes. We'll denote x_{1j} as the efficacy for brand j and x_{2j} as its mildness. The weights are larger for the attribute the customer cares most about (these weights should resonate with what you know now about MDS).

Decisions regarding price cuts, additional ad spending, or product improvements are structured in terms of likely profits from taking that action, and the model seeks to maximize that profitability. For example, in determining whether the product should be improved (or downgraded), the model begins with a statement of profitability, π:

$$\Pi_a(p, k_d, c) = (p - c)N_a M_a(p, c)D(k_d) - k_d$$

where p is our price, k_d are the dollars (or generally, "effort") spent in distribution channel d, c is the unit production cost, N_a is the market volume after the competitor enters the market, $M_a(p,c)$ is the potential market share (as a function of price and unit cost) after competitive entry, and $D(k_d)$ shows that sales are proportional to a distribution index, D.

The model then examines whether to enhance the brand along dimension 1 (efficacy) or 2 (mildness), depending on whether doing so means the brand approaches the new competitor (i.e., it gets positioned as more similar to the new brand) or the brand moves away from the new competitor (i.e., the product improvement distinguishes it from the new competitor). Other results obtained from the Defender model include the finding that when the market is segmented (that is, customers are heterogeneous in their tastes, which is true for most products), then a price increase is likely to be optimal.

Scan*Pro

As marketers, we're often interested in assessing ROI-like indices for our antics, I mean tactics. Too often, they're measured in isolation, as in "What did the ad campaign do?," or "What was the impact of the price promotion?" Yet when we step back a bit, of course we recognize that the marketing mix variables work jointly and are further contingent upon competitor actions and marketplace characteristics. With the advent of scanner data in grocery stores, a hugely impactful model, called Scan*Pro, was designed to examine multiple marketing effects simultaneously.[43] The model is stated:

$$S_{kjt} = \left[\prod_{r=1}^{n} \left(\frac{p_{krt}}{\bar{p}_{krt}} \right)^{\beta_{rj}} \prod_{i=1}^{3} \gamma_{lrj}^{D_{lkrt}} \right] \left[\prod_{t=1}^{T} \delta_{jt}^{X_t} \right] \left[\prod_{k=1}^{K} \lambda_{kj}^{Z_k} \right] e^{\varepsilon_{kjt}}$$

where S_{kjt} represents the unit sales of brand j in store k during week t. Sales are modeled as a function of: p_{krt}, the unit price for brand r in store k during week t, and $\bar{p}$, which is the mean, so $(p/\bar{p})$ is a price index. The β's are own-brand (r = j) and cross-brand ($r \neq p$) price elasticities (i.e., when we change price, what change is there in the demand for our brand r, and for our competitors' brands, all others but r). The D's are indicator variables for feature advertising (e.g., an ad appeared for the brand in the local newspaper sales inserts over the previous weekend) and in-store displays (e.g., end-of-aisle displays in grocery stores that set the brand apart from its competitors). If $D_{1krt} = 1$, it indicates that brand r is featured but not displayed by store k in week t (otherwise, it is 0); D_{2krt} indicates brand r is on display, D_{3krt} indicates

---

[41] The name is very "Star Wars," yes? See Hauser and Shugan (1983) and see Hauser and Gaskin (1984).

[42] Psychologically, we might worry that Joy cannot be excellent on both attributes; indeed it is dominated by Ajax on efficacy and Ivory on mildness. Yet recent research is showing that this "compromise" selection is very comforting. Most customers aren't seeking only efficacy or only mildness, and don't really want to purchase one thing thinking they'll be missing out on the other, and hence the compromise brand is better in that regard.

[43] Wittink et al. (1988), Andrews et al. (2008), Hanssens, Parsons, and Schultz (2003). Scan*Pro is now a service of Nielsen.

brand r is featured and on display. The γ coefficients correspond to the D's (γ_{1rj} for brands r and j being featured, γ_{2rj} for display, γ_{3rj} for both).

The second bracketed term contains X_t for the indicator variable that the observation is in week t. The δ_{jt} represents a seasonal multiplier for brand j in week t. The third bracketed term has Z_k to indicate that the data point is in store k. The λ_{kj} are store multipliers (e.g., store volume and traffic). Finally, the ε terms are ye ol' error terms.

I know, ay caramba. Let's do our usual first trick and take the natural log of both sides:

$$\ell n(S_{kjt}) = \sum_{r=1}^{n} \beta_{rj}\, \ell n\left(\frac{p_{krt}}{\bar{p}_{krt}}\right) + \sum_{i=1}^{3} D_{lkrt}\, \ell n(\gamma_{lrj}) + \sum_{t=1}^{T} X_t\, \ell n(\delta_{jt}) + \sum_{k=1}^{K} Z_k\, \ell n(\lambda_{kj}) + \varepsilon_{kjt}$$

and now the model may be fit via regular OLS regression. The terms in the first summation is really the primary focus— in particular, we'll grab out those β's to understand the brands' elasticities. The second set of terms (D_{lkrt}) will interest us to the extent we wish to assess the effectiveness of the in-store features and displays. The last two terms might be thought of as control variables that recognize that sales are different over weeks (X_t) and stores (Z_k), and of course the regression will seek to minimize the model error.

Adbudg

The advertising budgeting model, or Adbudg, seeks to offer guidance on the questions, "When should I spend my advertising dollars?," and "How much should I spend to achieve the desired sales response?"[44] The model is structured to get a band of realistic outcomes of the effects of ad spending. The scenarios span the following: 1) if we maintain current levels and activities in our advertising, we would expect to simply maintain share, assuming competitors aren't changing their activities, 2) If we were to increase our advertising budget, we would expect an increase in sales, but to what? 3) Conversely, if we decreased our ad spending, we could expect a decline in sales, but sales probably wouldn't drop to zero, so what level might we expect to see? The expectations of the possible rise or fall resulting from an increase or decrease in the spending is a guesstimate integrating past data and some assumptions and managerial judgment.

The model is also able to represent the likely effect of advertising over time as it occurs in your industry or with your brand. For example, if the relationship between advertising and sales tends to be s-shaped in your industry; that is, the effect of the ads get stronger with time, then that curve is incorporated into the model. In other industries, the relationship between advertising and sales shows a more concave structure; that is, the effect is strong and builds for a while, but at some point shows a downturn and decline, then that is the functional shape that will be represented in the model. Specifically, the heart of the Adbudg model looks like this:

$$share = \min + (\max - \min)\frac{adv^{\gamma}}{(\delta + adv^{\gamma})}$$

where the power term γ is the part of the model that allows for the functional flexibility. The advertising function is s-shaped when $\gamma > 1$, and the advertising function is concave for $0 < \gamma \le 1$. The "max" and min" variables are those estimates about how well we could do in terms of sales projected on the basis of an increase or decrease in our advertising. The term δ is the expected effect (or the known effect, if there are relevant historical data or data from test markets) of an increase in advertising at the 50% level, to calibrate.

Callplan

Callplan is a model designed to answer the question, "How much effort should a salesperson make on behalf of a particular client account or prospective account?"[45] To describe this model as simply as possible, we can formulate it to resemble the Adbudg model just described. The model is:

$$r_i(x_i) = \min + (\max - \min)\frac{x_i^{\gamma}}{(\delta + x_i^{\gamma})}$$

where x_i is the effort a salesperson makes toward customer account i. Effort is often measured simply as the number of calls the salesperson makes on that customer. The model predicts $r_i(x_i)$, the expected sales we'd see accrue to account i if x_i were the number of calls made on that customer.

Note that this model builds on Adbudg in that the input we're considering manipulating—advertising in Adbudg or effort in Callplan—has a subscript in Callplan, x_i. That subscript means that it's not a single level of effort (as it had

[44] Little (1970), also see Lilien and Rangaswamy (2003) for a great overview of this model and the next two.

[45] Lodish (1971).

been a single level of advertising, which makes sense for mass advertising). Rather, in Callplan, it's an amount of sales effort that varies with the customer.

Note also that this model presaged the current CRM philosophy—it helped managers determine which customers were worth their time and efforts and which were not quite as valuable. The overall sales effort was studied for its components, determining the number of calls a salesperson should make on particular current customers and on potential customers, depending on the costs of the trip, time requirements, likely profitability of each customer, etc.

Syntex

Syntex was the name of a hypothetical firm that served as the context for a model designed to determine the optimal size of a sales force.[46] The model is intended to be an advance over the then existing practice (which is probably still lingering now) of firms that calculate the number of salespeople they think they need by either comparing selling expenses (as a percentage of sales) to the average cost of a salesperson, or by comparing sales forecasts to an average revenue generated by a salesperson.

The Syntex model looks like Callplan. It is set to investigate scenarios of what level of sales might be expected if the size of the sales force were kept at status quo, or increased in size, or cut in size. We stipulate that the optimal number of salespeople will be different in different sales territories. Call the sales territory "i", the sales effort x_i, and r_i is the optimal number of salespeeps to assign to that area: $r_i(x_i) = min + (max - min)\frac{x_i^\gamma}{(\delta + x_i^\gamma)}$.

One might imagine generalizing the model still further, e.g., to include multiple γ_i's. Such an extension would be more sophisticated because a vector of γ's would allow for different advertising functions (s-shaped or concave) in different sales territories. (Of course the estimation of more model parameters usually requires more data.)

Some Thoughts about Adapting and Building Structural Marketing Models

We can respect the marketing models we've reviewed for at least two reasons. First, they were indeed useful in addressing the marketing questions for which they were designed. Second, and perhaps more impressively, these models had an important role in quantifying, systematizing, and generally making the field of marketing more rigorous, analytical, and scientific.

Yet those marketing models share a limitation of being rather narrow in scope. They need not be; there is no reason that we couldn't take any of the models and generalize them. For example, recall the indicator variable, D, in Scan*Pro. In the model, it captures whether a brand was on display in the store or not, and featured in recent advertising or not. That indicator variable could be modified to reflect whether the brand manager had sent an email coupon to loyalty card holders or not, and whether the brand's online community had engaged in more than 50 tweets the previous week, etc.

In reality, these models take on a life of their own, and they tend not to be modified. With time, this stasis renders the models increasingly dated and less useful. IRL, brand managers are frequently too busy to build models, and certainly too busy to calibrate them to verify that they're good models, not just capitalizing on their current data.

Furthermore, building models is challenging. There are numerous decisions to be made. The classic marketing models have included many elements, the forms of which are actually assumptions of their own.

For example, the Adbudg and related models used the range of "max – min." The computation of a difference might make particular sense for these models, but in other arenas, perhaps the ratio "min/max" would be more meaningful. Who's to say? In fact, you may recall that the diffusion model had it both ways—it contains both a "M – N_{t-1}" term as well as an "N_{t-1}/M" term (where M is not unlike "max" and N_{t-1} is not entirely different from "min").

Another example involves the choice of the shape of functions. For example, sometimes we'll see a model in which a cumulative normal curve (or even a z^2 term) is used (as in the diffusion model), whereas in others, the logistic function is used ($f_x = 1/(1 + e^{-x})$, (as in the generalized diffusion model). Given the similarities in their shapes, as depicted in Figure 11.1, perhaps this particular choice is immaterial. Perhaps the choice is selected as a function of other determinants—what kind of model is easier to fit, converges more reliably, requires data we can access, etc.

---

[46] Lodish et al. (1988); in addition to measuring sales potentials per territory, sales force compensation models are also big, e.g., salespeoples' preferences for pay and bonus structures (Mantrala, Sinha, and Zoltners, 1994).

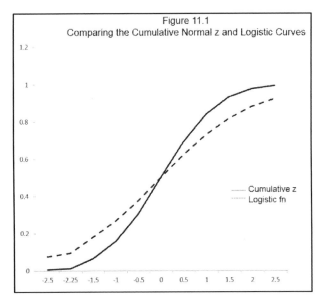

Figure 11.1
Comparing the Cumulative Normal z and Logistic Curves

——— Cumulative z
----- Logistic fn

The philosophy of this book is to spend more time with models whose derivations are not specific marketing questions. These statistical models can be and have been applied to many kinds of data sets that are multivariate, high-dimensional, or "big data." Thus, your spending time to learn cluster analysis, say, means you can use this valuable tool in many settings. If you spent as much time learning one of the classic marketing models, you'd be good to go when that particular marketing question arose in your company, but less capable in addressing other problems.

The 6 marketing models are also classics in that any marketing modeler should know them. They're foundational in that they kicked off the tradition of encouraging marketing managers to use decision making models, not necessarily instead of their intuitions but rather as a means to systematize their managerial instincts, so as to integrate the art of experience with the science of modeling. In addition, as we saw with the progression from Hotelling's Law to the Defender model, or from Adbudg to CallPlan and Syntex, models can build on former versions so as to extend and generalize the models' analytical capabilities and applicability.[47]

When these models were created, they were referred to as "analytical models" in contrast to econometrics or statistical models. These days, the term "analytical" is used so vastly and colloquially to mean something like thoughtful, data-based, involving detailed math, etc., that the analytical modeling approach has come to be referred to as "structural modeling." The idea underlying structural (formerly analytical) models is that the model is truly trying to capture the behavior of the entities being modeled—consumers, business customers, etc. Even the simple Hotelling set-up is an example of a structural model, because we can imagine a town planner dealing with two businesses in determining their Main Street addresses to optimize their profits. In contrast, the structural modelers say, in econometrics (the economist's part of the field of applied statistics) and statistical modeling, the emphasis is on analyzing data, describing and fitting the data well, predicting the current data set well and expecting that forecasting to do reasonably well in similar alternative data sets, and doing so while making relatively fewer assumptions than the structural modeling types make. Statisticians make assumptions about distributions like normality, for example, to be able to test hypotheses, but they don't tend to specify personifications of the model elements. For example, a statistician would approach the Hotelling scenario by saying, "How do we minimize the sum of squared distances over two points in space (the bakery locations) in 1 dimension?" or some such formulation. They wouldn't worry about bakeries and prices, or customers living to the west or east, or pies being equal ceteris paribus.

As is the case with much of life, the distinction is relatively blurred in reality. In addition, we should recognize and acknowledge that both approaches have their strengths, both can inform the other, and marketing models as a whole are stronger for the presence and interaction of both.

There are models beyond marketing too, of course. For example, there are a plethora of queuing models that can be useful to marketers who care about yield management (e.g., in services and operations); with just a little data, e.g., observing the average arrival rate of customers over some duration (e.g., hourly, daily, etc.), we can derive how many customers the system can serve at once, how many are likely to have to wait, and how long is their expected wait. Any element of marketing, or business more generally, can be encapsulated in a model, particularly if management can be creative about obtaining relevant data.

Big Data

The popular business press seems obsessed with "big data." It is standard to define big data in terms of "3Vs": volume, velocity, and variety.

---

[47] Marketers don't tend to name their models anymore, perhaps because the concept of modeling isn't as novel as when the pioneering models were formulated. One exception is that consultants continue to name models so they can sell them as rigorous-sounding products, and they can refer to the model as being complicated and analytical, but a proprietary black box, thereby precluding the divulgence of any specifics.

The V's

Regarding volume: the most obvious quality of big data is its quantity. Big datasets do not always contain a large number of variables, but they almost inevitably contain a huge number of observations; that is, there will be a huge number of rows in the spreadsheet. Consider the scale: 1 byte captures a single character, 1000 bytes is a kilobyte, 10^6 bytes is a megabyte, 10^9 bytes is a gigabyte, 10^{12} bytes is a terabyte, and those terms are familiar. Next, a petabyte (10^{15} bytes) has been likened to filling 20 million 4-drawer filing cabinets with documents or storing more than 10 years of HD-TV videos. The naming of big bytes continues: exabyte (10^{18}), zettabyte (10^{21}), yottabyte (10^{24}), xenottabyte (10^{27}), domegemegrottebyte (10^{33}). Amazon and eBay use about 100 petabytes for their data warehouses. The volume and scale of big data can indeed be impressive, and it's the first element that seems to overwhelm managers.

Regarding velocity, similarly, managers are astounded that massive waves of data keep coming and coming. For example, big data trackers note that Walmart captures some 1 million customer transactions per hour. Walmart is obviously huge, and that's only standard retail; many websites are larger in scale, updating at least as rapidly.

Regarding variety, the idea is that these days the "data" aren't just numbers that can be stored easily or directly into a spreadsheet. The data can be numbers (dates, quantities, prices of transactions), links (from promo offers to websites for more information to ultimate shopping carts and purchasing), and even different modalities such as photos or videos. For example, Facebook stores 50 billion photos for its users. Marketers know how to analyze purchase transactions or loyalty and membership programs and CRM databases, but it's less clear how one goes about analyzing photos and YouTube videos. Marketers are experimenting with text analysis of blogs, tweets, users' text on Facebook, and phone calls and text messages, but again, the analysis of information in social network posts and links is challenging.

Sometimes additional "V"s are offered, such as "value" (figuring out how to turn big data into information that is useful) or "veracity" (what is the quality or uncertainty regarding the data). Several of the challenges of big data include its storage and coordinating all of the company's databases. These are very real and quite substantial problems, but they are more ops in nature, and we marketers have neither the expertise to solve the issues nor the interest in doing so. In this book, the consideration is how the bigness of the data affects the analyses. One concern is the effect on statistical power, and another concern is that of data visualization.

Power

The sample sizes in big datasets are so large that the test of almost any parameter will be significant. That is, the null hypothesis will be rejected as unlikely, and the finding will be characterized as "real," not just attributable to sampling variability. It's easy to see why. Here are several examples:

- When we compute a correlation coefficient, we usually also whether it is significantly different from 0. To do so, we calculate a t-statistic (with N-2 degrees of freedom) of the form: $t = r\sqrt{\frac{N-2}{1-r^2}}$. Note that no matter how large r is, t grows as function of the square root of the sample size, N. So, for example, r = 0.5 on a sample of 100 results in a t = 11.43. A much smaller r = 0.05 on a larger sample of 10,000 results in a t = 100.12.

- We also use t's (or z's) in testing means. For some null value hypothesized for μ, we'd compute $t = \frac{(\bar{X}-\mu)}{(sd/\sqrt{n})}$. If we rearrange the terms a little, we obtain: $t = \frac{\sqrt{n}(\bar{X}-\mu)}{sd}$. That is, once again, we see that the likelihood with which this t is found to be significant is enhanced at the rate of the square root of N.

- You get the idea, but to be sure you understand that this relationship holds not just for the t-statistic, consider the X^2 for a simple 2-way cross-tab. Let's label the cells in a 2×2 table, a and b (for the frequencies in the first row), and c and d (for the frequencies in the second row). Then $X^2 = \frac{(ad-bc)^2(a+b+c+d)}{(a+b)(c+d)(a+c)(b+d)}$. We know that the sum of a+b+c+d = N, so $X^2 = \frac{(ad-bc)^2 N}{(a+b)(c+d)(a+c)(b+d)}$, thus we see that X^2 grows directly proportionally to N, the sample size.

What this principle and these examples illustrate is that statistical tests per se don't really convey a great deal of information in the world of big data. That's not to say we wouldn't run a regression, say, only that we could predict rather confidently that every effect will be significant. So in addition to t-tests and p-values, we supplement the analyses with estimates of "effect sizes." There are several indices that have been proposed to reflect the size of an effect, but the most frequently used is probably eta-squared, η^2, because its interpretation is like that of an R^2. It ranges from 0 to 1, and it reflects the proportion of variance in the dependent variable explained by the effect of the particular variable being examined. For instance, in a multiple regression of $\hat{y} = b_0 + b_1 X_1 + b_2 X_2$, any statistical computing package will give the estimates for the regression coefficients, their standard errors, the t-statistics and p-values. The computer will also provide the sums of squares for the whole model, the SS_{error} (and a Mean Square for the error which is SS_{error} divided by the degrees of freedom for error), and a total SS (if you have a choice between a "total" SS and a "corrected total" SS, use the latter). If we compute $\eta^2_{model} = {SS_{model}}/{SS_{total}}$, we'd know the proportion of variance in Y that X_1 and X_2 together explain. If we compute a "partial" eta-squared, $\eta^2_{X1} = {SS_{X1}}/{SS_{total}}$, we'd know the proportion of variance in Y that X_1 explains by itself. (If the computer does not provide the SS for each particular effect, such as SS_{X1}, it is easily found. Take the t-statistic testing the X_1 effect, square it and multiply it by the SS_{total}. That will equal MS for X_1 and given that we use one degree of freedom for one variable, the MS for X_1 is also equal to the SS for X_1. That is, $t^2_{X1} MS_{error} = MS_{effectX1} = SS_{X1}$. Then you have the pieces to calculate η^2_{X1}.) The η^2's may be interpreted like any proportion, e.g., if $\eta^2_{X1} = .4$ and $\eta^2_{X2} = .2$, we can state that the effect of X_1 is twice as strong as the effect of X_2.

Data Visualization

Big data are often presented in the form of diagrams and graphs and other visual charts. The pictures are often striking and beautiful. They are just as often not terribly informative and definitely imprecise. It's one thing to acknowledge, per the power discussion above, that any apparent difference in a plot will almost surely be significant. It's another thing to not even try to express precise sizes or accurate numerical differences.

In addition, for 25 years or more, perceptual psychologists have been studying perceptions and misperceptions that arise in the interpretation of data displayed in graphs. For example, in Figure 11.2, there are 3 forms of a pie chart, used frequently to depict market shares. At the left is a simple pie chart—it is perfectly acceptable. In the middle is a chart that someone thinks look more sophisticated because it is 3-d, however it is misleading because now the pie has 3-d volume in addition to 2-d area, and the smallest market share looks relatively smaller in the middle pie than in the pie to the left. The exploding pie chart at the right shares the problem that the extracted slice looks larger than its true relative proportion (in Figure 11.2, the areas are actually correct, but often the extracted slice is stretched to exaggerate the area even more).

Figure 11.3 similarly shows very simple and familiar charts—two histograms. In the chart to the left, there is a separate bar for each brand A and B. In the chart to the right, the bars are stacked. I don't know anyone who can read the stacked bars easily, quickly, or accurately.

Figure 11.4 shows schematic faces to reflect 3 variables measured on each of the 4 BRIC countries (data from the CIA Factbook). When schematic faces were introduced as a possible vehicle for displaying information, it was thought that the advantage would be a

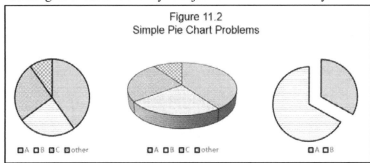

Figure 11.2
Simple Pie Chart Problems

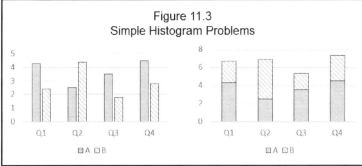

Figure 11.3
Simple Histogram Problems

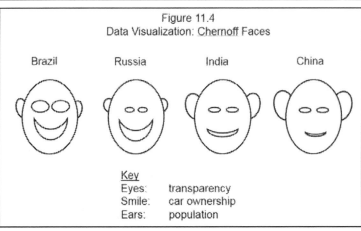

Figure 11.4
Data Visualization: Chernoff Faces

Brazil   Russia   India   China

Key
Eyes: transparency
Smile: car ownership
Ears: population

human interpreter's familiarity in perceiving faces. As with many things in life, the strength is also a weakness—as human beings, we make judgments about qualities of faces. For example, we don't trust people with little, beady eyes, and in Figure 11.4, sure enough, smaller eyes correspond to lower scores on corporate measures of transparency (or higher scores of corruption). Big, wide, open eyes are friendly, and in this case also correspond to straightforward business dealings. Similarly, we tend to find faces with smiles more attractive and welcoming. The schematic smile in Figure 11.4 corresponds to car ownership. Brazilians and Russians may indeed be happier, given that they own more cars, but on the face of it, car membership and happiness are not the same thing. Finally, we human beings seem to have negative connotations about big ears—we reference Dumbo (who is an elephant and so his ears might not be any bigger than the average elephant's!), or consider even the seventh dwarf, who sports a large pair of ears and whose name is

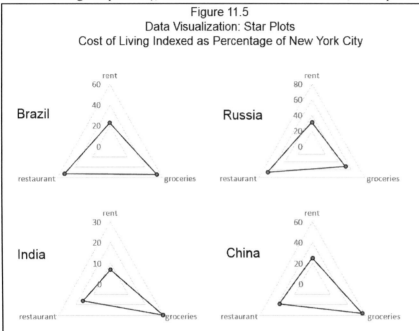

Figure 11.5
Data Visualization: Star Plots
Cost of Living Indexed as Percentage of New York City

Dopey. In the figure, India and China have big ears. We don't want to convey data in a manner that even subconsciously creates a undue negative impression.

Figure 11.5 displays a different vector of 3 numbers for each of the BRIC countries in a more neutral "star chart." The 3 legs of the triad are labeled, so we know how to interpret the taller or shorter spikes. These star charts are better than faces, and they're not misleading. Yet note that these star charts are not inherently superior to simple bar graphs—if our interest is "strengths and weaknesses within a country" we would create a histogram for each country, with 3 bars in it, one for each variable. If instead, our interest was in "relative expense across countries for each category of expenditure," then we would create 3 histograms, 1 for each consumption purchase with 4 bars in it, one for each country.

Data visualization is intended to help the perceiver interpret the displayed information efficiently. Care must be taken that the presentation is not misleading. We want the interpretation to be valid, not just quick.

A Framework to Organize and Choose among Modeling Techniques

After learning many kinds of multivariate statistical models in detail, it helps to pull back to see the big picture. Figure 11.6 presents a framework that shows the methods we've discussed and offers guidance as to when to use which kind of model. There are two ways to answer this question. First, as we've done, chapter by chapter, we look to see what

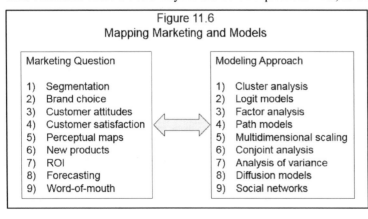

Figure 11.6
Mapping Marketing and Models

Marketing Question	Modeling Approach
1) Segmentation	1) Cluster analysis
2) Brand choice	2) Logit models
3) Customer attitudes	3) Factor analysis
4) Customer satisfaction	4) Path models
5) Perceptual maps	5) Multidimensional scaling
6) New products	6) Conjoint analysis
7) ROI	7) Analysis of variance
8) Forecasting	8) Diffusion models
9) Word-of-mouth	9) Social networks

kinds of questions the technique is designed to resolve—if you want groups, use cluster analysis; if you want a map, use MDS, etc.

To complement that perspective, Figure 11.7 offers another approach. The kind of statistical question you're asking, and the kind of data you're working with, determine which methods you should use and which methods you shouldn't or cannot use. Figure 11.7 is most of a 3×2×2 cross-classification of: 1) the number of variables you're analyzing, 2) whether you're asking a question that requires a prediction or you just want to know what are the patterns underlying the variables, and 3) whether the variables (particularly the dependent variable if you're in the predictive models part of the table) are categorical or continuous.

If you are only working with one variable (e.g., you've just received a new data set, and you want to get a feel for it by running basic descriptive statistics), then you can compute frequencies and percentages if that variable is categorical, or means and standard deviations if that variable is continuous. If you only have one variable, it's vacuous to speak of using one variable to predict another. (Of course, if you nevertheless use that one variable to predict itself, you should get a pretty high R^2.)

Figure 11.7 continues with scenarios having 2 or more variables. For example, the lower right cells indicate that if you're in a predictive mode, and you have a handful of independent variables, you can use regression if your dependent variable is continuous, and a logit or logistic regression if it's categorical.

Figure 11.7
Framework of Techniques

#variables:	variables are	Interdependence Models (variables have equal status)	Predictive Models (1 variable predicted from others)
1	categorical	frequencies, percentages, z-tests for proportions	
	continuous	mean (descriptive stats), one-sample t-test (test H_0: $\mu = c$)	
2	categorical	n_1 and n_2, percentages, z-test to compare p_1 and p_2, cross-tabs, X^2 test for independence, log linear models, odds ratio and Yule's Q	categorical dependent variable: logit model with one categorical predictor or logistic regression with one continuous predictor
	continuous	means (descriptive stats), two-sample t-test (H_0: $\mu_1 = \mu_2$), r_{xy} (are two variables related (in one group)), can use dummy codes for binary variables	simple regression with one predictor
$p \geq 3$	categorical	log linear models	logit model or logistic regression with two or more predictors
	continuous	means (descriptive stats), analysis of variance, experiments, r_{xy}, r_{xz}, r_{yz}, etc., stare at R, factor analysis, principal components, canonical correlations, δ_{xy} perceptions of d_{xy} for MDS, perceptions or deriveds d_{xy}'s for cluster analysis	multiple regression with more than one predictor; conjoint analysis takes the same form when the predictors represent combinations of manipulated product features

Resources to Help You Be a Model Modeler

In addition to guidance on appropriate methods, an altogether different concern for modelers is what data sets are to be crunched. Every company has its favorite databases and sources, but the smart modeler will access additional, supplemental sources of data to populate the variables in their models. Table 11.1 lists numerous data sources on many global phenomena, as well as several specialized resources focusing on China, India, Brazil, Mexico, other Central and South American countries, and Russia. Models only work in contexts, and marketing models should incorporate contemporary phenomena, which certainly include the growth of commercialization or at least customer bases in those countries.

Data like these remind us to zoom back and gain a broader perspective on our marketing problems. It's been said that an extremely useful model is simply to state that:[48]

brand sales = industry sales * brand market share.

This equation makes explicit that the marketing mix elements are important for share, and the macro-environmental effects are important across all competitors.

Table 11.2 lists data sets that focus on the U.S. as it continues to dominate business and certainly marketing. It also contains sources for data on health care, given the industry's size, growth, and relevance, and the basic demographic facts of aging baby boomers who will require assistance with health, wealth transfer, etc.

---

[48] Thanks to Prof. Hanssens (UCLA).

In Table 11.3, there are some sites for marketing research data sources. There are also resources for social networks and social media. These phenomena might not be all the rage in 10 years as they are now, but they are unlikely to go away.

Table 11.4 directs you to sites for software. Programs can be purchased and downloaded, and there is usually extensive documentation and help resources.

Final Words

In closing, I repeat the offer I made at the outset of this book: if anything in this book is unclear, or you wish there were materials on some other topics, send me an email and I'll see what I can do. You might also consult the multivariate stats books I've referenced below.

Thank you! Have fun!

Table 11.1: Global Data Sources

General:
- https://www.cia.gov/library/publications/the-world-factbook/
- http://www.imf.org/external/pubs/cat/subject.aspx
- http://www.nationmaster.com/statistics
- http://data.worldbank.org/
- http://www.census.gov/population/international/data/idb/informationGateway.php

China:
- http://www.stats.gov.cn/english/
- http://www.worldbank.org/en/country/china/data
- http://chinadataonline.org/
- http://www.chinatoday.com/data/data.htm

India:
- http://www.indiastat.com/default.aspx
- http://www.unicef.org/infobycountry/india_statistics.html
- http://www.nationmaster.com/country/in-india

Brazil:
- http://data.un.org/CountryProfile.aspx?crName=BRAZIL
- http://data.worldbank.org/country/brazil

Mexico:
- http://www.mexicodataonline.com/
- http://www.nationmaster.com/country/mx-mexico/lab-labor

Central and South America:
- http://www.latinamericamonitor.com/
- http://www.allmapdata.com/dun-bradstreet-business-databases-south-america.html

Russia:
- http://www.worldbank.org/en/country/russia

Table 11.2: U.S. Data Sources

United States:
- http://www.usa.gov/Topics/Reference-Shelf/Data.shtml
- http://www.census.gov/
- fedstats.sites.usa.gov/

Health Care:
- http://www.cdc.gov/nchs/
- http://www.ahrq.gov/data/
- http://www.census.gov/hhes/www/hlthins/
- http://www.healthpaconline.net/health-care-statistics-in-the-united-states.htm

---

Table 11.3: Marketing Data Sources

General:
- http://www.marketresearch.com/
- http://www.pewinternet.org/
- http://www.geolytics.com/resources/market-research-data.html
- http://www.internetworldstats.com/

Social Networking:
- http://www.socialnetworkingwatch.com/all_social_networking_statistics/
- http://www.ignitesocialmedia.com/social-media-stats

Social Media:
- http://socialmediastatistics.wikidot.com/
- http://www.mediabistro.com/alltwitter/social-media-key-statistics_b19061

Table 11.4: Software Sites

General statistical computing packages:
- SAS: www.sas.com/
- SPSS: www-01.ibm.com/software/analytics/spss/products/statistics/
- Stata: www.stata.com
- Mathematica: www.wolfram.com/mathematica/   (for xtreme geeks)
- Mplus: www.statmodel.com/
- Excel add ins:
  XLSTAT: www.xlstat.com/en/
  Unistat (for plots):   www.unistat.com/

Specialized software:
- Path models (Lisrel):   www.ssicentral.com/
- Networks (UCINET):   www.analytictech.com/ucinet/

Survey sites:
- www.surveymonkey.com
- www.zoomerang.com/online-surveys
- www.facebook.com/surveygizmo

References

Classic marketing models used in the chapter:

- Andrews, Rick L., Imran S. Currim, Peter Leeflang, and Jooseop Lim (2008), "Estimating the SCAN*PRO Model of Store Sales: HB, FM or Just OLS?," *International Journal of Research in Marketing*, 25, 22–33.
- Hanssens, Dominique M., Leonard J. Parsons, and Randall L. Schultz (2003), *Market Response Models: Econometric and Time Series Analysis,* 2nd ed., Boston: Kluwer Academic Publishers.
- Hauser, John R., and Steven P. Gaskin (1984), "Application of the 'Defender' Consumer Model," *Marketing Science* 3 (4), 327–351.
- Hauser, John R., and Steven M. Shugan (1983), "Defensive Marketing Strategies," *Marketing Science* 2 (4) 319–360.
- Hess, Sidney W., and Stuart A. Samuels (1971), "Experiences with a Sales Districting Model: Criteria and Implementation," *Management Science* 18 (Dec.), 41–54.
- Hotelling, Harold (1929), "Stability in Competition," *Economic Journal* 39 (153), 41–57.
- Little, John D. C. (1970), "Models and Managers: The Concept of Decision Calculus," *Management Science* 16 (April), B466–B485.
- Mantrala, Murali K., Prabhakant Sinha, and Andris A. Zoltners (1994), "Structuring a Multiproduct Sales Quota-Bonus Plan for a Heterogeneous Sales Force: A Practical Model Based Approach," *Marketing Science* 13 (2), 121–144.

- Wittink, Dick R., Michael J. Addona, William J. Hawkes, and John C. Porter (1988), "SCAN*PRO: The Estimation, Validation and Use of Promotional Effects Based on Scanner Data," Internal Paper, Cornell University.

Overview texts on marketing models:
- Bierman Jr., Harold, Charles P. Bonini, and Warren H. Hausman (1986), *Quantitative Analysis for Business Decisions*, Homewood, IL: Irwin.
- Kerin, Roger A., and Rob O'Regan (eds.) (2008), *Marketing Mix Decisions: New Perspectives and Practices*, Chicago, IL: AMA.
- Lilien, Gary L., and Philip Kotler (1983), *Marketing Decision Making: A Model-Building Approach*, New York: Harper & Row.
- Lilien, Gary L., and Arvind Rangaswamy (2003), *Marketing Engineering: Computer-Assisted Marketing Analysis and Planning*, 2nd ed., Upper Saddle River, NJ: Prentice-Hall.
- Lilien, Gary L., Arvind Rangaswamy, and Arnaud De Bruyn (2007), *Principles of Marketing Engineering*, Trafford Publishing.
- Wierenga, Berend (ed.) (2010), *Handbook of Marketing Decision Models*, New York: Springer.

Visual display of information:
- Few, Stephen (2006), *Information Dashboard Design: The Effective Visual Communication of Data*, Canada: O'Reilly.
- McCandless, David (2009), *Information is Beautiful*, New York: Harper Collins.
- Tufte, Edward R. (2001), *The Visual Display of Quantitative Information*, 2nd ed., New York: Graphics Press.
- Tufte, Edward R. (1990), *Envisioning Information*, New York: Graphics Press.
- Tufte, Edward R. (1997), *Visual Explanations: Images and Quantities, Evidence and Narrative*, New York: Graphics Press.
- Wainer, Howard (2011), *Picturing the Uncertain World: How to Understand, Communicate, and Control Uncertainty through Graphical Display*, Princeton: Princeton University Press.
- Wainer, Howard (2000), *Visual Revelations: Graphical Tales of Fate and Deception from Napoleon Bonaparte to Ross Perot*, New York: Psychology Press.
- Wainer, Howard (2004), *Graphic Discovery: A Trout in the Milk and Other Visual Adventures*, Princeton: Princeton University Press.

General multivariate statistics books:
- Dillon, William R., and Matthew Goldstein (1984), *Multivariate Analysis: Methods and Applications*, New York: Wiley.
- Everitt, Brian S., and Graham Dunn (1992), *Applied Multivariate Data Analysis*, New York: Oxford University Press.
- Lattin, James, Douglas Carroll, and Paul Green (2002), *Analyzing Multivariate Data*, Duxbury Press.
- Manly, Bryan F. J. (1986), *Multivariate Statistical Methods: A Primer*, London: Chapman and Hall.
- Morrison, Donald (1976), *Multivariate Statistical Methods*, 2nd ed., New York: McGraw-Hill.
- Seber, George A. F. (1984), *Multivariate Observations*, New York: Wiley.
- Tabachnick, Barbara G., and Linda S. Fidell (2006), *Using Multivariate Statistics*, 5th ed., Allyn & Bacon.

27925498R00083

Made in the USA
Lexington, KY
08 January 2019